Edward Ford, George Hewitt Hodson

**A history of Enfield in the County of Middlesex;**

including its Royal and ancient manors, the chase, and the Duchy of Lancaster,

with notices of its worthies, and its natural history, etc

Edward Ford, George Hewitt Hodson

**A history of Enfield in the County of Middlesex;**
 *including its Royal and ancient manors, the chase, and the Duchy of Lancaster, with notices of its worthies, and its natural history, etc*

ISBN/EAN: 9783337025090

Printed in Europe, USA, Canada, Australia, Japan

Cover: Foto ©ninafisch / pixelio.de

More available books at **www.hansebooks.com**

# A HISTORY OF ENFIELD

### IN THE COUNTY OF MIDDLESEX,

#### INCLUDING ITS

## Royal and Ancient Manors,

### THE

## Chase,

#### AND

## THE DUCHY OF LANCASTER,

#### WITH

### NOTICES OF ITS WORTHIES,

#### AND ITS

### NATURAL HISTORY, ETC.

#### ALSO AN ACCOUNT OF

## The Church and the Charities

#### AND

### A HISTORY OF THE NEW RIVER.

*The Church History, by the Rev. GEORGE H. HODSON, Vicar,*
*And the General History by EDWARD FORD, Esquire.*

*///*

PRINTED FOR SUBSCRIBERS ONLY, AND NOT PUBLISHED.

*(PRICE ONE GUINEA.)*

ENFIELD PRESS:—PRINTED BY J. H. MEYERS.

1873.

# CONTENTS.

## GENERAL HISTORY.

# ERRATA AND ADDENDA.

*p.* 15, *l.* 7, for son, read descendant.

*p.* 22, *l.* 17, for 335 acres, read 3˙35 acres.

*p.* 30, *l.* 4, for Albermarle, read Albemarle.

*p.* 54, (Note) Transfer to page 53.

*p.* 62, Additional Note.—The sovereign of Hungary was always "King." In the 14th century Louis of Hungary, surnamed "the Great," was succeeded by his daughter Mary "King of Hungary," and when, in 1740, Maria Theresa, driven from every other part of her dominions took refuge in Hungary, and threw herself and her child on the loyalty of her subjects, they unsheathed their swords and swore to devote "vitam et sanguinem pro *rege* nostro Maria."

*p.* 67, add,—The Right Hon. John Bright, Aug. 1873.

*p.* 73, *l.* 7, for command, read commend.

*p.* 82. Every reader will recall the concluding scene of the Lady of the Lake, where

——— "in the room
Fitz-James alone wore cap and plume."

*p.* 134, *l.* 7, Edmond Godesman was the last chantry priest, and received a pension at the dissolution of chantries.

*p.* 173, *l.* 23, for laying, read lying.

*p.* 211, *l.* 4, for July 9th, 1835, read October 15th, 1831.

*p.* 212, *l.* 12, for emeritas, read immeritas.

*p.* 213, [vulturnus—cornix—snowdrop—curfew.]

*p.* 271, *l.* 14, for £10, read 10 marks.

*p.* 273, *l.* 27, for Jugland's, read Juglans.

*p.* 302, *l.* 5, for presentum, read presentem.

*p.* 308, *l.* 17, for January 31st, read January 1st.

*p.* 319, *l.* 25, But in the Chauntry Roll (Hen. VIII. and Edw. VI.) in the Public Record Office, under Enfield, we find:—— "Landes and tenements being in the townes of South Benfleet, Hadley, and Thundersley, given for the maintenance of a brotherhood priest there, whereof Sir John Bridgeman received for his salary, vii£."

" Go, lityl boke, be simple of mannère,

" And specially let this be thy prayère,

" Unto all 'hem that thee will rede or hear,

" Where thou art wrong—after ther' help to call

" Thee to correct, in any parte or all.

—— " Praie 'hem also, with thine humble servise

" Thy boldènesse to pardon in this case;

" For els thou art not able in no wise

" To make thyself appear in any place,

—— " Consideryng by good advisament

" My grete unconnyng and my simplenesse.

*Chaucer.*

# THE PREFACE.

WHEN this volume was first announced, the intention was simply to edit a new edition of Mr. Tuff's " Historical Notices," for the benefit of his widow. The general interest however that was taken in the work, and the encouragement given by the constantly lengthening list of subscribers, were so far beyond what had been anticipated, that the Editors felt something more would be expected of them than a mere reprint of the little book as originally proposed.

They have attempted to meet this expectation, so far as the more important duties of one writer, and the literary inexperience of the other,* would permit, and they offer the following pages as a HISTORY OF ENFIELD, " endeavoured "—to use the expression of old Fuller— according to their ability. Any such work must be necessarily imperfect, and when the life-long antiquarian researches of Mr. Gough, and of Mr. Lysons, have been at fault, many errors no doubt still remain.

---

* I shall be excused for adding, that any value or interest which my share in the work may possess, is in great measure due to the labour and research of my son, John W. Ford, to whose filial assistance in this, as in other matters, I am so much indebted. [E. F.]

Much information has been gleaned from both these writers, and from the later history of Dr. Robinson (whose references in particular have been of great value). Where, however, their statements are at variance with other evidence, and the Editors have attempted to correct inaccuracies, or to remove obscurities; or where, what appeared redundant has been replaced by matter which they thought would be more generally interesting, they have endeavoured to steer between the two extremes, so aptly described by Hen. VIII. in proroguing Parliament on Christmas Eve, 1545.—"Some be too stiff in their "old mumpsimus, others be too busy and curious in their "new sumpsimus." (NOTE.) Whatever may be the defects of their unpretending production, it will be a gratification to them and to the Subscribers, to know that its original object has succeeded far beyond their expectations, and that a sum of nearly one hundred pounds will be realized, which it is intended to invest for the widow of Mr. Tuff, on whose behalf it was undertaken.

No probable sale could have defrayed the cost of the engravings, so skilfully executed by Mr. Pearson,—many of them have been contributed free of expense by different subscribers;—for the interesting illustrations of the New River, the Editors are indebted to the liberality of Mr. Smiles and Mr. Murray, of Albemarle Street, and for those of the Bohun and Tiptoft families to the London and Middlesex Archæological Society. It is a grateful duty to express their thanks to these donors, to the

different landed proprietors who have lent their title
deeds for examination (from which much curious informa-
mation has been obtained); to the officials of the British
Museum, whose courteous attention never fails to the
most troublesome enquirer; and lastly, to the "troops of
friends" who have done so much to encourage and assist
their faithful and obliged servants,

THE EDITORS.

---

NOTE.—The curious reader may be gratified to see this proverbial
allusion, (which has perhaps been more frequently quoted than
explained) traced to its source. The anecdote is first told by Sir
Richard Pace, Dean of St. Paul's, the friend and correspondent of
Erasmus, and Secretary of State. It occurs in a rare volume,
"Ricardi Pacei, invictissimi Regis Angliæ primarii secretarii, ejusque
"apud elvetios oratoris De Fructu qui ex doctrina percipitur Liber.
"In inclyta Basilea.—A.D. 1517." Where Pace speaking of the
hard usage to which the letter S had been subject, tells the story of
an ignorant English priest who had disused it for thirty years, and
during that time (in the office of the mass) had read *mumpsimus*
instead of *sumpsimus*, and when his error was pointed out to him by
a scholar, replied that he did not choose to change his own old
"mumpsimus" for *his* new "sumpsimus."

"Sane proba hæc mea ancilla [S] omnium literarum fuit infortu-
"natissima. Nam et quidam indoctus sacrificus Anglicus eam,
"possessione sua annis triginta expulit, nec puduit illum tam longo
"tempore *mumpsimus* legere loco *sumpsimus*. Et quum moneretur
"a docto, ut errorem emendaret, respondit se nolle mutare suum
"antiquum mumpsimus ipsius novo sumpsimus."—p. 80.

# HISTORY OF ENFIELD.

----

"I know each lane, and every alley green,
"Dingle, or bushy dell of forest wild;
"And every bosky bourn from side to side,
"My daily walks and ancient neighbourhood."

*Masque of Comus.*

----

THE parish of Enfield is situated about nine miles from London * and is bounded by Edmonton, East Barnet, Hadley, South Mimms, Northaw, and Cheshunt, and by the River Lea, which separates it from Waltham, in Essex. It contains 12653·096 acres, of which 223 are public roads, 122·5 water, and about 100 railways. It extends from east to west about 8½ miles, and 3¼ from north to south by the main road, but between 5 and 6 in other places.

Few districts in the vicinity of London retain so much of rural and sequestered character, owing no doubt in part to its formerly tedious and circuitous means of access.

----

* The old mile-stone,—opposite the Market-house,—was inscribed, "9 miles and a-half and 32 poles, from Shoreditch Church."

Since the opening of two new lines of railway however, this isolation cannot much longer continue. The beauty and variety of the scenery, the upland Chase, still so nobly timbered, and the more cultivated lowlands, watered for many a mile by the windings of the New River and the Lea; and the long-sustained character of the parish for health and longevity (rating the second in England) are drawing the attention of the country-loving public, to this picturesque and interesting neighbourhood.

From the more elevated situations, extensive prospects may be obtained in all directions over the adjoining counties; from Camlet-moat, and from the Ridgeway-road, across the broad expanse of the Chase; far down into Hertfordshire, from the wood at Forty Hall; and away into the heart of Buckinghamshire, from above Potter's-bar; and the long range of Epping and Hainault forests from everywhere.

The bridle-road across Hadley-common, perhaps the last remains of genuine forest scenery in Middlesex, leads to the highest ground in the parish, whence looking south, distant gleams of the Thames and the white sails of its shipping may be seen in the far horizon.

Norden (MS. Harl. 370) describes it as "a parish standing on the edge of the Chace, of such extent that if it were measured by the ring it would be found at least 20 miles in extent, some time parcell of the Duke of Lancaster's lands—now Queen Elizabeth's. The Chace, called Enfield Chace, taketh its name of this place." To this he

uncivilly adds, "It is called of some Enfen, and so
" recorded in regarde of the fenny scytuation of some
" parte thereof, upon the marshes or meerish ground,
" which, though now brought to be good meadow and
" profitable pasture, it hath in time past been fenny."

This statement, however, is not supported by any
authority. The termination " field," is the past participle
of the-verb fællan, to fell, and opposed to woodland,
as land where the trees have been cleared. Domesday
Book calls it Enefelde, and the variations in subsequent
records are very trifling,—Endfield, Enfeld, Enefield,
and Enfield, and less frequently Envild.

This place formerly conferred the title of Baron, on
the Earl of Rochfort, whose ancestor, the first Earl,
married Joan, daughter of Sir Henry Wroth, of Durants,
and was created Baron of Enfield by William III. in
1695. It now gives the title of Viscount to the Earl
of Strafford, whose son and heir is M.P. for Middlesex.

The parish is included within the "Hundred" of
Edmonton, a division which originated in the old military
constitution, the name being given to a district which
chose one hundred men for counsel and defence, though
it is stated by Tacitus that the number did not always
correspond with the name. The meetings of the hundred
were held monthly, "quum aut inchoatur luna aut
"impletur." Every free member of the community
above twelve years old was bound to enrol himself in a
hundred, which should be surety for him, and in case of

an accusation, should bring him to justice. The leader of the men of the hundred was called the "comes stabuli," since degenerated into that subordinate police officer the *constable*.

The administration of justice was also in the hundred, the finding a verdict being entrusted to a committee of twelve of the principal thanes. The decision of two-thirds of this jury was a valid one, those outvoted being *subject to a pecuniary mulct*.

## DIVISIONS OF THE PARISH.

The parish is divided into four quarters, viz.—the Town, Chase, Bull's Cross;—and Green Street and Ponder's End.

*Town Division.*—Enfield Old-park, London-road, Essex-road, Sydney-road, Raleigh-road, Cecil-road, Church-street, Enfield-town, Silver-street, Nag's-head-lane, Baker-street, Clay-hill, Parsonage-lane, and the east side of Chase-side.

*Chase Division.*—Windmill-hill, the west side of Chase-side, and the whole of Enfield-chase.

*Bull's Cross Division.*—Forty-hill, Bull's-cross, Turkey-street, Enfield-wash, Lock-lane, the Lock, Freezywater, White-webbs, and Crew's-hill.

*Green Street and Ponder's End Division.*—Green-street, Enfield-highway, and Ponder's-end.

It appears by the minute book of the Vestry, 1691 (the earliest one preserved) that there were then, and for several years subsequently, four Churchwardens and four Overseers for four quarters, viz.: "Enfield *Green*," now "the Town" quarter, Bull's-cross quarter, Green-street quarter, and Ponder's-end quarter; and five Surveyors, for Enfield-green, Parsonage-ward, Bull's-cross, Green-street, and Ponder's-end respectively. In 1703, one Churchwarden served for Green-street, Ponder's-end, and Bull's-cross. From that time, Green-street and Ponder's-end seem to have been permanently united for Church-wardens;—but not for Overseers, till 1710.

## PRIVILEGES AND EXEMPTIONS.

There is a singular document in existence, with reference to Fairs and Markets. There was originally a grant by Richard II., and subsequently confirmed by Henry IV. and VI., and other Monarchs, down to George III., a copy of which can be had on application to the Steward of the Duchy of Lancaster, which exempts the inhabitants of Enfield from toll, pannage, passage, lastage, tallage, tollage, carriage, pesage, picage, and terrage, for their goods, wares, and merchandizes, in all fairs, markets, villages, and other places throughout England, (out of the Duchy of Lancaster, in the County of Middlesex.) It is stated, however, that this exemption has been resisted in Covent-garden and Whitechapel markets.

There was also a charter of exemption from arrest, granted by Richard I., but it has not been acted upon for many years, and is now considered obsolete.

An exemption from toll at Warebridge was also granted to the inhabitants of Enfield by Queen Elizabeth, and subsequently confirmed by George III. All these charters are preserved among the parish records.

# MANORS, COURTS-LEET, COURTS-BARON, &c.

" Out of monuments, names, words, proverbs, traditions, private
" recordes and evidences, fragments of stories, passages of bookes,
"and the like, we doe save and recover somewhat from the deluge
" of time."

*Bacon—Advancement of Learning,—Book II.*

———

The following is a list of the Manors for which Courts-
leet and Courts-baron are held on particular days, for the
purpose of settling all fines, heriots, services, reliefs,
profits, perquisites of courts, waters, waste grounds,
fisheries, royalties, liberties, franchises, &c., viz.—

The Manor of Enfield.

The Manor of Durants, or Durant's Harbour.

The Manor of Elsynge, alias Norris, or North Farm.

The Manor of Suffolks.

The Manor of Honylands and Pentriches, alias Capels.

The Manor of Goldbeaters.

The Manor of Worcesters,—and

The Rectory Manor.

———

Of these Manors the most important are those of Enfield and of Worcesters, both of which were formerly in the possession of the Crown, each having its own park and palace.

It is material that this circumstance should be distinctly pointed out, as it has led to some confusion in the statements of both Gough and Lysons, which have been copied by Dr. Robinson and all subsequent writers. The Manor-house of Worcesters, was Elsynge-hall, alias Enfield-house;—this was built by the Earl of Worcester in the 15th century, and enlarged by his nephew, Sir Thomas Lovell, after which, it was sometimes known by the name of Lovell-place. This was the royal residence of Edward VI., of Queen Mary, and Queen Elizabeth, and was pulled down in the time of Charles II.

"The palace," as it is still called, and a part of which yet remains, was the Manor-house of Enfield, and appears to have been built by Edward VI. at the time when he gave the Manor to his sister Elizabeth, who resided here whilst Princess, but held her court at Elsynge-hall, after she came to the throne. Norden records with exultation, "the stately and most princely pallaces of Queene "Elizabeth," and speaks of "Hir Majesties parkes "exceeding all the kingdome of Fraunce, (if the discourse "be true betweene an Heraulde of England and a "Heraulde of France) where it is affirmed that there are "in all that region but two parkes,—in Mydlesex there "are ten of Her Majesties,—Enfield parkes two."

## MANOR OF ENFIELD.

In the reign of Edward the Confessor, the Manor of Enfield belonged to Asgar, Master of the Horse. When the survey of Domesday was taken, it was the property of Geoffrey de Magnaville, or Mandeville, a powerful Norman, who had accompanied William to England.

His son William de Mandeville, gave to the Priory of Hurley, in Berks, the tithe of nuts, "in parco suo de "Enfeld in frank-almoine," and to Trinity Priory, Aldgate, "XL carucates *bushii* per ann. in bosco de Enefeld. He married Margaret, daughter of Eudo Dapifer, (Steward to the Conqueror), by whom he had a son, Geoffrey, created Earl of Essex, by King Stephen.

"Circa hæc tempora ROBERTUS HUDUS et PARVUS "JOANNES, latrones famatissimi in nemoribus latuerunt - - "Latronum omnium humanissimus et princeps erat." [Majoris Britan. Histor.]

Dr. Stukely says, that "Robin Hood took to this wild "way of life, in imitation of his grandfather, Geoffrey de "Mandeville, who, being a favourer of Maude, Empress, " King Stephen took him prisoner at St. Albans, and "made him give up the tower of London, Walden, "Plessis, &c., after which he lived in plunder."

In resentment for this reduction of his power and influence, he committed (says Camden) the most violent ravages on the King and his party, and proceeding to seize and pillage Ramsey Abbey, was shortly afterwards mortally wounded at the Castle of Burwell, which he had laid siege to. He was carried off by some of the Knights Templars, who, putting him in the habit of their order, carried his corpse into their orchard at the Old Temple. But as he died under sentence of excommunication, they would not give him Christian burial, but wrapping him up in lead (canali plumbeo inclusum) hung him up on a crooked tree. At length the sentence was taken off by the application of the Prior of Walden, to the Pope, and the Templars buried the body obscurely in the porch before the west door.

This haughty baron inherited above one hundred Manors, with the constableship of the tower of London. The Monks of Walden have taken care to embalm the memory of their munificent founder, and though they acknowledge him to have committed the greatest outrages, he was with them one of the bravest and best of men. " Erat enim vir militaris ac Deo devotus, cujus cordis " arca virtutibus nunquam erat vacua." He married Roisia de Vere, daughter of the Earl of Oxford, by whom (according to Dr. Stukeley) William Fitzooth was brought up, and he marrying their daughter, Joanna, became the father of Robert Fitzooth, commonly known as Robin Hood.* The sons of Geoffrey de Mandeville dying

---

* The traditional bow of Robin Hood, (which is stated by Ritson to have been preserved with peculiar veneration) is in

without issue, the bulk of his possessions devolved to
Henry de Bohun, in right of his wife, Matilda, sole
daughter and heiress of Geoffery Fitz Piers, who was
himself, through his wife, Beatrice de Say, representative
and heir of the Mandevilles.   Henry de Bohun, constable
of England, was created Earl of Hereford, and was one
of the Barons of Runnymede.   He died in 1220, on his
voyage to the Holy Land, and was succeeded by his son
Humphrey, second Earl of Hereford, and Earl of Essex,
and distinguished by the title of " The Good."   By his
marriage with Maude, daughter of the Earl of Eu, in
Normandy, he had a son, Humphrey, who died before

---

possession of J. W. Ford, Esq., and would tax the strength of any
modern archer to string it—to say nothing of drawing it with "a
cloth-yard arrow " to the head.

Whatever exaggeration may attach to the stories of Robin Hood
shooting an arrow "a measured mile," there can be no doubt that
the distances reached by the old bowmen were far beyond anything
which modern skill or strength could approach.  Drayton says that
they used to shoot at marks full 800 yards, and the statute 33 Henry
VIII. cap. 9, made it penal for any one who had reached the age of
24, to shoot at any *less distance* than 220 yards.

Strutt mentions that at the end of the last century he was at a
meeting of the London Toxophilites, "in their ground near Bedford
Square," when the Turkish Ambassador, who was present, complained of the shortness of the enclosure, and going out into the
adjoining fields, he shot several arrows "more than double the
length of the archery ground," being above a quarter of a mile.

*Counter Seal of Humphrey de Bohun,*
*4th Earl of Hereford, and 3rd Earl of Essex.*

The principal shield in this seal bears azure—a bend argent—
cotised and between six lioncels or.  On either side is a small shield
charged with the arms of Mandeville, Earl of Essex— quarterly or.
and gules—from which arrangement the usage of quartering is said
to have been derived.

The de Bohun *swan* was a badge of the Mandevilles, who bore
this device, along with the Nevilles, in token of their descent from a
common ancestor Adam de Swanne, or Sweyn, a Dane.

Geoffrey Mandeville, Earl of Essex, was buried in the Temple
Church, where may be seen his effigy, with a shield, on which his
arms are sculptured—being the earliest instance known of a
monument with an armorial bearing.

*Gough's Sepulchral Monuments,—p.* 104, *Introd.*

his father, leaving a son, Humphrey, who married
Matilda, daughter of William de Fienles, and had one
son, Humphrey de Bohun, who, in 1302, married
Elizabeth Plantagenet, daughter of Edward I. The
eminent position of the Bohun family at this time is
apparent both from the alliance and the cause that led to
it, as set forth in an important document, which states,
that there having been great dissention between the King
and the Earl's father, the peace and tranquillity of the
realm might be secured by the proposed marriage·

*Counter Seal of John de Bohun,*
*5th Earl of Hereford, and 4th Earl of Essex.*

Shortly after this event, he surrendered all his honours and
lordships to the King, who granted them again to him
and his heirs.  His eldest son, John, succeeded him,
who married Alice, daughter of the Earl of Arundel, and
was succeeded by his brother Humphrey, who, in 1347
obtained the royal licence to fortify and embattle his
manor houses in Essex, Middlesex, Wilts, and Gloucester-
shire; of these ten castles, one was at Enfield.  His
nephew, Humphrey, was the eleventh and last who bore
that name.  He died in 1372, leaving two daughters,
Alianore and Mary de Bohun, the two most noble and
wealthy heiresses in the realm.  Alianore married
Thomas de Woodstock, seventh son of Edward III.,
Earl of Buckingham and Essex, afterwards Duke of
Gloucester, who was murdered at Calais by the command
of his nephew Richard II., in 1397.  "I was informed,"
(says Froissart) "that he was on the point of sitting down
"to dinner; when the table had been laid and he was
"about to wash his hands, four men rushed from an
"adjoining chamber, and throwing a towel round his
"neck, strangled him by two pulling at one end and two
" the other.  When he was quite dead they carried him
" to his bed and undressed him, placing him between two
"sheets, and covering him with a furred mantle,
" gave out that he had died of a fit of apoplexy."  His
unfortunate widow survived her husband for a period of
about two years, and was buried in St. Edmund's Chapel,
in Westminster Abbey, according to the directions of her

BRASS TO ALIANORE DE BOHUN, WESTMINSTER ABBEY, A.D. 1399.

will. The monumental brass upon her tomb, and that of Joice Lady Tiptoft, in Enfield Church, are among the best and most interesting specimens of these memorials, and will be more fully described hereafter.

After the death of Alianore,* in 1399, the Manor of Enfield was inherited by her sister Mary, who was married to Henry of Lancaster, the son of John of Gaunt, afterwards King Henry IV. The Manor thus vested in the crown was annexed to the Duchy of Lancaster, of which it still continues to be parcel.

The site of the original Manor-house of Enfield has been the subject of much antiquarian research. Camden says, that "almost in the middle of the Chase there are the ruins and rubbish of an ancient house which the common people from tradition affirm to have belonged to the Mandevilles, Earls of Essex." This site, called Camlet-moat, is a large quadrangular area, overgrown with briars and bushes. When measured in 1773, the length was 150 feet. At the north-east corner is a deep well, paved at the bottom, in which it is pretended lies an iron chest full of treasure, which cannot be drawn up to the top, and that the last owner to whom the Chase belonged being attained of treason, hid himself in a hollow tree, and falling into this well perished miserably. This tradition is probably a distorted version of the account

---

* This unfortunate Duchess is introduced by Shakespeare as one of the dramatis personæ in his Richard II.

of Geoffry de Mandeville, which has been given above. Mr. Lysons (whose attentive investigations were assisted by the late Mr. Gough) considers however that this spot was more probably the site of the principal lodge and the residence of the chief forester.* The tiles scattered over the area, the well and the traces of the enclosures and avenues, would seem to be rather the works of the 15th or 16th centuries than of any earlier period.

It appears from Dugdale's Baronage, and from MS. in the British Museum, that Humphrey de Bohun, Earl of Hereford, obtained in 1347, the King's license to fortify his Manor-house in Enfield, as mentioned in page 20, the words of the grant are, "mansum manerii de Enefelde muro et petra et calce firmare et kernellare,"—dated at Guildford, Dec. 22,—21 Edward III.

In a meadow to the east of the Church near Nag's-head-lane, there is an oblong area of 3⅕5 acres, (marked 1946, 1947 on the ordnance map) surrounded by a deep and wide moat with high embankments. The south side is 132 yards long, with a vallum 12 yards high, and the north side 160 yards long with the vallum 15 yards high, and 16 yards wide at the base. The east and west sides are 135 yards long, the vallum on the west side showing an entrance in the middle, corresponding with another in

---

* It seems to be so indicated in a "sketch of the outlines of the Chase, 1658," in the centre of "the great square convenient for the deer to feed in." ·

the inner vallum, which is 40 yards long at the east and
west, and 96 yards at the north and south. The moat is
from 10 to 12 yards wide, except on the north, where
it is 32 yards wide. At the north-west corner is a
mount, indicating a small keep, and opposite to it on the
other side of the moat is a deep well. It is probable
that this moated place, which was included in some
demesne lands, might have been the site of Humphrey
de Bohun's castle, and that when the manorial residence
was removed it acquired the name of Oldbury, by which
it is still known.

From the records of the Duchy it appears that the
Manor of Enfield was leased to private individuals in the
early part of the 16th century, and that the lease reverted
to the crown at the latter end of Henry VIII.'s reign.
During this time the original Manor-house of Bohun
had fallen into decay, and the royal children were brought
up at Elsinge Hall (alias Enfield House) belonging to the
Manor of Worcesters.

At the death of King Henry VIII. his son Edward
was resident in the Castle of Hertford, and his daughter
Elizabeth at Enfield. The Earl of Hertford, the young
King's maternal uncle, accompanied by Sir Anthony
Browne, the Master of the Horse, undertook the charge
of conducting the new sovereign to the metropolis.
They repaired to Hertford Castle, and, without apprising
Edward of all that had occurred, removed him (probably
on Saturday, the 29th of January, 1547) to Elsynge Hall.

Here, in the presence of his sister, Edward was informed of
his father's death, and of his own accession to the crown.
On the following Monday he was conducted from Enfield
to the Tower of London.*

It was in the garden at Elsynge Hall that the Earl of
Hertford took the opportunity of communicating to his
companion, the Master of the Horse, *his intention to
assume the office of Protector*, in contravention to the late
King's will, which had designated eighteen executors
with equal powers.

We are told, that "after communication in discourse
of the state," Sir Anthony "gave his frank consent to the
proposal;" upon which, as we learn from a letter,† of

---

* In the State Paper Office is a letter from the Earl of Hertford
to the Council—"From Envild this Sunday night att xj of the
clok." He writes, "We intend the King's Matie. shal be a
horsbak to-morrow by xj. of the clok, so that bi iij. we trust His
Grace shal be att the Tower."

† "Myne old master, the master of th' orsses, albeit, as is
commonly known, he did much dissent from the proceedings in
matters of religion, yet was I long sins by himself right well assured
that he, commoning with my Lordes Grace *in the garden at Endfielde*,
at the King's Majesties cooming from Hartforde, gave his franke
consent, after communication in discourse of the state, that His
Grace should be Protector, thinking it (as indede it was) both the
surest kynde of government and most fyt for this commonwelth."—
*Letter of William Wightman to Cecill, Literary Remains of King
Edward VI. (printed for the Roxburghe Club, 1558) p. ccxlvii.*

"Remember what you promised me in the gallery at Westminster,
before the breath was out of the body of the King that dead is.
Remember what you promised immediately after, devising with me
concerning the place which you now occupy. I trust in the end to
good purpose, however things thwart now."—*(Letter of Paget to
the Protector Somerset.)*

SOLA SALVS SERVIRE DEO
SVNT CETERA FRAVDES

Paget's, Hertford had previously "devised" with Secretary Paget, who was now left at Court to arrange matters with the other counsellòrs.

Edward VI. did not again return to Enfield, and in 1552 he settled the Manor of Enfield on his sister Elizabeth,* at which time he probably built (or re-built on the site of a former structure) the house now known as "The Palace," for her use, as is shown by the initials E. R. on the walls and chimney pieces, and the words "benevolentia regis." Dr. Robinson erroneously states that it was "built in the reign of Henry VII., by Sir Thomas Lovell, *as one may gather from the arms*," citing Camden as his authority. The reference in Camden is clearly to Elsynge Hall, and Gough's edition explicitly says "the arms of Lovell do not appear on the Palace." Notwithstanding the great alterations it has undergone the interior still preserves some vestiges of its ancient magnificence, and a part of one of the large rooms on the ground floor remains nearly in its original state, with

---

* In April, 1557, "the Princess was escorted from Hatfield Hall, Hatfield House, to Enfield-chase, by a retinue of twelve ladies, in white satin, on ambling palfries, and twenty yeomen, in green, on horseback, that Her Grace might hunt the *hart*. On entering the Chase she was met by fifty archers, in scarlet boots and yellow caps, armed with gilded bows, each of whom presented her with a silver-headed arrow, winged with peacocks' feathers; and by way of closing the sports, the Princess was gratified with the privilege of *cutting the throat of a buck*."

its fine fretted pannels of oak and its ornamental ceiling
with pendants of four spreading leaves, and enrichments
of the crown, the rose, and the fleur de lis.  The chimney
piece is of stone beautifully cut and supported by Ionic
and Corinthian columns, decorated with foliage and birds,
and the rose and portcullis crowned;—with the arms of
England and France quarterly in a garter, and the royal
supporters, a lion and a dragon.

Below is the motto "Sola salvs servire Deo sunt
cætera fraudes." The letters E. R. are on this chimney
piece, and were formerly on each side of the wings of the
principal building.  The monogram is clearly that of
Edward VI., as the same room contains part of another
chimney piece which was removed from one of the upper
apartments, with nearly the same ornaments, and the
motto, " Vt ros svper herbam est benevolentia REGIS,"
alluding no doubt to the royal grant.  Several of the
ceilings in the upper rooms are decorated in a similar
manner to those below.

It appears that the Queen leased the Manor-house,
"the Palace," in the year 1582, to Henry Middlemore,
Esq., for fifty-one years, and that it did not revert to the
crown during her reign.

It was alienated in 1629, by Charles I., to Edward
Ditchfield, and others, trustees for the City of London,
who afterwards conveyed it to Sir Nicholas Raynton, and
it has ever since remained private property. Sir N.
Raynton let the house to Sir Thomas Trevor, one of the

VT · ROS · SVPER · HERBAM · ✚ ✚ · EST · BENEVOLENTIA · REGIS · ✚

L. M. Parker Sculpt.

Barons of the Exchequer, in whose tenure it seems to
have been from 1635, till his death in 1656. About the
year 1660, "the Palace" was let to Dr. Robert Uvedale,
Master of the Grammar School, who, being much
attached to the study of botany, had a large and curious
garden in which he cultivated a choice collection of
exotics. Among others he had a cedar, said to have
been brought in a portmanteau from Lebanon, by one of
his pupils, and planted by himself, which has since
become much celebrated for its beauty and size, being
probably the largest in England, and but little inferior in
girth to the largest tree on Mount Lebanon.

It was destined to be cut down by the late Dr.
Callaway soon after he purchased the Palace,—the saw-
pit was actually prepared and the trench dug round it
ready for the axe, but at the earnest request of the late
Mr. Gough and Dr. Sherwen the tree was spared.
Although it has suffered much from storms and high
winds, it is still a magnificent tree, and forms a conspicuous object from many parts of Enfield.

In 1792 a great part of the original Palace was pulled
down, and several dwelling houses built upon the site.
It formerly consisted of a centre and two wings facing
the west, with bay windows and high gables. The wings
bore the arms of England, with supporters, and the letters
E. R., the same as on the chimney piece before mentioned.

After the death of Eliab Breton, the descendant of
Sir N. Raynton, this property was purchased by Daniel

Lister, Esq., in whose family it still remains. It was for many years in the tenantcy of the late Dr. May, as a first class boarding school, and it still retains all its deserved reputation under its present accomplished master, W. Nutter Barker, B.A., F.R.A.S.

In the time of Edward the Confessor, the Manor of Enfield was valued at £50, and bore the same value in the survey of Domesday. In the reign of Edward I. (1303) it was valued at only £34 3s. 1d. In that of Edward III. (1337) its extent and value are thus described:—" A capital messuage, 13s. 4d.; a garden of herbs, 5s.; a dove house, 5s.; four hundred and twenty acres of arable in demesne, sixpence an acre; sixty-three acres of meadow, 3s.; and thirty-nine other acres of meadow, one shilling only; twenty-four acres of pasture, 3s.; a park called " The Frith," or Old Park, whence twenty acres of underwood, worth 3s. an acre might be sold annually; another called the Great Park, or Chase, which was of common pasture and no underwood, worth 50s. per annum. There were fish ponds also,* whence fish might be sold every seventh year to the amount of 15 marks."

To this Manor belongs a view of frankpledge; courts leet and baron are held in Whitsun-week, and on

---

* Old Pond, New Pond, Sloper's Pond, Ranmey Reach Pond, and Monkey Mead Pond, all long since drained and filled up.

November 5th, when a constable and two headboroughs
are chosen for the town quarter, with a brander and
aleconner; a constable, headborough, and brander, for
Bull's-cross quarter; and two headboroughs, a brander,
and a hayward for Green-street. The annual fines did
not exceed £16. The Court Rolls were burnt by
accident many years ago, and the present books begin
in 1705.

The value of the fee simple of these quit rents was
deducted from the allotments under the Enclosure Act,
and their estates exonerated and for ever discharged,
from the 29th September, 1803.

---

### THE OLD PARK.

" In the early surveys of the Manor of Enfield, the
Old Park (so called in contradistinction from the Little
Park or New Park, near White-webbs) is sometimes
called the Frith,* and sometimes 'Parcus Intrinsecus,' or
the Home Park, to distinguished it from the Chase,
which was called 'Parcus Extrinsecus,' and sometimes
the Great Park."

" It was formerly the home park of the ancient
Manorial Palace of Enfield, at which the Princess

---

* FRITH is used by Chaucer for a wood, an open space among
woods.

Elizabeth resided.* The park, with 'the hop garden,' (designated on the Ordnance Map as Old Park Farm), and the 'warren,' was granted by Charles II. to George Monk, first Duke of Albemarle, in 1660. It was bequeathed by Christopher, the second Duke, together with the whole of his great estates, to his cousin and godson, Christopher Rawlinson, Esq., of Cark-hall, Lancashire, (son of Curwen Rawlinson, M.P. for Lancaster, who married Elizabeth, daughter of Nicholas Monk, Bishop of Hereford)—in the event of his surviving the Duchess. Her Grace being taken ill, Mr. Rawlinson was called to London, but was seized by the small-pox on the road, and died one month before the Duchess. He was buried in the north transept of St. Alban's Abbey, where a marble monument was erected to his memory. The property thus escheated to the Crown; it was again granted by King William III., in the first year of his reign, to the Earl of Rutland, and was sold in 1736 by Grace, Countess of Granville, to Samuel Clayton, Esq.,

---

· * To this time belongs an incident which is recorded by George Puttenham in his *Art of Poesie*, and which is "characteristic of the majesty of her thoughts as well as her actions." When she came to the crown, a knight who had behaved insolently to her when Lady Elizabeth, fell upon his knees and besought her pardon, expecting to be sent to the tower. "Do you not knowe" (she good-humouredly replied) "that we are descended of the lion, whose nature is not to harme or prey upon the mouse, or any other such smalle vermine."

ENFIELD-OLD-PARK, THE SEAT OF EDWARD FORD, ESQ. J.P.

for £7000, at which time it consisted of 230 acres, to which 33 acres were added by the Enclosure Act of 1777. In 1825, the mansion house and 200 acres were purchased by the late Mrs. Winchester Lewis, and a part was afterwards resold. It is now the property and residence of her son-in-law, Edward Ford, Esq., a descendant of the Rawlinson family. The house appears, from the survey of 1650, to have been then a Ranger's Lodge, at which time it was occupied by Mr. Crosby, and valued at £8 per annum, and from the remains of massive foundations in every direction, must have been of considerable extent; but the greater part of the original structure has long since been pulled down, and the remainder transformed into a comparatively modern residence.*

The park is richly wooded with oaks, the growth of centuries, from which three hundred and ninety-seven were selected and felled for the Navy, in the time of the Commonwealth.

The lawn, in front of the house, is mentioned by Camden as the site of an ancient Roman Oppidum, and is surrounded on three sides by a circular entrenchment, from which various interesting relics have, at different times, been obtained."

---

* There still remain in the Library the original open chimney and hearth, with fire dogs, and a curious old "reredos," with figures of the time of James I.

## CHASE PARK.

Chase Park, the residence of Mrs. Adams, was originally parcel of the Old Park. The former house which stood near the entrance lodge from Chase Green, was purchased of Mr. Clayton, in 1811, by Mr. Thomas Cotton, along with thirty-four acres of land, for £7027. In 1822, he sold it to the late Mr. Browning, who pulled it down and built the present mansion in its stead. Ten years afterwards Mr. Browning conveyed the estate to his son-in-law, William Carr, Esq., who had previously purchased of Mrs. Winchester Lewis, fifty-six acres of adjoining land, when the whole property was thrown together, and the present park laid out.

About the same time the New River Company, under a mutual agreement, formed the ornamental sheet of water in front of the house, on which the proprietor has the right of fishing and keeping a boat.*

In the year 1859, the estate, which then contained seventy-six acres, was purchased for £15000, by the late Francis Bryant Adams, Esq., the husband of the present owner.

---

* The New River Company having failed in procuring powers from Parliament to construct a drain to divert the surface water of the adjoining lands, for which the parochial authorities had refused permission, obtained leave from Mr. Carr to take the drain through his estate, which was done at a cost of £2000, the lake being excavated by the Company in return for the permission granted to them.

CHASE-PARK, THE SEAT OF MRS. ADAMS.

## CHASE SIDE HOUSE.

The estate of Chase Side House was originally a part of the Old Park, which formerly extended as far as Enfield, and included " the Palace," with its gardens and curtilage. After these had been alienated by the Crown in the year 1629, parts of the freehold adjoining the street were sold for building purposes to various individuals.

This part of the town was then known by the name of " Enfield Green," (the present Green being at that time unenclosed chace), and within this century several trees were still standing, marking the former boundary of the Old Park. The last of these, a noble old elm, stood in the middle of the open space at the top of the town. It was greatly injured by a bonfire on the 5th of November, 1836, and finally blown down by the great hurricane on the 29th of the same month.

Amongst the oldest of those houses which can be now identified, was the George Inn,* originally a private dwelling house, and a house marked upon the old map of 1658, where Chase Side House now stands, which was possibly that of Sir Robert Jason, who had " a mansion at Enfield Green, in 1686."

This house was bought in 1826 by the late Mr. Steadman, who afterwards purchased an additional

---

* The title-deeds of Mr. Mathison comprise the original conveyance of this house from Edward Heath to Thos. Taylor, in 1666.

quantity of land, lying within the bend of the New
River, from the late Mr. Clayton, and subsequently he
re-built a great part of the house as it now stands,
removing the wrought iron gates and the piers, with their
fine floriated vases of cast lead, from the front facing the
road, and placing them within the grounds as an entrance
to the walled garden.

Mr. Steadman's widow, afterwards so well known as
Mrs. Everett for her hospitality and beneficence, and for
the liberality with which the beautiful grounds were
constantly thrown open whenever they could contribute
to the public benefit or amusement, died 1865, and the
property was purchased in 1867, by Phillip Twells, Esq.,
M.A., the present proprietor.

The estate consists of thirty-five acres within a ring
fence.

A young oak in these grounds has an interesting history,
which is worth recording. General Pallisier had sent
over some acorns from Algiers to Louis Philippe, by whom
they were presented to the Queen, and Her Majesty
distributed several to different ladies about the Court.
One of these was given by Miss Skerrett to Mrs. Everett,
who planted it on the lawn, where it has reached a height
of twenty feet, the stem being a foot in diameter, and the
spread of the branches eighteen feet. The leaf, which
somewhat resembles that of the beech, remains on the
tree till May, when the young leaves appear, thus giving
it all the advantages of an evergreen.

CBS. ... ESQ. PY SEAT OF PHILIP T... ES. ESQ. J.P.

# ENFIELD CHASE.

"next Enfield—
"A Forrest for her pride, though titled but a Chace,
"Her Purlewes, and her Parks, her circuit full as large
"As some perhaps whose state requires a greater charge,
"Whose Holts that view the East, do wistly stand to look
"Upon the winding course of Lee's delightful Brook."

*Drayton's Polyolbion—16th Song.*

On the north side of Enfield Town there is an extensive tract of land called Enfield Chase, anciently in the possession of the Mandevilles, and afterwards of the Bohuns, their successors, but now belonging to the Duchy of Lancaster, since the marriage of Henry IV. to Mary, daughter and ultimate heiress of Humphrey de Bohun.

Enfield Chase first occurs under that name in the reign of Edward II., previously to which it was generally called the "Great Park,"—"parcus extrinsecus," or the outer park. It extends into several adjoining parishes, and is supposed by Lord Lyttleton to have been a tract of the ancient forest of Middlesex.

The Chase, together with the Manor of Enfield, was given by Richard III. in 1483, to Stafford, Duke of Buckingham, as a reward for his services in raising him to the crown; but it is doubtful whether he ever took possession, as he soon conspired, with the Bishop of Ely, to dethrone the King, and being betrayed by his own servants, he was taken to Salisbury and beheaded in the Market-place, without any arraignment or trial.

The Chase remained in the possession of the sovereign till the death of Charles I., when it was seized by the Commonwealth as public property, and by an order of the House of .Commons, was surveyed in the year 1650, when it was reported to contain 7,900 acres, and its value £4,742 8s. per annum. . At this time there was an abundant quantity of deer, which were valued at £150. The oak timber (exclusive of 2,500 marked for the use of the navy) was valued at £2,100. The horn-beam and other wood at £12,100.

In November, 1652, it was resolved, " that Enfield Chase should be sold for ready money;" pursuant to which resolution it was divided into parcels, which were sold to various purchasers, and a considerable part was inclosed, and several houses built. The proposed division, according to the plan made in 1650, called " *Oliver Cromwell's Division;*" was as follows:—

| | A. | R. | P. |
|---|---|---|---|
| To persons entitled to common rights in the Parish of Enfield, and Enfield Old Park ... ... ... ... ... | 1329 | 2 | 0 |
| To ditto of Edmonton ... ... ... | 917 | 0 | 0 |
| To ditto of Hadley ... ... ... | 240 | 0 | 0 |
| To ditto of South Mimms and Old Fold Farm ... ... ... ... ... | 913 | 0 | 0 |
| Total Allotment to the Commoners ... | 3399 | 2 | 0 |
| Roads over His Majesty's Allotment ... | 140 | 0 | 0 |
| The remainder to the King ... ... | 4360 | 0 | 0 |
| The whole contents of the Chase... ... | 7899 | 2 | 0 |

Much discontent was excited among those who claimed
the right of common which caused "divers riots and
unlawful assemblies," and also "manslaughter and other
outrages." These were suppressed under an order of the
House of Commons (July 18th, 1659,) by the Sheriff and
Magistrates, " all military officers and forces whatsoever
" being required to aid and assist the said Sheriff and
" Magistrates." Four files of foot being sent against the
insurgents were so far from being able to suppress them,
that they seized ten soldiers and made them prisoners, on
which " Mr. Sheriff Bateman, according to order of
" Parliament, went down, attended by some troops of
" horse in a readiness, when quiet was at last restored."

In the Bodleian Library, Oxford, there may be found
an original survey of the Chase, intituled, "A Description
" of Enfield Chase, situate in the Parish of Enfield, and
" County of Middlesex, as the same is now divided
" between the Commonwealth and the Commons, by
" Edmund Rolfe and Nicholas Gunter, in the year 1658."*
It was on a thick parchment, with rollers. There are
some seats mentioned in this survey, with the names of,
their possessors at that time, viz.—Captain Nelthorp's.
(called the West Lodge), Captain Dauge's (called the
East Lodge), and Captain Kempe's (called the South

---

* A duplicate, or probably the original, of this document, much
decayed and obliterated by age and damp, is in the possession of
the Vestry Clerk.

Lodge). Adjoining the Chase, on the south, were the seats of Captains Colvill, Malyn, Spinage, Blake, and Gladman. On the east, Forty House, one mile from Enfield, the seat of the Wolstenholme and Breton families ; and adjoining the Edmonton allotment, the seats of William Allton, Esq., Mr. Megg, and Edmund Peeke, Esq. (called Belmont), and Sir William Ashurst's, near South Mimms allotment, the seat of Colonel Web.

The following is a schedule of the division marked on this map, with the quantity of land contained in each.

| | A. | R. | P. | | A. | R. | P. |
|---|---|---|---|---|---|---|---|
| Greene Oak Plane | 126 | 0 | 0 | The Great Scoots | 109 | 1 | 0 |
| Faire Feedings ... | 131 | 1 | 0 | The Little Scoots... | 26 | 3 | 0 |
| Great Monkey Mead | 101 | 2 | 0 | East Camelot ... | 86 | 1 | 0 |
| Long Hill... ... | 95 | 1 | 3 | Noddin's Well Hill | 88 | 3 | 0 |
| Great Broad Slade | 99 | 3 | 0 | Leezing Beech ... | 103 | 2 | 0 |
| Little Broad Slade | 24 | 2 | 0 | Horsey Plane ... | 149 | 0 | 0 |
| Little Monkey Mead | 34 | 2 | 0 | Marke Plane ... | 138 | 3 | 0 |
| High Beech ... | 43 | 2 | 0 | Capt. Coville's ... | 6 | 3 | 0 |
| On South Mimms | | | | Merry Hill ... | 67 | 2 | 0 |
| Common ... | 17 | 2 | 0 | Red Clay ... ... | 65 | 2 | 0 |
| New Pond Plane.. | 138 | 3 | 0 | Matthew's Plane | 95 | 2 | 0 |
| Fenny Slade ... | 80 | 2 | 0 | Matthew's Breake | 71 | 2 | 0 |
| Plumridge Hill ... | 172 | 0 | 0 | South Coney Burrow | 62 | 0 | 0 |
| Faire Thorne ... | 131 | 0 | 0 | Great Hooks Hill | 117 | 0 | 0 |
| North Camelot ... | 80 | 0 | 0 | Little Hooks Hill | 65 | 3 | 0 |
| West Camelot | 110 | 3 | 0 | Mote Plane ... | 109 | 2 | 0 |
| Camelot Hill | 115 | 3 | 0 | Hart Green ... | 56 | 1 | 0 |

| | | | | | | | |
|---|---|---|---|---|---|---|---|
| West Barvin* | ... | 61 | 3 | 0 | Little Lodge Hill | 16 | 2 | 0 |
| South Barvin | ... | 97 | 2 | 0 | Den's Lawne ... | 6 | 3 | 0 |
| East Barvin | ... | 69 | 1 | 0 | Enfield Common | 1522 | 1 | 30, |
| Pond's Course | ... | 102 | 2 | 0 | Common of the | | | |
| Cow's Face | ... | 105 | 0 | 0 | Old Parke ... | 31 | 1 | 30 |
| Stroud Head | ... | 114 | 0 | 0 | Edmonton Com- | | | |
| North Coney | | | | | mon ... ... | 1224 | 2 | 15 |
| Burrow | ... | 74 | 0 | 0 | Hadley Common | 186 | 1 | 30 |
| Deep Slade | ... | 115 | 1 | 0 | Sir F. Allen's ... | 45 | 0 | 28 |
| Lodge Hill | ... | 86 | 2 | 0 | South Mims Com- | | | |
| Old Lawne | ... | 34 | 3 | 0 | mon ... ... | 1077 | 3 | 20 |

There was a survey of the Manor of Enfield in 1686,.
(deposited in the office of the Duchy of Lancaster),
which states that on a former perambulation, the Chase.
had been found to contain 7,600 acres, of which 500 had.
been since inclosed in Theobald's-park. This inclosure
was made by King James I.† while he resided at

---

* This word (erroneously printed "Baroin" in Robinson's
History) is the same as *burrow*, or *warren*, being the past participle
of **Perian** (protegere.)
"Foxis han borwin or dennes, and briddes of the eir han
"nestis, but mannes sone hath not where he shal reste his hede."—
[*Mattheu viii*, 20. *Wicliffe's translation*.]

† The King gave the Parish, for these 500 acres, the estate called
King James's Charity, at North Mimms, which was sold by the
Parish under the authority of a private Act of Parliament.—*See the
Account of the Charities*.

Theobald's.* At this time the Chase was abundantly
stocked with deer; but the army of the Parliament,
during the civil war, destroyed the game, cut down the
trees, and let the ground out into small farms. In this
state it continued until the restoration, when young trees
were planted, and the Chase was again stocked with
deer.

Upon one of the surveys it was presented that the fines
for the Manor of Enfield were certain, and not arbitrary.
Every heir paid, on his admittance, one year's quit-rent
as his fine for his copyhold, and every one admitted
upon surrender paid two years' quit-rent for his fine.

"There are no heriots belonging to this Manor, either
to freehold or copyhold lands; but every heir, upon
descent, paid to His Majesty, for a relief, one year's quit-
rent for his freehold land." There are no other rents

---

* In the year 1606 Sir Robert Cecil (who was the second son and
successor of his father, Lord Burleigh, in the possession of the manor
of Theobalds), entertained King James I. and Frederick III., King
of Denmark, there. "The King, having become enamoured of this
"place from its proximity to an extensive tract of open country favour-
"able to the diversion of hunting (his favourite amusement), he pre-
"vailed upon his Minister to exchange it with him for his Palace of
"Hatfield, in the County of Herts. The King, having obtained
"possession of this manor, enlarged the park by taking in part of
"adjoining Chase, and surrounded it with a wall of brick ten miles
"in circumference."—*Clutterbuck's Hertfordshire.*

and services except fealty and suit of court, and the following curious fine:—

" Item, of Henry Hunsdon, for two parcells of meadow in South marsh, whereof the one containeth three roods, and the other half an acre, both of them abutting south upon the demesnes of the mannour of Worcesters, called the nine acres, sometime John Banks, — per annum. *A Red Rose at Midsummer.*"*

There was another survey of the Chase in 1698, when the Earl of Stamford was Chancellor of the Duchy, by Hugh Westlake, Esq., Surveyor of the Woods, in the south part of the Duchy, in order to a fall of timber, by which several new ridings were to be formed, and a square lawn of 300 acres for the deer to feed in. The money arising from the sale of this timber was for the King's use, who granted it to the Earl. In consequence of this, 261 acres of wood were to be cleared, for which one John Shelley contracted at £1,044, with bond and penalty £2,000.

The ridings marked out when the Chase was to be divided into farms at the time of the Commonwealth,

---

* Hatton Garden was held by Sir Charles Hatton, of the Bishop of Ely, by a similar tenure, of "*A Red Rose at Midsummer,*" the Bishop reserving to himself and his successors, the privilege of walking in the garden and gathering twenty bushels of roses yearly.

still distinguished by hedges and ditches, were* Cockfosters, and the Ridgeway from the gravel pits by East
Lodge to Ganna-corner.

In the year 1766 the largest oak on the Chase was
felled, which measured thirty feet long, and contained
three tons, or about two loads, reckoning a ton and a
half to a load; the diameter of the butt end was three
feet.   It was sold for £10.

In the year 1777, an Act of Parliament passed for
dividing the Chase, intituled, "An Act for dividing the
Chase of Enfield, in the County of Middlesex, and other
purposes therein mentioned," and assigning allotments to
such parishes and individuals as claimed right of common
which rights were in the survey of 1650 thus defined:—
*herbage, mastage for swine, green boughs to garnish horses,
thorns for fences, and crabs and acorns gathered under trees.*

Upon this occasion an accurate survey was made by
order of Thomas, Earl of Clarendon, Chancellor of His
Majesty's Duchy of Lancaster, intituled, "A survey and
admeasurement of Enfield Chase, shewing the boundaries
thereof, and the lines and quantities of the allotments
assigned and set out to the several parishes and estates

---

* An obliging antiquarian correspondent writes, that the
name of "Cock Fosters" is a corruption of Bicoque Forestier—
Bicoque (bi-kok) petite ville de peu de consideration, petite maison,
—a hut, a hovel.—Vile oppidulum.   "Bicoque—a little paltry
"town," &c.—(Cotgrave.)

in lieu of their respective rights; with the roads directed
to be made on the division of the said Chase, made and
taken in obedience to an order of the Right Honourable
Thomas Earl of Clarendon, Chancellor of His Majesty's
Duchy of Lancaster, in the months of August and
September, 1776, by F. Russell, His Majesty's Surveyor
General of the south parts of the said Duchy, and Richard
Richardson, Land Surveyor, his deputy, and since
corrected, according to the Act of Parliament of the
seventeenth year of King George III. for the division of
the said Chase;" when the Chase was found to
contain, including the roads, lodges, and encroachments, 8,349 acres, 1 rood, and 30 perches, or thereabouts, which were divided and allotted in the
following manner:—

To the King, 3,218 acres, 2 roods, 20 perches; to the
Lodges, 313 acres, 3 perches; to be enfranchised, 6 acres,
2 roods, 1 perch; to the Tithe-owners, 519 acres,
32 perches; to the Manor of Old-fold, 36 acres, 3 roods,
24 perches; to the Proprietors of the Old Park, 30 acres,
15 perches; to the Parish of South Mimms, 1,026 acres,
3 perches; to the Parish of Hadley, 240 acres; to the
Parish of Edmonton, 1,231 acres, 2 roods, 6 perches; to
the Parish of Enfield, 1,732 acres, 2 roods, 6 perches.
The greater part of this allotment, viz., 1,530 acres,
remained as waste land until 1801, when the inclosure
took place, over which the inhabitants had right of
common. 200 acres of the 1,732 acres, 2 roods,

6 perches, were cultivated, and on an average, in 1795, were worth 30s. an acre, but let out on lease for ninety-nine years, at 35s. an acre, in 1778, producing £333 14s. 8d. per ann. One-half of the produce was appropriated in aid of the quota to the Land-tax, the other to the reduction of the Poor-rates, and these 200 acres were tithe-free.

The calculations for Tithes were as follow :—

|  | A. | R. | P. |
|---|---|---|---|
| The Chase contained . . . 8036 | 8036 | 1 | 27 |
| The Lodges . . . . . 313 | 313 | 0 | 3 |
| Total, including roads . . 8349 | 8349 | 1 | 30 |

|  | A. | R. | P. |  | | |
|---|---|---|---|---|---|---|
| Titheable part of Enfield allotment . . . | 1532 | 2 | 6 | | | |
| Edmonton ditto . . | 1231 | 2 | 6 | | | |
| Hadley ditto . . . | 240 | 0 | 0 | | | |
| Roads on the residue . | 153 | 1 | 8 | | | |
|  |  |  |  | 3157 | 1 | 20 |

To be clear of tithes . . . 5192 0 10

One-tenth of which for tithe is . . . 519 0 32

The allotments to Hadley, South Mimms (to which the Manor of Old-fold belongs), and Edmonton, were annexed by the Act to those parishes, which left 5,824 acres in the Parish of Enfield, and made the whole extent of this parish to be about 12,254 acres ; and at the time this survey was made, the greater part of the Chase was covered with wood.

The officers belonging to the Chase were, "the Chancellor of the Duchy of Lancaster ; a Master of the Game, Forester, Ranger, Keepers, Woodward, Steward, Bailiff, Verderers (who were annually chosen in the King's Court of the Manor of Enfield, a sort of Supervisor of the Wood), Receiver-General of the Duchy of Lancaster) Auditor of ditto, Attorney-General of ditto, Clerk of the Revenues of ditto."

The joint offices of ranger, forester, keeper of the lodges, master of the game, and chief steward of the manor, having been vested successively in the persons of John Dudley, Earl of Warwick, Sir Thomas Wroth, John Ashley, Esq., Robert Lord Cecil, William Earl of Salisbury, Charles Viscount Cranbourne, Charles Lord Gerard of Brandon, George Villiers (the younger), Duke of Buckingham, the Right Hon. Henry Coventry, and Adam Loftus, Viscount Lisburne, were, in the year 1694, granted to Sir Robert Howard for fifty-six years, who, the same year, assigned all his right in the grant to Sir William Scawen, of Carshalton, for £1,245.

When the Chase was ordered to be sold by the Parliament, during the interregnum, the sum of £1,051 1s. 8d. was ordered to be paid to the Earl of Salisbury, who then held the above offices, for his interest therein, and in the custody of the parks,* which claims were allowed on the 25th of December, 1651, by the House of Commons.

---

*See Journals of the House of Commons.

In the year 1714 James Bridges (afterwards Duke of Chandos), purchased the above offices for the unexpired term, and they were afterwards vested in the Marquis of Buckingham, in right of his wife, who was the daughter and sole heir of the late Duke of Chandos.

The whole district, called Enfield Chase, was dis-chased from the 1st of January, 1779.

The form of the Chase was very irregular—its north and longest side was nearly straight, as was also its west side ; its south and east sides were full of angles ; its greatest length was about four miles and a half from east to west, that is, from Parsonage-lane to Ganna-corner ; from north to south, from Cattle-gate to Southgate, about four miles. Its shortest length, from east to west, that is, from Potter's-bar to Hadley-town, two miles and three-quarters. On the north side it abuts on Northaw-common, with which it communicates by Cattle-gate, Stock-gate, Cooper's-lane, and Potter's-bar. On the east it adjoins Enfield parish, its outlets to which are White-webbs, Clay-hill, Cocker, or Crook-lane, New-lane, Parsonage-lane, and Enfield-green, or the Town ; on this side also it extends into Edmonton parish, communicating with it by Winchmore-hill and Southgate.

On the west side it runs up to the north road, on the edge of which stands Hadley, and part of the Chase hereabouts, under the name of Gladmore-heath, or Monken-mead-plane, was, in 1471, the scene of a decisive battle, commonly called " the Battle of Barnet," between

the houses of York and Lancaster. Although this battle
has been generally considered to have been fought on
the road to Barnet, yet it seems pretty certain that it was
fought on that part of Enfield Chace formerly called
" Monken, or Monkey-mead," which was near Hadley
and South Mimms Common, and probably the armies
extended across the Barnet-road, from which circumstance, and the rebel army having marched directly
from Barnet to the scene of action, it derived the
name of the " Battle of Barnet," though it was
actually fought on Enfield Chace. Cannon were
used in this battle—" Bothe parties had goons and
" ordinaunce, but the Erle of Warwicke had many
" moo than the Kynge."—[*Fleetwood's M.S. printed by
the Camden Soc. p. 62*].

" In this battle the Erle of Warwyke and the Markes
" Montague were slain. The Duke of Excetre faugth
" manly, and was gretely despolede and woundede, and
" lefte naked for dede in the felde ; and so lay ther from
" vij. of clokke tille iiij. after none, which was taken up
" and brought to a house by a manne of his owne, and
" a leche brought to hym. After that the felde was don,
" Kynge Edwarde commanndyd bothe the erle of
" Warwike's body and the lord Markes' body to be putt
" into a cart, and the seide ij. bodyes to be layede in the
" Chyrche of Paulis on the pavement that every manne
" myghte see them, and so they lay iij. or iiij days."—
*The Warkworthe Chronicle ( Camden Soc).*

On the south and south-west, the Chace abuts upon Southgate and Barnet; the outlets to which are by Southgate and Bohun,* Bohon, or Bourngate. It is reported to have had four Lodges, though properly there were but three, that is to say, the East Bailey-lodge, the West Bailey-lodge, and the South Bailey-lodge; the last of which,

SOUTH LODGE,

is situated a mile and a-half west of Enfield Town, and was for some years the occasional residence of the Earl of Chatham, to whom it was bequeathed with a legacy of £10,000. Some parts of the grounds are said to have been planted by his own hand. A story is told of his desiring the owner of a windmill, which stood on a post at the top of the Windmill-hill, to paint that side next South Lodge at his expense. The miller did so, but when his Lordship on his next return from London looked out of the window and saw the mill unpainted, he sent for the miller to remonstrate with him, when the miller informed him that *the wind had changed*, but that he was quite ready to paint that side also on the same terms. The mill in question was pulled down many years ago, and the present one erected on its site. The enclosure annexed to this lodge in 1635, was stated to be sixty-five acres, two roods.

---

* Probably so called from Humphrey de Bohun.

## WEST LODGE.

West Lodge was pulled down and re-built by the late Archibald Paris, Esq., in 1832, the walls having given way several inches in one night. Evelyn thus writes of it, June, 1676:—"I went with my Lord Chamberlain to see "a garden at Enfield Town (probably Dr. Uvedale's), "thence to Mr. Sec. Coventry's Lodge on the Chase. It "is a very pretty place, the house commodious, the "gardens handsome, and our entertainment very free. "That which I most wondered at was, that in the compass "of twenty-five miles, yet within fourteen of London "there is not an house, barne, churche, or building, "besides three lodges. To this lodge are three great "ponds, and some few enclosures, the rest a solitarie "desert, yet stored with not lesse than 3,000 deer. "These are pretty retreats for gentlemen, especially for "those who are studious and lovers of privacy."— *(Evelyn's Diary, p.* 419.*)*

## EAST LODGE.

East Lodge is described in the survey of 1650, as a brick building, covered with tiles, and was occasionally used by Charles I. as a hunting seat. At the time of the Commonwealth it was sold to John Nelthrope, Adjutant-General, and towards the end of last century it was occupied by Alexander Wedderburne, who succeeded Lord Thurlow as Chancellor, and was created Earl of

D

Rosslyn. It was afterwards, for many years, the residence of the Elphinstones. The house was pulled down and rebuilt by G. J. Graham, Esq., the present occupant. The enclosure annexed to this lodge in 1686, was thirty-eight acres.

The Chase was formerly considered to have been a sheep-walk, belonging to the family of Coningsby, of Wales, one of whom having been complained against for having too many sheep, brought up a parcel of goats, which did great damage. This circumstance it seems gave rise to the right of sheep-walk on the Chase, annexed to certain farms in its neighbourhood, for a certain time of the year. Norden says, "there ariseth a "profit unto the poore inhabitants there, by the use of " the Chase, where they have common of pasture for all " kinde of cattle, pannage, and wood;" but the Parish, it seems, thought otherwise, finding itself over-burthened by numerous and disorderly poor, who availed themselves of the privilege of the Chase to support dissolute lives of idleness and beggary. The deer were stolen and exposed for sale with the greatest audacity; venison could be purchased cheaper than mutton; the poachers were sometimes transported, but at the expiration of their time returned to their old habits.*

---

* Nov. 1, 1762.—John Batt, of Potter's Bar, was committed to Bridewell, for cutting young beech trees on the Chase, and carrying them away in a cart. He was sentenced to be publicly whipped in

The Parish was entitled, under the Inclosing Act of
1777, to a certain portion of the Chase, amounting "to
1,732 acres, 2 roods, and 6 perches, together with the
encroachments, timber trees, and other trees, tellers and
sapplings thereon," which were vested in the Churchwardens, for the time being, and their successors, in trust,
for the sole benefit of the owners and proprietors of
freehold and copyhold messuages, lands and tenements,
within the Parish; their heirs and assigns, and their
lessees, tenants, and undertenants, for the time being
entitled to right of common or other rights within the
Chase, according to their several estates and interests
therein. In 1801 they obtained "an Act for dividing
" and inclosing the open and common fields, common
" marshes, and lammas grounds, Chase allotment, and
" other commonable and waste lands within the Parish,"

---

the market place, at Enfield, once every month during his imprisonment.—(*Gent. Mag.*)

"On Wednesday, the 14, a woman, an old offender, was conveyed
" in a cart from Bridewell to Enfield, and publicly whipped at the
" cart's tail by the common hangman, for cutting down and
" destroying wood in Enfield Chase. She is to undergo the same
" discipline twice more."—(*Public Ledger*, 1764.)

As late as 1810, a public house, kept by one Brocksop, stood
on the site of Mr. Logsden's coach factory, which had been the
recognised depôt for venison, for those who made no enquiries,
according to the old forest adage,

" Non inquirendum est, unde venit venison."

(41 Geo. III. 1801); and the same have been divided
and allotted accordingly, among the tithe owners, lords
of manor, and proprietors of freehold and copyhold
lands, and others entitled thereto.

At the present time it is nearly all inclosed, and but
little of its original appearance remains to arrest the
attention. The deer from the Chase, which were very
numerous, were taken to the estate of the Earl of Bute,
at Luton-park, Bedfordshire.*

The "Ancient Chase," has been converted into tillage,
so that almost all traces of its ancient state have
disappeared under the axe and plough. The first
attempts to improve it after the division, were, in
general, unsuccessful, and it was not until a large amount
of capital and labour was expended, that any great
progress began to be made in its cultivation; the great
obstacles at first were, the expence of clearing away the
wood, which, at the time of the enclosure, bore (oak
excepted) a very low price, and the poverty of the soil,
which was mostly a thin gravel intermixed with clay.
The methods adopted were draining, paring, burning,
and manuring with marle, which has been found in great
abundance and of a fine quality.

At the time of this enclosure, a large portion of the

---

* The last red deer killed on Enfield-chase, was shot by William
Mellish, Esq., M.P., and its horns are in the possession of
E. Ford, Esq.

TRENT-PARK, THE SEAT OF R. C. L. BEVAN, ESQ. J.P.

Chase remained in Woodland, a rude yet beautiful district, browsed by deer and suited to the pastimes of its former possessors.

The neighbourhood lost much of its picturesque attraction when the enclosure took place, but a sylvan wild of this extent situated in the vicinity of the metropolis was a dangerous source of mischief.

While the moral benefit derived from the change can scarcely be doubted, the advantages in an agricultural point of view are unquestionable. Perhaps the only parts of the Chase now remaining, are at Hadley-common, the "Rough Lot," at Trent Park, and Winchmore-hill wood.

### TRENT PARK.

Trent Park, the seat of R. C. L. Bevan, Esq., was formerly the residence of Sir Richard Jebb, Bart., to whom George III. granted a lease of 200 acres, of which he afterwards purchased the freehold. On conferring the dignity of baronet on Dr. Jebb, His Majesty gave the estate the name of Trent Place, in commemoration of the great medical skill by which the life of his brother had been preserved in his severe illness at Trent in the south Tyrol.* The estate, which consists of above a

---

* Before the decease of Sir Edward Wilmot, physician in ordinary to His Majesty, George III. being indisposed, ordered Dr. Jebb to be sent for, and being informed that it was etiquette to send for the physician in ordinary, he replied, "don't tell me of your ordinary or "extraordinary, I will have Jebb,"—and this confidence Sir Richard ever afterwards enjoyed.

thousand acres, covered with magnificent timber, the growth of centuries, gives -some idea of what Enfield Chase must have been in its primeval state.

The moated site of the reputed Manor House of Enfield,* before referred to, called Camlet Moat, is in this park. The scene is thus described by Sir Walter Scott, in "The Fortunes of Nigel :"

"The sun was high upon the glades of Enfield Chase, "and the deer with which it abounded were seen sporting "in picturesque groups among the ancient oaks of the "forest, when a cavalier and a lady sauntered slowly up "one of the long alleys which were cut through the park "for the convenience of the hunters. The place at "which he stopped was at that time a little more than "a mound, partly surrounded by a ditch, from which it "derived the name of Camlet Moat. A few hewn stones "were there, which had escaped the fate of many "others that had been used in building different lodges "in the forest for the royal keepers. These vèstiges "marked the ruins of the abode of a once illustrious "but long-forgotten family, the Mandevilles, Earls of "Essex, to whom Enfield Chase and the extensive "domains adjacent, had belonged in elder days. A wild

---

* The house is said (Gent. Mag., 1737, p. 643) to have cost Sir R. Jebb upwards of £19,000.

BEECH-HILL-PARK, THE SEAT OF CHARLES JACK, ESQ.

" woodland prospect led the eye at various points through
" broad and apparently interminable alleys, meeting at
" this point as from a common centre."

This moat is said also to have been the lurking place
of the notorious highwayman and robber, Dick Turpin,
whose grandfather, one Nott, kept " The Rose and
Crown," by the brook (Bull Beggar's-hole), Clay-hill.
The moat was distant but a few miles from the scene
of Turpin's exploits (Finchley-common), whence he
could easily conceal himself in such a place, in the then
wild state of Enfield Chase.

### BEECH HILL PARK.

Beech Hill Park, containing above 270 acres, was first
enclosed by Francis Russell, Esq., Secretary to the Duchy
of Lancaster, and the Board of Control for India. He
had the merit of first suggesting and drawing up the plan
for the enclosure of Enfield Chase, in recognition of
which, and his other services, he obtained a grant of this
beautifully situated estate, where he built the present
house, and surrounded it with extensive plantations.

After his death, September 1st, 1795, the property was
purchased by the late Archibald Paris, Esq., who added
greatly to its extent, and for some years farmed upwards
of 2000 acres on the Chase.  In 1841 it passed into the
hands of the late General Sir Edward Barnes, (G.C.B.
and M.P. for Sudbury), for some years Commander-in-

Chief in India, and Governor of Ceylon, and it was afterwards purchased by the present proprietor, Charles Jack, Esq. For many years after the enclosure, the land on the north side of Beech Hill retained much of its original character, but the last remnant of the old Chase woodland on this estate was cleared by Sir Edward Barnes, in 1845, and the timber sold to the Great Northern Railway, which was then constructing, for sleepers and fencing.

### CHASE LODGE.

Chase Lodge was formerly the residence of Thomas Holt White, Esq., a nephew of the Rev. Gilbert White,* the gentle author of " The Natural History of Selborne," and himself an accomplished scholar, well known as a commentator on Shakespeare, and the editor of Milton's

---

* The father of Gilbert White married Anne, daughter of the Rev. Thomas Holt, rector of Streatham, after whom Mr. Holt White was named. It is to be hoped that the good taste of the inhabitants will preserve the nomenclature of Holt White's-lane, and Hill, by which they have so long been known. The unhappy ignorance of some proprietors in a neighbouring parish has changed the picturesque and descriptive name of "Hanger," to "St. Anne's Road !" thus obliterating the last memorial of the old forest or "Hangre," of Tottenham, in a name which it had borne for above seven centuries, from the time of Malcolm, King of Scotland.

CLAYSMORE, THE SEAT OF JAS WHATMAN BOSANQUET, ESQ. J.P.

"Areopagitica, a speech for the Liberty of Unlicensed Printing." The estate was purchased in 1862, by Admiral Tindal (only surviving son of Chief Justice Sir Nicholas Tindal) whose residence it now is.

### CLAYSMORE.

Claysmore was purchased in the year 1847, by James Whatman Bosanquet, Esq., the descendant of an old Protestant family, in Languedoc, from whence, on the revocation of the edict of Nantes, they escaped to England—" per damna, per cædes "—and were naturalized by Act of Parliament. The estate is composed partly of an allotment from the Chace made to Mrs. Hume, who built the present residence, and partly of other enclosures lying between the "Rose and Crown," and the "Fallow Buck." Ten acres situated at "Morehatch" were conveyed in 1765, by Mary Turpin, probably connected with the family of the notorious Dick Turpin, whose grandfather is said to have kept the "Rose and Crown." The gipsy character of the original population of this district may still be traced in the features of some of the peasantry, and gipsy encampments are yet sometimes seen along the lanes beyond the "Fallow Buck."

In 1847 the present owner, in co-operation with the Vicar and other gentlemen, having established a school at Claysmore, appropriated, with the sanction of the Bishop, a building near Turpin's land, which had been fitted up as a private chapel by the former owner, for the performance of afternoon Sunday service, where one of the Curates preached to a congregation of seventy or eighty people.

This chapel, as well as another building in which the fine library of the late Lord Chief Justice Tindal had been placed by his executors, were burnt, with their contents, by the acts of incendiaries; and not less than five other fires occurred in the neighbourhood about the same time.

The late owner of the property, Mr. Edward Harman, a gentleman of cultivated taste, greatly enlarged and improved the residence, especially by the addition of a gallery, sixty feet in length, with a carved oak screen and panelling, and windows of stained glass, together with a corridor adjoining, seventy feet long. The large window at the end of the room (expensively set in copper) contains some fine specimens of the art in the 13th century, and one of those in the corridor is composed of sixteen compartments, technically known as " German Circles," dated from 1565 to 1622, the central figure (of James the less) being a gem of its kind. The picturesque character of the grounds is mainly due to the taste of Mr. Harman, who greatly added to their beauty by extensive plantations, and a well placed sheet of water. A long avenue of elms, lately opened by Mr. Bosanquet, forms a striking feature from the garden terrace.

### HILL LODGE.

Nearly adjoining the above estate is Hill Lodge, the residence of Sir Rowland Macdonald Stephenson, a compact property, consisting of about twenty-three acres, and commanding a beautiful and extensive view across the Chase, towards the Ridgeway and Trent Park.

## THE DUCHY OF LANCASTER.

"It must be granted, I am DUKE of Lancaster."

*Richard II., A. 2, S. 3.*

The Duchy of Lancaster, of which (says Sir Ed. Coke) it shall be necessary to show the beginning and erection, dates from 1352, when Henry Plantagenet (named Grismond, from the place of his birth) was created Duke of Lancaster by Edward III. Duke Henry died of the plague in 1361, and his daughter Blanche, who was married to the celebrated John of Gaunt, became sole heir to his estate.

" At the Parliament, holden 36 Edward III., the King, in full parliament, did gird his son John with a sword, and set on his head a cap of furre, and upon the same a circle of gold and pearls, and named him Duke of Lancaster, and thereof gave to him and to his heires males of his body, and delivered him a charter."

" In full Parliament, 50 Edward III., the King erected the county of Lancaster into a county palatine. It is called comitatus Palatinus, not *à comite*, but *à comitatu*, and *à palatio regis*, because the owner thereof hath 'jura regalia,' as fully as the King had in his palace, from whence all justice, honours, franchises, and privileges, flowed.

" Humphrey de Bohun, Earl of Hereford, the first and last of that name had issue, two daughters,—Eleanor, married to Thomas, Duke of Gloucester, and Mary, married to the Earl of Hertford, Bolingbroke, afterwards Henry IV.; and by 2 Henry V. it was enacted that all mannors and hereditaments which descended to Henry V. from the said Mary, his mother, should be dissevered from the Crown of England, and annexed to the Duchy of Lancaster. The Duchy thus separated from the Crown, was by Act of Parliment assured to Edward IV. and his heirs, Kings of England; and afterwards it was enacted, 1 Henry VII. that the King and his heirs (without adding ' Kings of England') should hold and enjoy the Duchy of Lancaster *separately from the Crown of England*, the Duke still having ' jura regalia;' and in this state doth the Duchy stand to this day, the King having the Duchy as Duke, and not as King, and the title and possession belonging to his person and not to the Crown." (Coke's Institutes.)

It may be added, on the authority of the late Lord Chief Baron Pollock, that the reigning Sovereign is always the " Duke " of Lancaster. " King and Queen (Rex and Regina) are separate titles, but Duke (Dux) has no feminine, Duchess being originally only a title of courtesy given to a Duke's wife.* Whoever therefore holds a Dukedom, whether male or female, is a Duke, and as the Dukedom of Lancaster is held with 'jura regalia,' no homage is done or can be required in respect of it, and the holder is not necessarily a vassal of the Crown; therefore the sovereign can, and does, hold this Dukedom of Lancaster."

---

* The word appears to have been coming into use in the time of Skinner, who gives "Duke" "Dux," and adds "Fr. duchesse, dux fæmina."—(ETYM. ANGLIC.)

An attempt was made by the wives of the bishops to claim the courtesy title of "lady" in the reign of Elizabeth, and again in that of James I., who is said to have negatived the pretension in terms more energetic than courteous,—"I made the carles lairds; but wha the de'il made their carlines leddies?"

# THE DUCHY COURT.

The Court to the Duchy has the power of deciding all cases belonging to it. The officers are a chancellor, vice-chancellor, attorney-general, Queen's serjeant and counsel, receiver-general, clerk of council and registrar, coroner, &c.*

The following is a list of the Chancellors to the present time :—

| NAME. | REIGN. | Date of Appointment, &c. |
|---|---|---|
| Sir Henry de Haydok ...... | 34 Edw. III. | Chancellor of Henry, first Duke of Lancaster. |
| Ralph D. Ergham, Clerk ... | 46 Edw. III. | Bishop of Sarum |
| Thomas de Thelwall, Clerk. | 51 Edw. III. | Created Chancellor of the County Palatine in the month of April |
| Sir John de Yerborough, Clerk | 1 Richard II. | |
| Sir Thomas Stanley ......... | 6 Richard II. | November 10, *pro. tem.* |
| Sir Thomas Scarle ............ | 6 Richard II. | November 29th. |
| Sir William Okey ............ | 7 Richard II. | October |
| John de Wakering ............ | 1 Henry IV. | |
| William Burgoyne, Esq. ... | 1 Henry IV. | |

* "This Court owes its origin to Henry IV., who, deposing Richard II., usurped the Crown, and, possessing the Duchy of Lancaster in right of his mother, was seized thereof as Duke, as well as King. But imagining his right to the Duchy better than that to the Crown, he resolved to secure the same by separating it from the Crown ; which being effected, he erected this Court for its use, wherein all matters of law and equity belonging to the Duchy, or County Palatine of Lancaster, are heard and decided by the Chancellor thereof."—*Pulleyn's Etymological Compendium.*

| NAME. | REIGN. | Date of Appointment, &c. |
|---|---|---|
| Sir Thomas Stanley ......... | 6 Henry IV. | May 15th. |
| John Springthorpe, Clerk ... | 11 Henry IV. | March 30th. |
| John Woodhouse ............ | 1 Henry V. | April 4th. |
| John Woodhouse, continued | 1 Henry VI. | January 20th. |
| William Troutbecke, Esq.... | 2 Henry VI. | June 10th. |
| Walter Sherington, Clerk ... | 9 Henry VI. | February 16th. |
| | 17 Henry VI. | May 7th—Chancellor for life. |
| William Tresham ........... | 20 Henry VI. | July 3rd—Chancellor in reversion. |
| William Tresham ...... ..... | 26 Henry VI. | November 1st. |
| John Say, Esq. ............... | 27 Henry VI. | June 10th. |
| John Say, Esq., continued... | 1 Edw. IV. | June 16th. |
| Sir Richard Fowler, Knt. ... | 11 Edw. IV. | June 10.—Also Chancellor of the Exchequer. |
| Sir John Say, Knt............. | 17 Edw. IV. | November 3rd. |
| Thomas Thwaites ......... .. | 18 Edw. IV. | April 2.--Also Chancellor of the Exchequer. |
| Thomas Metcalfe ............ | 1 Richard III. | July 17th. |
| Sir Reginald Bray, Knt. ... | 1 Henry VII. | September 13th. |
| Sir John Mordant, Knt...... | 19 Henry VII. | June 24th. |
| Sir Richard Empson, Knt. . | 21 Henry VII. | October 3rd. |
| Sir Henry Marney, Knt. ... | 1 Henry VIII. | May 14th. |
| Sir Richard Wingfield, Knt. | 14 Hen. VIII. | April 14th. |
| Sir Thomas Moore, Knt. .. | 17 Hen. VIII. | December 31st.—Made Chancellor of England. |
| Sir William Fitz Williams, Knt., afterwards Earl of Southampton. | 21 Hen. VIII. | November 3rd. |
| Sir John Gage, Knt. ......... | 35 Hen. VIII. | May 10th. |
| Sir William Pagett, Knt. ... | 1 Edw. VI. | July 1st. |
| Sir John Gate, Knt. ......... | 6 Edw. VI. | July 7th. |
| Sir Robert Rochester, Knt. . | 1 Queen Mary | |

| NAME. | REIGN. | Date of Appointment, &c. |
|---|---|---|
| Sir Edward Walgrave, Knt. | 4 and 5 Philip and Mary. | June 22nd. |
| Sir Ambrose Cave, Knt. ... | 1 Elizabeth. | |
| Sir Ralph Sadler, Knt. ...... | 10 Elizabeth. | May 16th. |
| Sir Francis Walsingham, Knt. | 19 Elizabeth. | June 15th. |
| Sir Thomas Henage, Knt... | 32 Elizabeth. | |
| Sir Robert Cecil, Knt. ...... | 37 Elizabeth. | October 7th. |
| Sir John Fortescue, Knt. ... | 43 Elizabeth. | September 16th. |
| Sir Thomas Parry, Knt., and John Daccomb, Esq. | 13 James I. | May 27th. |
| Sir John Daccombe, Knt.... | 14 James I. | June 5th. |
| Sir Humphrey May, Knt. | 15 James I. | March 23rd. |
| Edward Lord Newburgh .. | 5 Charles I. | April 16th. |
| William Lord Grey of Wake, and William Lenthall, Esq. | | February 10th, 1644. |
| John Bradshawe ... .......... | | August 1st, 1649. |
| Thomas Fell  ................ | | 1655. |
| Sir Gilbert Gerard, Bart. .. | | May 14th, 1659. |
| Francis Lord Seymour ...... | 12 Charles II. | July 9th. |
| Sir Thomas Ingram, Knt.... | 16 Charles II. | July 21st, |
| Sir Robert Carr, Bart. ... .. | 23 Charles II. | February 22nd. |
| Sir Thomas Chickeley, Knt. | 34 Charles II. | November 21st. |
| Robert Lord Willoughby, of Ersby. | 1 William and Mary. | March 21st. |
| Thomas Earl of Stamford. .. | 9 William III. | May 4th. |
| Sir John Leveson Gower, Bart | 1 Queen Anne. | May 12th. |
| James Earl of Derby ..... ... | 5 Queen Anne. | June 10th. |
| William Lord Berkley, of Stratton. | 9 Queen Anne. | September 21st. |
| Henage Earl of Aylesford ... | 1 George I. | November 6th. |
| Richard Earl of Scarborough | 2 George I. | March 12th. |

E

| NAME. | REIGN. | Date of Appointment, &c. |
|---|---|---|
| Nicholas Lechemere, Esq.... | 3 George I. | June 19th. |
| John Duke of Rutland ...... | 1 George II. | July 17th. |
| George Earl of Cholmondeley | 8 George II. | May. |
| Richard Lord Edgecumbe.... | 16 George II. | December 22nd. |
| Thomas Earl of Kinnoull. ... | 34 George II. | February 27th. |
| James Lord Strange ......... | 3 George III. | December 13th. |
| Thomas Lord Hyde, after-wards Earl of Clarendon. | 11 George III. | June 14th. |
| John Lord Ashburton ........ | 22 George III. | April 17th. |
| Edward Earl of Derby. ...... | 23 George III. | August 29th. |
| Thomas Earl of Clarendon.. | 24 George III. | December 31st. |
| Charles Lord Hawkesbury... | 27 George III. | September 6th. |
| Thomas Lord Pelham ...... | 44 George III. | November 9th. |
| Lord Mulgrave ......... ... | 44 George III. | June 6th. |
| Earl of Buckinghamshire ... | 45 George III. | January 14th. |
| Dudley Lord Harrowby ..... | 45 George III. | July 10th. |
| Edward Earl of Derby ...... | 46 George III. | February 12th. |
| The Right Hon. Spencer Perceval. | 47 George III. | March 30th. |
| Earl of Buckinghamshire ... | 52 George III. | May 23rd. |
| The Right Hon. Charles Bathurst. | 52 George III. | June 23rd. |
| The Right Hon. Nicholas Vansittart, afterwards Lord Bexley. | 4 George IV. | February 13th. |
| Earl of Aberdeen, K. T. ... | 9 George IV. | January 26th. |
| The Right Hon. Charles Arbuthnot | 9 George IV. | June 2nd. |
| Lord Holland.................. | 1 William IV. | November 25th. |
| The Right Hon. Charles Watkin Williams Wynn.. | 5 William IV. | December 26th. |
| Lord Holland ................. | 5 William IV. | April 3rd. |
| Earl of Clarendon ............ | 4 Victoria. | October 31st. |

| NAME. | REIGN. | Date of Appointment, &c. |
|---|---|---|
| The Right Hon. Sir George Grey, Bart. | 5 Victoria ... | June 23rd. |
| Lord Granville Charles Henry Somerset. | 5 Victoria ... | September 3rd. |
| Lord Campbell ............... | 10 Victoria ... | July 6th. |
| Earl of Carlisle ............... | 13 Victoria ... | March 6th. |
| The Right Hon. Robert Adam Christopher | 15 Victoria ... | March 1st. |
| The Right Hon. Edward Strutt, now Lord Belper | 16 Victoria ... | December 30th. |
| Earl Granville .................. | 18 Victoria ... | June 21st. |
| Earl of Harrowby ............ | 18 Victoria ... | March 31st. |
| The Right Hon. Matthew Talbot Baines | 19 Victoria ... | December 7th, 1855. |
| James Duke of Montrose ... | | February 26th, 1858. |
| The Right Hon. Sir George Grey, Bart., G.C.B. | | June 22nd, 1859. |
| The Right Hon. Edward Cardwell, M.P. | | July 25, 1861. |
| The Right Hon. George William Frederick, Earl of Clarendon. | | April 7, 1864. |
| The Right Hon. George Joachim Goschen, M.P. | | January 26, 1866. |
| The Right Hon. William Reginald Earl of Devon | | July 10, 1866. |
| The Right Hon. Colonel John Wilson Patten, M.P. | | June 26, 1867. |
| The Right Hon. Thomas Edward Taylor, M.P. | | November 7th, 1868. |
| The Right Hon. Lord Dufferin, K.P., K.C.B. (now Earl of Dufferin). | | December 12th, 1868. |
| The Right Hon. Hugh Culling Eardley Childers, M.P. | | August 9th, 1872. |

*Right Ho. John Bright*

*Aug 1873*

## THE MANOR OF WORCESTERS.

In the wardrobe accounts of Edward II. it is mentioned that "the King kept his Christmas this year (1318) at the palace of Westminster," and on that day the following knights received sumptuous presents of plate from the King, viz., "Sir Bartholomew de Enefeld," &c., &c. His son, John de Enefeld, died in 1350, seized of a manor in this parish, and his widow, Margaret, married John Wroth, who purchased the manor in 1374, of her son, Francis de Enefeld. John Wroth leaving no issue on his death, the manor descended through Sir John Tiptoft, to his son, the learned Earl of Worcester, Lord High Treasurer, who lost his head on the scaffold for his adherence to the House of York, "when (says Fuller) the axe did at one blow cut off more learning than was left in the heads of all the surviving nobility." His son dying without issue, the manor devolved to his sister Philippa, wife of Thomas, Lord Roos, who died in 1461, and their son Edmund (whose monument in the Parish Church is hereafter described) also dying childless, in 1508, the estate came to his brother-in-law, Sir Thomas Lovell, K.G., Privy Counsellor and Treasurer to Henry VIII. He was made Chancellor of the Exchequer in the first year of Henry VII., and in 1502 became Treasurer of the Household, and President of the Council. He was one of Henry VII.'s executors, and Steward and Marshall of the House to Henry VIII. He built the gateway of

Lincoln's Inn, on which he placed the King's arms, along with the Earl of Lincoln's and his own. His badge of the-rose and the wing,—which will be more fully discussed in the account of the Parish Church,—appears in the vaulting of the choir of St. George's Chapel, Windsor, as well as on his stall-plate.

Sir Thomas Lovell died at his house here (Elsynge Hall) May 25th, 1524, and was buried in the priory of Haliwell, Shoreditch, within the chapel founded by himself, with great funeral pomp. The following curious items occur in the records of the Herald's College, at the close of a long description of the ceremonies " down at the buryall of the most noble knyght, Sir Thomas Lovell, banneret, and knyght of the most Noble Order of ye Garter, on whose soule God pardon."

" Item,—It is remembered that the day he came from Enfyld to Holywell, there followed a carte with ale and torches, for to refresche the poore people, and the torches were renewen by the way.

" Item,—There was every day, while he was at Enfylde, 200 poore folks, and them that had pence-a-piece, and bread and meat.

" Item,—There was said the day of his buryall at Holywell, 140 masses.

" Item,—There was served that day to people that were ther, 400 messes of mete and above."

Sir Thomas Lovell, by his will, dated October 14th, 1522, gave the Manor of Worcesters to Thomas Manners,

Lord Ros, afterwards first Earl of Rutland, who married Elizabeth, daughter of Sir Robert Lovell, his brother.

In 1540, the Earl of Rutland gave the manor, along with the *capital messuage of Elsygne Hall*, to King Henry VIII., and it was settled by Edward VI. upon his sister Elizabeth. It was afterwards granted by the Crown to Robert Cecil, first Earl of Salisbury, who died seized of it in 1612.

Lysons and Dr. Robinson state, that "it is not certain at what time it was alienated by the Cecils," but by the deeds at Forty Hall, it appears to have been conveyed by the second Lord Salisbury, (July 4th, 1616) to Sir Nicholas Raynton, and by "An abstract of all ye landes "and tenements appertaining to ye estate of N. Raynton, "Esq., which are in Endfield in ye Co. Middlesex, being "carefully collected by compairing up ye tennants, and "by perusing severall writeings, &c., about ye year 1656." The property at this time consisted of,—"Imprimis, Forty "Hall, one antient howse lately ‚new-built, called and "knowne by ye name of Forty Hall, with close adjoining, "enclosed by a brick wall, and containing by estimation, "six acres," with sundry meadows and closes duly specified, containing 344 acres, 1 rood, 36 poles. "Also "in ye possession of ye said N. Raynton, Esq., one "very ancient house called ENFIELD HOUSE, (otherwise "ELSYNGE HALL) with ye court yards, gardens, orchards, "&c. adjoining, one antient tenement att "Wight-webbs 'adjoining to Endfield Howse. And ye piece of land

FORTY-HALL, THE SEAT OF JAMES MEYER, ESQ. J.P.

"called ye Warren, and ye close or park, called ye Little
"Park, containing 375 acres," &c.

### FORTY HALL.

The present mansion or manor house of Forty Hall,
above referred to, was built by Sir Nicholas Raynton,
from the designs of Inigo Jones, about the year 1629, as
appears from the dates on the leaden pipes. The date
of 1632 may also be seen near the top of the buildings
(probably that of its completion.)

It was at this time copyhold, but after its purchase by
Sir N. Raynton, it was enfranchised and merged in the
Manor of Worcesters.

In 1787, on the death of Eliab Breton, who had
married the heiress of the Raynton and Wolstenholme
families,* the whole estate comprising above 1800 acres,
and then considered the finest and most compact in
Middlesex, was sold in sixty-five lots for £50,000.

---

\* Mr. Breton died at Forty Hall, December 19th, 1785, in his
76th year, and his widow died January 20th, 1790, aged 80. "She
"was the surviving co-heiress of the Wolstenholme and Raynton
"families, whose estate at Enfield (one of the finest in Middlesex)
"she conveyed to her husband, and after his death, saw it dismem-
"bered under Mr. Christie's hammer through the misconduct of
"their offspring."—*Gent. Mag., Jan.* 1790.

Forty Hall, with 159 acres adjoining, was purchased by
. Mr. Armstrong, and on his death in 1799, by James
Meyer, Esq., for £11,940. It is now the property and
residence of his great nephew, James Meyer, Esq., and
consists of above 280 acres within a ring fence.

"The interior accommodations of the house (says Dr.
Robinson) are numerous and pleasant, and the rooms are
well-proportioned and superbly decorated." The beautiful tracery work of the pannelled ceilings is especially
deserving of notice. The fine collection of pictures
contains "A Holy Family," by *Rubens;* "The Miracu-
lous Draught of Fishes," by *D. Teniers;* "The Carnival
in the Square of St. Mark's," by *Canalletti;* "The Three
Marys," by *Annibal Caracci;* "The Toilet," by *Gabriel
Metzu;* "Uriah conveying the letter from David," by
*Raphael,* from the Orleans collection, erroneously as-
cribed by Dr. Robinson to Albert Durer; "The Tower of
St. Mark's," and "A Companion of the Doge's Palace," by
*Canaletti;* "Christ purifying the Temple," by *Bassano;*
and two landscapes by *Both,* from the Lansdowne
collection. There is also a fine portrait of Sir Nicholas
Raynton in his civic robes (1643) supposed to be by
*Dobson,* the pupil of *Vandyke.*

The fine old gateway of the stables is still standing,
and is a characteristic example of the effect which Inigo
Jones could give to the simplest design by the judicious
management of light and shadow, and the solid durability
of appearance which distinguish all his works.

GATEWAY BY INIGO JONES, AT FORTY-HALL.

## ESLYNGE HALL,

OTHERWISE

## ENFIELD HOUSE, OT LOVELL PLACE.

---

" Where throngs of knights and barons bold
In weeds of peace high triumphs hold
Of wit or arms, while both contend
To win HER grace whom all command."

L'ALLEGRO.

---

Great antiquarian and historic interest attaches to the
now forgotten site of Elsynge Hall, once the scene of
royal magnificence, and thronged with the sage counsel-
lors and the brilliant courtiers of Elizabeth.

Elsynge Hall was for several years the residence of
Edward VI. and his sister during their childhood, and
Holinshed relates how, in 1543, " on New Year's-day the
" noble Scottish prisoners departed from London, and
" roade to Enfield to see the Prince, and dined there
" that day, greatly rejoicing to beholde so proper and
" towardly an ympe."

There can be no doubt that this was the residence of
Queen Elizabeth after she came to the throne. It is
distinctly stated by Norden to have been " builded by an
Earle of Worcester," and is described by him as being
a " Howse or Palace of Queen Eli.," in his map of
Myddlesex (1593), where it is represented as surrounded

by a park-paling enclosing the "New-park," and about a mile distant from the town, where he places another similar enclosure for the Old-park, which adjoined the Manor House of Enfield. Both these parks are marked in the same way in Saxton's map (1579), in Speed's (1608), and in the famous atlas of Blaeu, the pupil of Tycho Brahe (a sheet of which is worth its weight in gold).

In the account of Sir Thomas Lovell's funeral, the house is stated to have been "a good myle distant from the Parische-churche." Weever ranks it among the princely houses heritable by the Crown; and Vallance, in his tale of Two Swannes, calls it "Enfield House yt longs unto our Queene."

In the memoirs of Carey, Earl of Monmouth, it is stated that in the year 1596, the Queen came from Theobalds to dinner to Enfield House, and had toils set up in the park to shoot at bucks after dinner.

The Court was resident here in the summer of 1561, and went up to St. James's in July, on which occasion such was the state of the roads, that "the hedges and ditches were cut down to *make the next way* for her." The Court was again here from September 8th, to the 22nd, 1561, and from July 25th to 30th, in 1564, and in July, 1568, as will be more particularly alluded to in the life of Sir Walter Raleigh.

When the Manor of Worcesters was granted to the Cecils, Elsynge Hall was reserved to the Crown, but in

1641 it was sold by Charles I. along with the "Little Park" and "the Warren" adjoining, (part of the Duchy of Lancaster) to Philip, Earl of Pembroke and Montgomery.

It was the celebrated widow of this nobleman, who was said by Dr. Donne, to "know well how to discourse of all things, from predestination down to *slea-silk*," and who wrote the spirited letter to Sir J. Williamson, Secretary of State, who had presumed to propose a candidate for her borough of Appleby:—

"I have been bullied by an usurper, I have been neglected by a court, but I will not be dictated to by a subject. Your man shan't stand.

ANNE, Dorset, Pembroke, and Montgomery."

It is the fashion of these enlightened days to doubt every thing best worth believing, and the authenticity of this letter is doubted by Lodge, chiefly on the ground that "no instance can be found of the verb *stand* being used at that time in the sense to which it is here applied." It may be found so used in the life of Bishop Sanderson, at least seven times, speaking of his "standing" for the place of procter, in 1614.

The baptism of five of her children is recorded in the parish registers.

Elsynge Hall has long been pulled down, but its site is still discernable towards the bottom of the avenue at Forty Hall, between the house and the Maiden-bridge-brook. Here, in dry seasons, the outlines of an extensive fabric may be traced on the ground by the withering of the grass;—the remains of foundations have frequently been dug up, and about the year 1830, under a lime tree in the avenue, an unfortunate bullock fell through the decayed brickwork into a vault below.

In addition to Forty Hall and the Manor of Worcesters, Sir Nicholas Raynton purchased "a copyhold house, "described in the survey of Enfield (says Dr. Robinson) "as sometime Hugh Fortee's, and late Sir Thomas "Gurney's," to which he curiously adds that Sir Hugh Fortee built the mansion called Forty Hall, between the years of 1629 and 1632, and gave name to it. Hugh Fortee died in the previous century, and it is certain that " Forty Hill " was known by this name at least as early as 1564. In a deed of that date (penes H. C. B. Bowles, Esq.) a parcel of land is described as being bounded on the east by the road leading from Friday Street "versus ffortie."

### MYDDELTON HOUSE.

Myddelton House was purchased in 1724 by Michel Garnault, whose descendant, Daniel Garnault, died unmarried in 1809, leaving the estate, together with his shares in the New River, to his sister Anne, wife of the late Henry Carington Bowles. The present villa was built in 1818, by this gentleman, on the site of the old house known as Bowling Green House, and was named after Sir Hugh Myddelton, the patriotic but ill-requited

MYDDELTON HOUSE, THE SEAT OF H. C. B. BOWLES, ESQ. J.P.

projector of the New River. The estate, containing about 100 acres, was formerly parcel of the Manor of Worcesters and of Goldbeaters.* It is now the property of H. C. B. Bowles, Esq., J.P., and includes a site of some historic interest, from its connection with the Gunpowder Plot. "A tradition which (says Lysons) is perhaps not much to be depended upon," states that White Webbs House was hired by the conspirators for the purposes of their plot.

This tradition is, however, fully substantiated by existing title deeds, and by the following extracts from the documents of the State Paper Office, which also identify the locality beyond any doubt.

In the confession of "John Johnsonne (alias Guido Fawkes), he further saith that the Wednsday before his "apprencon he went forthe of the towne to a house in "Enfielde Chase on this side of Theobalds, where he "stayed till Sonday night following." (9—10 November, 1605.)

The report to the council of the search of "White Webbs House," says, "the search ended in the discovery "of Popish books and relics, but no papers or munitions,

---

* Goldbeaters was a reputed Manor under the Manor of Worcesters, and has now become extinguished and merged in various freeholds. In an abstract of a survey of Enfield, 1572, lands called Goldbeaters are described as belonging to *Dr. Huicke*, with a quit rent of 7s. 7d. to the Queen.

" and the house was found to be full of trap doors and
" passages." In the examination of " James Johnson,"
it was stated by him that the house " had been taken of
" *Dr. Hewicke,* by his master, Mr. Meaze, of Berkshire,
"(the Jesuit father Garnet) for his sister, Mrs. Perkins
"(alias Mrs. Ann Vaux) that Mrs. Vaux had spent a
" month there, and mass had been said by a priest, whose
" name deponent did not know."

On the 25th February, 1606, Johnson described the
taking and furnishing of the house, and said that Ann
Vaux had kept it up at her own expense, and that Garnet
was the man who had visited it under the names of
Meaze and Farmer.

On March 21st, 1606, a letter written in lemon juice—
which is still in existence—was intercepted from Mistress
Vaux to Garnet, then prisoner in the Tower. It was
accompanied by a *pot of marmalade,* and had the signifi-
cant endorsement (in common ink,) " I praye you prove
" whether these spectacles doe fytte your sight." Lysons
states, " from some papers communicated by Mr. Gough "
that Queen Elizabeth, in 1570, granted a mansion called
White Webbs House, to *Robert Huicke,* her physician
in ordinary (and principal of St. Alban's College, Oxford).
And a deed in the possession of H. C. B. Bowles, Esq. of
the same year, contains the grant of " all the vaultes and
all the conduit * and pipes of lead laid within the said

---

* *Vide* White Webb's Park.—(p. 83).

Chase at the charges and expenses of our servant (*Robert Huycke*) for the leading and conveying water into the "Nowe Howse" of our said servant, "abuttinge in parte uppon the saide Chase, which mansion house is within the parish of Endfield in our saied co. of Midd.," and for supplying water to the mansion house, gardens, ponds, and orchards.

Old White Webbs House, which was evidently of considerable extent, was pulled down by Mr. Garnault, in 1790. Its site extended from the fields numbered 254, 255 (in the large ordnance map of the parish) across White Webbs-lane (formerly known as Rome Road) to those numbered 392, 396, the property of H. Wilkinson, Esq. The remains of the fish ponds and orchards are still discernable, and the ale house known as the King and Tinker probably still retains some portions of the old out-buildings. With this little beershop is popularly identified the ballad of King James and the Tinker, the incident of which is supposed to have occurred during the residence of James I. at Theobalds.

This old ballad deserves a place in the History of Enfield, from having suggested the details of one of the most beautiful descriptions in modern poetry.

"It has long been a favourite subject with our ballad-"writers (says Bishop Percy) to represent our Kings "conversing by accident or design, with the meanest of "their subjects. Besides the song of the 'King and the "Miller,' we have 'King Edward IV. and the Tanner,'.

" ' King Henry and the Soldier,' ' King James I. and
" the Tinker,' &c." (*Reliques of Ancient Poetry.*)

" The earliest of these stories (writes Professor Child)
" seems to be that of ' King Alfred and the Neatherd,' in
" which the herdsman's wife plays the offending part, and
" the peasant himself is made Bishop of Winchester."

The verses are not given in any collection of old
ballads, though they may be found in a few chapbooks
and broadsides. The following text has been collated
with a reprint of the Percy Society.

### KING JAMES AND THE TINKLER.

And now, to be brief, let's pass over the rest,
Who seldom or never were given to jest,
And come to King Jamie, the first of our throne—
A pleasanter monarch sure never was known.

As he was a-hunting the swift fallow deer,
He dropt all his nobles, and when he got clear,
In hope of some pastime, away he did ride,
Till he came to an ale-house hard by a wood-side,

And there with a Tinkler he happened to meet,
And him in kind sort he so freely did greet ;
" Now pray thee good fellow, what hast in thy jug,
Which under thy arm thou dost lovingly hug ?"

" By the mass !" quoth the Tinkler, " 'tis nappy brown ale,
And for to drink to thee friend, I will not fail,
For although thy jacket looks gallant and fine,
I think that my two-pence as good is as thine."

"By my soul! honest fellow, the truth thou hast spoke,"
And straight he sat down with the Tinkler to joke;
They drank to the King, and they pledged to each other,
Who had seen them had thought they were brother and brother.

As they were a-drinking, the King pleased to say,
"What news, honest fellow? come, tell to me, I pray;"
"There's nothing of news, except that I hear,
The King is a-hunting the fair fallow deer,

And truly I wish I so happy may be,
While he is a-hunting the King I might see;
For though I have travelled the land many ways,
I never have yet seen a King in my days."

The King with a hearty brisk laughter replied,
"I tell thee, good fellow, if thou canst but ride,
Thou shalt get up behind me, and thee I will bring
To the presence of Jamie, thy sovereign King."

"But he'll be surrounded with nobles so gay,
And how shall we tell him from them, Sir, I pray?"
"Thou wilt easily know him, when once thou art there,
The King will be covered, his nobles all bare."

Then up got the Tinkler, and likewise his sack,
His budget of leather and tools at his back;
They rode till they came to the merry green wood,
His nobles came round him, and bare-headed stood.

The Tinkler then seeing so many appear,
He slyly did whisper the King in his ear,
Saying, "They are all clothed so gallant and gay,
"But which amongst them is the King, Sir, I pray?"

F

The King did with hearty good laughter reply,
" By my soul, my good fellow, its thou or its I,
The rest are bareheaded, uncovered all round,"
— With his bag and his budget he fell to the ground

Like one that was frightened quite out of his wits,
Then up on his knees he immediately gets,
Beseeching for mercy—the King to him said,
" Thou art a good fellow, so be not afraid ;

Come, tell me thy name !"  " I am John of the Dale,
A mender of kettles, and lover of ale."
" Then rise up, Sir John, I will honour thee here,
And make thee a knight of five hundred a year."

This was a good thing for the Tinkler indeed,
Then unto the Court he was sent for with speed ;
Where store of great pleasure and pastime was seen
In the royal presence of King and of Queen.

Sir John of the Dale, he has land, he has fee,
At the court of the King, who so happy as he?
Yet still in his hall hangs the Tinkler's old sack,
And the budget of tools which he bore at his back.

WHITE-WEBBS-PARK, THE SEAT OF HENRY WILKINSON, ESQ.

WHITE WEBBS PARK.

The estate of White Webbs Park was purchased by
Dr. Wilkinson, on the sale of the property of Mr. Breton,
in 1787. It was then known by the name of White
Webbs Farm, and was enclosed within the pale of Forty
Hall Park, from which it is divided only by the New
River and the brook. At this time it consisted of 134
acres, but has been increased by successive purchases
and allotments, to 250 acres, 100 of which are woodland,
and covered with old oaks and underwood, the remains
of the original Chase or forest.*

The top of the hill is crowned by a dark mass of
Scotch firs, and the whole forms a conspicuous and
beautiful object from the surrounding country.

In an open glade at the bottom of this wood stands a
small brick building, enclosing a circular tank or well of
five feet diameter, always full of the purest water, and
transparent to the bottom. This is the old "Conduit-
house" before mentioned, as having been granted by
Queen Elizabeth to her physician, Dr. Huicke, for the
supply of his mansion-house at White Webbs. The
texture and form of the bricks, which are unusually thin,

---

* A fine old badger, probably the last wild one in Middlesex, was
killed in these woods in the summer of 1848, and is preserved at
Forty Hall.

and the peculiar "old English bond" of the brickwork indicate great age; and the corners of the building have been completely worn away by the rubbing of deer and cattle during upwards of three centuries.

The present mansion was built in 1791, by Dr. Wilkinson, and has been much enlarged by his grandson, Henry Wilkinson, Esq., whose fine taste has enriched it by a collection of works of art of the highest beauty and rarity. A short descriptive catalogue is subjoined of some of these which are specially interesting, either from their associations or their intrinsic excellence.

----

*Outer Hall.*—Carved ebony cabinet, surmounted by engraved bronze tazza. Terra-cotta group of boys in masques by *Flaxman.* The Entombment, by *Clodion,* (signed). The Adoration of the Shepherds, from *Verona.* Colossal busts of Sculpture and Poetry, in white marble, from the Palace of the Duchesse de Berri, by *Orazzia Marinari* (1680). Two Figures in Suits of Damascene Armour. Triptic of the Adoration of the Shepherds, in ivory, with carved ebony frame.

*Inner Hall.*—Buhl clock finely engraved, from Strawberry-hill. Marble bust of Aurelius. Bust of Cassius, the head of bronze, the bust in dark marble. White Marble Vase, with death of Hector on pedestal, with supporting nymphs and sphinxes in grey marble, (height eight feet). Two rosso antico busts on red marble

OLD CONDUIT-HOUSE AT WHITE-WEBBS.

pedestals. Terra-cotta figure of Night. Two deep blue jewelled enamelled Sevres Jardinieres (1790—5).

*Dining Room.*— *Gainsborough,* — Portraits of his Daughters. *Sir T. Lawrence,*—Son of Colonel Hill, full length. *Velasquez,*—Two full lengths, Dukes of Monti Leoni, from the Auldjo collection. *Sant,*—St John, after *Raphael.* Plaque of the Massacre of the Innocents in della Robbia ware. Marble alto relief of David and his men eating the shew-bread, by *Donatelli.* Terra-cotta bust of Titian, taken in his life time by his friend Alessandrio Vittoria, the Venetian Senator. Antique bust of a Roman Lady, with drapery of agate. Oval silver Salver in deep repoussé work, Androcles and the Lion. Brazen Wine Cooler, engraved, by *Orazzia Fortezza di Sabenico.* Table, supported by Sphinxes, old Florentine mosaic.

*Morning Room.*—Flora, by *Marin.* Sevres Plate, made for George III., companion plate from the royal manufactory, Vienna. Limoges Enamel of Paulus III. in marble frame. Old Dresden Clock of the finest white paste, with four caryatides. Ancient Buhl Commode. Ebony and Ivory Inlaid Cabinet. Three Portraits in Enamel, by *Bone.* Portrait of the Empress Catherine of Russia, and companion Portrait, by *Rosalba.* Capo di Monte, Dresden and Berlin Tazzas, Ivories, and Miniatures, by *Cosway.* Carved Ivory Tray, with the arms of the Dauphin, set with Turquoises. Fine Venetian Glass set in coral.

*Library.*—Enamel, by *Bone.* Ditto of the Holy Family. White Marble Clock, by *Clodion.* Bronze of young Bacchus.

*Passage.*—Portrait of Camilla del Orto, by *Tintoretto.* Portrait of Wilson, by himself (from Wanstead-house). Large bronze bas relief of Hades (from the Strozza collection). Terra-cotta St. Andrew on the Cross (by *John of Bologna*). Black basaltic bust of a Boy (from the Marquis Spinola's Palace.) Terra-cotta bust, by *Raphael.*

*Drawing Room.*—Cabinet, nine feet high of white China enamel. Carved ebony ditto, with Group in Della Robbia ware. Two ditto, inlaid with ivory, with vases of early Capo di Monti (from the Duke of Hamilton's collection.) Bronze bust of the grand Condé (1621) on marble pedestal, by *Thorwaldson.* Buhl Table, from Strawberry Hill. Tazza of Rock Crystal. Illuminated missal from Newstead Abbey; Ditto bound in embossed silver and velvet. Plate of Limoges Enamel. Carved Ivory Magdalen. Miniatures, by *Cosway* and *Hopner*, &c. Rock Crystal Tazza, with the passage of the Red Sea exquisitely engraved. A Child and Parrot, by *Greuze.* Cameo of Semiramis (from Strawberry Hill). Louis XIV. and Madame de Chianges, by *Petitot.* Miniature of Alfieri, with autograph of Lord Byron. Etui, with Mounts and Enamel of the Duchesse de Montpensier, by *Petitot.* Dish of Limoges Enamel, with Lot and his Daughters. Ancient carved Ivory Group, cut out of a single tusk. Six Limoges Enamel Cups and

Saucers. Two Bronzes, from the collection of the late Duke of York. Castor and Pollux, in White Marble, from the collection of the Duke of Cambridge. Ewer and Basin of deep blue Sevres. Antique Cup of Cat's-eye, with jewelled stem. Two Miniatures, by *Cosway*. Ditto of Charles I. and his Queen Henrietta. Ditto of Lady Jersey, by *Sir Thomas Lawrence*. Four Plates from the Royal Vienna Manufactory. Cups and Saucers of Sevres, Capo di Monti, old Dresden, Berlin, Buen Retiro, and Vienna. A jewelled Limoges Triptic—the birth of Christ. · Sofa and four Chairs of old Tournay tapestry. Embroidered ditto, with Screen and Footstool from the petit Trianon, fromerly belonging to Marie Antoinette. Twelve magnificent old Venetian Glasses, from the palace at Naples ;—six others of the suite are in the possession of the Duchess of Wellington. Two Bronze busts of Sextus V. and Clement VII., of the highest art and workmanship.

*Staircase.*—Hermandino, Duke of Mantua, by *Paul Veronese*. John Locke, by *Sir G. Kneller*. Elizabeth, Duchess of Norfolk, by *Zuccharo*. Madame du Deffand. Large Majolica Plaque of the twelve Disciples in the porch of the Temple, (A.D. 1525.) Virgin and Child in della Robbia ware. Bronze bust of Columbus. Portrait of the Marquis Grimani, by *Tintoretto*. Marble bust of a Roman Lady, the drapery in agate. St. Peter and St. Paul, della Robbia. Large Spanish Cabinet of Tortoise-shell and Mother-of-pearl. Lofty Ebony Cabinet, with the arms and portraits of the Visconti family. Head of Charity, by *Sir J. Reynolds.* Landscape by *Gainsborough.* Large Limoges Enamel in Ebony Frame. The Annunciation, carved in Amber, with border of Lapis Lazuli. Two terra-cotta plaques, by *Marin.* Miniatures of Charles I. and Henrietta Maria, with ten Nobles, in Tortoise-shell frame.

*Study.*—Table of old Roman mosaic. Antique Desk of Tortoise-shell and Mother-of-pearl. Two oak Cabinets from Fonthill.

*Japan Room.*—Old Dresden Clock, with Landscapes. Chest of rare old Marquetry, with Limoges Enamel.

*Red Dressing Room.*—Terra-cotta plaque of the Holy Family, by *Giorgio Marchioli,* 1620.

*Green Dressing Room.*—Four magnificent plaques of old Capo di Monti, representing the four seasons. Two oval ditto of Night and Morning, in Ebony Cabinet.

ROSELANDS,

The seat of James Pateshall Jones, Esq., is situated on the south side of Turkey-street. The estate, which is watered by the New River, contains upwards of fifty acres, and includes the house and grounds, which were for more than a century the property and residence of the late Mr. Phineas Pateshall and his ancestors, and afterwards of his grandson, the present owner, who purchased the adjoining estates in the year 1859, and blended the two properties. In the following year the public road,

ROSELANDS, THE SEAT OF JAS. PATESHALL JONES, ESQ.

which wound round the front of the house, was diverted, under an order of the Quarter Sessions, and carried in a direct line across Mr. Jones's land, at his own expense, by which a great improvement, public as well as private, was effected.

The families of Pateshall and Jones (who have more than once intermarried), are among the oldest residential proprietors in the -parish. Phineas Pateshall appears from the Duchy Records, as quoted by Dr. Robinson, to have held a house and land "at Bull's Cross, near Card's Bridge," in 1686, as copyhold of the Manor of Enfield in the Duchy of Lancaster.

Philip Jones, of Barnard's Inn, the great-grandfather of James Pateshall Jones, died at his house in Green-street, Enfield, now the residence of the Rev. Thomas Jones, his grandson. He was an auctioneer of great eminence in London, and his father, Thomas Jones, was the first individual who practised that profession in this country. (*Gentleman's Magazine,* 1778.)

## MANOR OF DURANTS.

The Manor of Durants belonged in the reign of Edward I. to Richard de Plessitis, at which time it appears to have been valued at £21 1s. 11½d.

In default of male issue it devolved to Thomas Durant, whose only daughter, Maude, married John Wrothe, and the Manor of Durants, to which that of Gartons was at an early period annexed, descended to their son, William

Wrothe, who died 20 March, 9 Hen. IV.* after which it continued in the Wrothe family for many generations. " Sir Thomas Wrothe was," says Fuller, "of the Bedchamber, " and a favourite to King Edward the Sixth, who, (as I " am informed) at his death, passed out of the armes of " him, his faithfull servant, into the embraces of Christ, " his dearest Saviour. Soon after Sir Thomas found a " great change in the English Court, but no alteration as " many did (to their shame) in his own conscience, in " preservation of which he was fain to fly beyond the " seas." It was observable (he adds), that the family of this man who went away for his conscience, was the only family in Middlesex out of all those mentioned by Norden, which was not extinct in his time (1660). A curious letter from his son, Sir Robert Wrothe, who died June 26, 1605, is preserved among the Lansdowne manuscripts, which vividly depicts the state of the country round London at the close of the sixteenth century.

Sir Robert Wrothe to Mr. Michael Hickes. Intelligence concerning
robbers who frequented Layton Heath in Essex.

*(M.S. Lansd.* 87 *Art.* 60 *Orig.)*

My very good frende, Mr. Hickes, I am informed that now, towardes these darke evenings, there are sertaine lewde fellowes, sumtimes horsemen, somtimes footemen, disguising themselves with beardes that they carry aboute them in their pockets, which doe

---

* " Ex bundello Inquisitionum anno 2 Regis Hen. V. num. 4, in Turre Lond.

frequente and use aboute Layton heath and at or about Snaresbrooke in your brother Colstone's walke. I have appoynted sum espiciall spyall of them to bewray them and to know them, either by theire horses apparell or otherwise, and I hope in time to have them discifared. Yet for better surety thereof, I pray you lett me intreate you to speake to your brother Colstone that with some secresy he woulde take such order with sum of the discreatest keepers he hath that towardes eaveninges they woulde have an eye upone the heath and about Snaresbrooke for such kinde of persons, and to discry them by their horses or otherwise if they can. They come not above one or two in company until they meete about the heath, and when they have obteyned that they come for, they sever themselves in the like maner, and sum times sum of them ride over by Temple Mill, where I pray you take likewise secret order with the miller that he woulde keepe his gate shute up in the nighte ; besides sumtimes they ride over by Hackney ; and yf they doe discry any of them that I may have notice thereof, and I doubte not but to have them quickly apprehended, for I have notice of sum of their hauntes. And so, with my commendations to your good wiffe, I will bid you farewell.

Lucton the 16th of October, 1599.

Your assured frende,

ROBERT WROTHE.

One of them usethe to ride on a whit mare. Let them have a diligent care if they doe see any such man. To my verie loving friend Mr. Michaell Hicks,* at his house at Duckett or elsewhere.

---

\* Mr. Hickes, afterwards Sir Michael Hickes, was Lord Burghley's secretary.

The old Manor House of Ducketts, in the parish of Tottenham, and formerly said to have been in Hornsey, still remains with part of its surrounding moat ; a fine old stone chimney piece of the 16th century, bearing the Tudor rose in the centre of its frieze was removed a few years ago, and is now in the possession of J. W. Ford, Esq.

The family of Wrothe became extinct with Sir Henry Wrothe, the grandson of Sir Thomas, to whose exile, during the reign of Queen Mary, Fuller again refers in his dedication to Sir Henry of part of his Church History.

"Hence it is that I have seen in your ancient house
"at Durance, the crest of your armes (viz., a lion's head
"erased) with the extraordinary addition of sable wings,
"somewhat alluding to those of bats, to denote your
"ancestour's dark and secret flight for his safety. How-
"ever, God brought him home again on the silver wings
"of the dove, when peaceably restoring him in the dayes
"of Q. Elizabeth to his large possessions."

On the death of this Sir Henry Wrothe, in the year 1673, the manor was sold by his executors for the sum of £8,900, to Sir Thomas Stringer, whose son, William, dying in 1723, bequeathed the estate to his wife Margaret, daughter of Lord Chancellor Jeffreys. After various successive changes it was purchased in 1793 by Newell Connop, Esq., in whose family it still remains.

The Manor House stood on the east side of the high-road between Ponder's-end and Green-street, but it was burnt down at the end of the last century, at a meeting of tenants by imprudently heaping logs on the hall fire. The entrance was by a large gateway, with a postern, flanked by extensive barns and outbuildings, and approached by a bridge of one arch, across the moat which surrounded it. Judge Jeffreys is said to have occasionally resided here with his daughter, and two or

OLD GATEWAY TO DURANT'S MANOR-HOUSE.

three portraits of him were formerly in the picture gallery, one of which was for many years to be seen at the White Hart Inn at Ponder's-end, but it has long since disappeared.

### ABBOT OF THORNEY'S LANDS.

In the reign of Hen. VI. the Abbot of Thorney had lands in this parish known as Cranes, which were then valued at seven marks per ann. In 1686 they were the property of Sir Thomas Stringer, and they still belong to the Manor of Durants.

### MANOR OF ELSYNGE.

The Manor of Elsynge, or Norris, appears to have no connexion beyond its name with Elsynge Hall. It is said to have been situated in Welsh's-lane (now Lock-lane), and was held of the king in capite by Stephen Wilforde, who died in 1547. The property was sold in 1708 by Richard Wilforde to Robert Mackeris, whose representatives hold one-third, the remainder being held by the Connop family of the Manor of Enfield at a fee farm rent of tenpence.

### MANOR OF SUFFOLKS.

The Manor of Suffolks, also situated near Ponder's End, was, in the middle of the fifteenth century, held under the crown by Sir Richard Parr, comptroller of the household. In the year 1798, it was sold to Newell Connop, Esq., and became merged in the Manor of Durants.

MANOR OF CAPELS.

Honeylands and Pentriches, *alias* Capels, are joint manors, and were formerly part of the possessions of Sir Giles Capel, who, in exchange for other lands, conveyed them to the crown in 1547. Capel House, the residence of James Warren, Esq., is situated at Bull's Cross, near the site of the old manor house, which along with the estate was sold by Queen Elizabeth in 1562 to William Horne, merchant, and after passing through the hands of various successive purchasers, became (in 1793) the property of the late Rawson Hart Boddam, Esq., some time governor of Bombay. Mr. Boddam pulled down the old manor house, reserving little more than the stables, and transferred its name of Capel House to his own villa, which is said to occupy the site of some of the out-buildings of the Palace of James I. at Theobalds. Tradition says that an old cross formerly stood near this spot, from which the name of Bull's Cross* is derived. The old manor house stood near a field now called North Field, where there are still the vestiges of an old garden, with three remarkable old trees—a willow, a plane, and a poplar.

Capel House, with its estate of thirty-one acres, was purchased in the year 1840 by James Warren, Esq., the uncle of the present proprietor.

---

* Called "Bedell's Cross" in a conveyance of land to John fforde, 23 Ed. IV (1483).

CAPEL-HOUSE, THE SEAT OF JAMES WARREN, ESQ.

ENFIELD-COURT, THE SEAT OF COL. A.P.F.C. SOMERSET, J.P., D.L.

### ENFIELD COURT.

Enfield Court is the residence of Colonel Alfred Plantagenet Frederick Charles Somerset, J.P., and Deputy Lieutenant. The estate, which contains about eighty acres, is partly freehold and partly copyhold of the Manor of Worcesters, and was devised to Colonel Somerset by his godfather, the late General Martin. At the Battle of Waterloo, Lord John T. H. Somerset (a younger son of the Duke of Beaufort), then an officer in the 23rd Light Dragoons, saved the life of his comrade, Gen. Martin, by his gallantry, and on the birth of his son (5 Sept., 1829), the general undertook the office of sponsor, and dying unmarried in 1852, left this estate and the bulk of his large property to his godson.

. The original structure dates from the latter end of the seventeenth century, since which time it has received many successive additions; the southern wing having been rebuilt by the present owner in 1864, at which time the grounds adjoining the street were planted; the public footpath which formerly ran between the house and the lawn being diverted with the consent of the Vestry, and under an order of the Quarter Sessions. The Riding House, which was erected in 1858, is a spacious building 63 feet in diameter, and well known to the public from the liberality with which it has at all times been freely lent for their use or recreation. The garden on the west front of the house still bears traces of having

been originally laid out in the time of William III., with
its broad terrace walk four hundred feet in length, and
what were once the clipped yews and hollies of the Dutch
style of gardening. At the bottom of this walk stands
the quaint and picturesque summer-house, a small
building two stories high; and an oblong fish-pond,
crossed by a bridge, the remains of the former canal.
The accompanying engraving is copied from a curious old
painting taken in the last century.

LINCOLN HOUSE.

On the west side of the road at Ponder's-end, opposite
South-street, stands an ancient mansion called Lincoln
House, said to take its name from the Earls of Lincoln,*
of whom Henry and Thomas, the second and third earls,
resided here from 1600 to 1612. From the arms which
were formerly in the windows it appeared to have been
the property of Henry Howard Viscount Bindon, and
afterwards of Sir Thomas Coventry, Lord Keeper, and of
George Villiers, first Duke of Buckingham. The house
was a buttressed brick building, with marks of great
antiquity. Under one of the windows between two marble
pillars there was in 1750 a tablet inscribed R.L. 1520.

---

* LYSONS.—Mr. Gough, however, says that this house was the
house of the *Bishops* of Lincoln, "or of that other William of
"Wickham, Bishop of that diocese, who was born here."

*(Gough's Camden, Vol. ii., p. 107.)*

OLD-SUMMER-HOUSE AT ENFIELD-COURT.

The interior of the house, which was very irregular,
contained several ornamental ceilings. The hall and
other rooms were wainscoted, apparently of the date of
James I., and the windows richly ornamented with stained
glass. One of these contained the arms of Howard with
seven quarterings (gules, a bend between 6 cross crosslets
fichée argent) with the supporters and crest of Howard
and a viscount's coronet—motto " Quod videri vis esto"—
underneath "Henry Howard, 1584." Another shield
bore "Sable, a fesse ermine," between three crescents,
or, with the Coventry crest, and below "Thomas
Coventrye Miles Dñus Custos magni sigilli Angliæ
anno 1627." On a third was the arms of Villiers
quartered with Pakeman, Bellers, Howby, and Kirkby.
A great part of the house was burned down a few years
ago, and has been rebuilt.

### BRIDGEN HALL,

Late the residence of John Smart, Esq., was built by
William Bridgen, of an ancient family in Bridgenorth,
Shropshire, many years Alderman of Farringdon Within.
He contested the Mayoralty with Beckford in 1761, when
the latter was elected. He became Lord Mayor in 1764,
and died at Bridgen Hall, October, 1779, his death being
accelerated by attending, at the request of his friend
John Wilkes, the election of Recorder to the City, when
he gave a casting vote for Serjeant Adair. He was buried
in the Parish Church of Enfield, his pall being supported

G

by six Aldermen, the Recorder attending as chief mourner.
His nephew Edward Bridgen, F.R.S., was treasurer to the
Society of Antiquaries, and married Martha, daughter of
Richardson, whom she is said to have assisted in writing
Clarissa.* Bridgen Hall was for many years the residence
of William Linwood, Esq., the brother of Miss Linwood,
so justly celebrated for her "sutile pictures," some fine
examples of which, including a Madonna della Sedia after
Raphael, are in the possession of David Henry, Esq., at
Forty-hill. Such was the trouble taken by Miss Linwood
to obtain the nice gradations of tone and colour, that she
took her worsteds over to Paris to the Gobelins manufactory, and there dipped them with her own hands into
the different vats of dye to ensure the exact shades
and tints which her work required. These wonderful
specimens of needlework comprised many copies from
old masters, some of which had the highest artistic merit.
The most remarkable perhaps was the "Salvator Mundi,"
from the original by Carlo Dolci, belonging to the
Marquess of Exeter. For this work, said to be the finest
copy in existence of that celebrated picture, the Emperor
Alexander offered her three thousand guineas. It is now
in the collection of Her Majesty at Windsor.

---

* "Mr. Richardson is dead of an apoplexy, and his second
"daughter has married a merchant." 20 July, 1762. Boswell's
Life of Johnson, vol. 1. p. 359.

### THE OLD ROMAN ROAD.

The ancient Roman Road, delineated on the old country maps as the ancient Ermen-street, or military road, led through part of the Chase in its passage to Hertford ; coming from Cripplegate, or Moorgate, it passed through Newington, thence through several green lanes to the east of Hornsey, entered Enfield Chase, and proceeded thence through Hatfield to Hertford. This was the road by which the Londoners marched with King Alfred at their head against the Danes, in the year 895, to a strong hold or fortification built by them at Hertford. After the low lands towards the River Lea had been drained, the Lord of the Manor of Edmonton first made the road from Hornsey through Tottenham and Edmonton, and so on to Enfield, whence it was continued to Bull's Cross, Hoddesdon, and Ware. "After the Barons' war (says Camden) against King John was waxed hot, the town of Ware turned London highway to it, whereas before it was but a little village, and known by a friery."

The public highways, staked out by the Commissioners under the Act of Parliament, 41 George III., chap. 143, called the " Enfield Inclosure Act," of the width of forty feet, are Ponder's-end-road, over Southbury-field, the East Barnet-road, the Ridgeway-road, the Hadley-road, Parsonage-road, New-lane-road, Theobald's Park-road, and East Lodge-road, &c., the expenses of their formation and repair for two years being defrayed by the sale of part of the enclosed land, after which time they were to be kept up and repaired by the parish. Such, however, was the state of these roads within the last fifty years, that the late Lady Elizabeth Palk, who resided at the Rectory, was accustomed, when she intended to call on Mrs. Elphinstone, at East Lodge, to send out men two or three days in advance, to fill the ruts with faggots to enable her carriage to pass. Within living memory it was possible to travel from Hadley Church through Enfield Chase, Epping and Hainault Forests, to Wanstead without ever leaving the green turf, or losing sight of forest land.

---

NOTE.—There are in Enfield 3 miles 4 furlongs, 110 yards, of turnpike roads which have been thrown, by the late Act, upon the parish, the repairs of which are estimated at £1,480 per annum.

## MARKETS AND FAIRS.

King Edward I. by a Charter, dated 1303, granted licence to Humphrey de Bohun, and his wife (Elizabeth, Countess of Holland and the King's daughter), and their heirs, to hold a weekly market on Mondays, at Enfield.

James I., also, by writ of Privy Council, dated the 17th of April, 1619, granted to certain parties therein named, and their assigns, one market in Enfield every Saturday. It appears that the latter grant established a Court of Pie Poudre, and all liberties, free customs, tolls, stallage, &c., a market-house, shambles, shops, and stalls, in trust for the poor. The site of the market-place, with the market-house and the profits, and the houses formerly standing on the west side, belong to the Parish, and are vested in trustees for any general use that concerns the Town and Parish. The market, however, from various causes, fell into decay; though several attempts have subsequently been made to revive it.

The present Market-cross was erected by subscription in 1826, at a cost exceeding £200, from the design of the late Mr. John Hill.

The Market-house was formerly a wooden building of an octagonal form, supported by eight columns and a central pillar. There were also a portable pillory and stocks in the Market-place, both of which have been long removed. The present stocks are in the iron railing surrounding the police station.

The Charter (of which a translation is appended) also granted a license to hold two annual fairs, of three days each, beginning respectively on the 14th of August and the 29th of November.

"A.D. 1303, 8th April,

31st Edward I., at Lenton.

"Edward, by the Grace of God, King of England, Lord of Ireland, Duke of Guienne, to his Archbishops, Bishops, Abbotts, Priors, Earls, Barons, Justices, Sheriffs, Reeves, Ministers, and all his Bailiffs and faithful people, greeting—

Know ye, That we have granted, and by this our Charter have confirmed unto our trusty and beloved Humphrey de Bohun, Earl of Hereford and Essex, and. Elizabeth, Countess of Holland, our very dear daughter, his wife, that they and the heirs of their bodies begotten for ever, may have a market every week, on Monday, at their Manor of Enfield, in the County of Middlesex, and 2 Fairs there every year, namely, one to last three days, to wit :—on the eve and on the day, and on the morrow of St. Andrew the Apostle ; and the other Fair to last during other three days, to wit :—on the eve and on the day, and on the morrow of the Assumption of the Blessed Virgin Mary ; unless such markets and such fairs be a nuisance of the neighbouring markets and neighbouring fairs. Therefore we will, and strictly command for us and our heirs, that the said Humphrey and Elizabeth, and the heirs of their bodies begotten for ever, shall have the aforesaid markets and fairs at their Manor of Enfield, with all liberties and free customs, to like markets and fairs pertaining, unless such markets and fairs be to the nuisance of the neighbouring fairs, as aforesaid, these being witnesses :—

The Venble. Father Antony, Bishop of Durham.

Th omas Earl of Lancaster.

William de Castellon.

Robert de la Warde, Steward of our Household.

Eustace de la Hacche.

Phillip de Varney.

John de Merk, and others.

Given under our hands at Lenton, on the 8th of April, in the 31st year of our reign, by the King himself.

Y de BROKENFORD, relating."

Of these the St. Andrew's Fair was once much celebrated as a fair for cheese, immense quantities of which were brought from Essex and other places, but it is now chiefly resorted to by horse dealers and cattle jobbers.

The August Fair, which, from some unknown cause, had latterly been held in September, had long ceased to answer any legitimate purposes of trade, and had become a source of immorality and disorder, and a growing nuisance to the inhabitants. This was so generally felt that in the year 1868 a memorial was signed by 100 of the leading inhabitants and tradesmen, including the names of all the magistrates, clergy, and ministers, stating the above facts, and praying that such steps should be

taken as were needful for its suppression. This memorial
was submitted to the Duchy of Lancaster, the Secretary
of State, and the Commissioner of Metropolitan Police ;
in consequence of which the Commissioner applied for a
summons to the Chief Steward to show the right and title
of the Duchy to hold such fair. Her Majesty having
graciously waived any claims under the supposed
authority of the Charter, the Steward was directed (on
application to the Duchy), to abstain from offering any
objection which might prevent the Justices from adjudi-
cating, and when their judgment was pronounced against
the legality of the Fair, Her Majesty was pleased to
acquiese in that decision. In consequence of this judgment, the following notice was posted by the directions
of the Commissioner :—

### " POLICE NOTICE! UNLAWFUL FAIR!

" Notice is hereby given, that, in pursuance of the Act
passed in the third year of the reign of Her Majesty
Queen Victoria, intituled " an Act for further improving
the police in and near the Metropolis," the Fair usually
holden upon certain ground called Enfield Town, owned
by the Duchy of Lancaster, and occupied by Edward
Letchworth, Chief Steward of the Manor of Enfield, in
the Duchy of Lancaster, and situate in the Parish of
Enfield, in the County of Middlesex, has been declared
unlawful, and a copy of the declaration by the Justices of
the Peace for the district of Enfield to that effect is

hereunto subjoined ; any attempt, therefore, to hold such Fair in future will subject offenders to a penalty not exceeding *ten pounds*, or in default of payment to *three months' imprisonment* in the House of Correction.

E. Y. W. HENDERSON,
*The Commissioner of Police of the Metropolis.*
*Metropolitan Police Office,*
4, *Whitehall Place, 24th August,* 1869."

COPY OF DECLARATION under 2 and 3 Vict., cap. 47, sec. 39.

" METROPOLITAN POLICE DISTRICT TO WIT.

"Whereas it hath been duly made to appear to us, James Meyer, Edward Ford, James Whatman Bosanquet, and Henry Carington Bowles Bowles, Esquires, four of Her Majesty's Justices of the Peace acting in and for the district of Enfield, in the county of Middlesex, sitting at the office for Petty Sessions at Enfield Town, in the said county of Middlesex, and within the Metropolitan Police District, that the Commissioner of Police of the Metropolis did direct Alexander Manson, one of the Superintendents belonging to the Metropolitan Police Force, to summon Edward Letchworth, the Chief Steward of the Manor of Enfield, in the Duchy of Lancaster, in the said county, and acting for the said Duchy of Lancaster as the owner of certain ground called " Enfield Town," situate in the Parish of Enfield in the said county and district aforesaid, whereon a certain Fair called the " Enfield Fair," has been usually holden on the 22nd, 23rd, and 24th days of September in each year without lawful authority, to show the right and title of such owner to hold such Fair ; and whereas on this thirteenth day of August, 1869, Edward Letchworth, the Chief Steward of the Manor of Enfield, in the Duchy of Lancaster, acting as such for the said Duchy of Lancaster as the owner of the said ground, having been duly summoned to appear before us this day, as is now proved before us as having been duly served with the said summons (not less than eight days before this day), and now being duly called does not appear before us, the said Justices sitting in Petty Sessions aforesaid, in pursuance of the said summons, and in that behalf issued, to show the right and title (if any) of such owner to hold the said Fair ; and we, the said Justices, having heard the case, and no sufficient cause to believe that the said Fair has been lawfully holden having been shown to us, we do hereby declare such Fair altogether unlawful.

Given under our hands, at the office for Petty Sessions at Enfield, in the County of Middlesex, this thirteenth day of August, one thousand, eight hundred and sixty-nine.

HENRY C. B. BOWLES.

(Signed)      JAMES MEYER.

EDWARD FORD.

J. W. BOSANQUET.

Some little opposition was excited by the publication of this notice, and an attempt was made to hold the Fair as usual, when one of the booth-holders was taken into

custody.  On the hearing of the case, an elaborate judgment was pronounced by Philip Twells, Esq., re-affirming
the illegality of the Fair, as declared by the Justices, and
committing the defendant to one day's imprisonment.
The defendant was accordingly walked into the cell at
the Station-house, and then liberated.

This being the last fair in the Metropolitan district
which was suppressed under the provisions of the Act,
some interest may attach to this record of the proceedings,
which we have, therefore, given in full.

## THE ENFIELD RACES.

The "Enfield Races," formerly held on the marshes at the bottom of Green-street, were first established in the year 1788, and on the 23rd and 24th of September two £50 plates were run for. These races were carried òn for some years, but failing in interest they were discontinued after several attempts to revive them. It was at these races, on September 1st, 1790, that the notorious pickpocket, George Barrington (whose real name was Waldon), was apprehended for robbing Henry Hare Townsend, Esq., of Bruce Castle, Tottenham, of a gold watch. He was taken before the Bench at the Angel at Edmonton, and committed; tried on the 16th September, and sentenced to seven years transportation. Being a man of some education and considerable abilities he became, after the expiration of his sentence, superintendent of the convicts, and chief officer of the police at Paramatta. On the opening of a theatre at Sidney in 1796, he composed the prologue, containing the well-known lines :—

> True patriots all !—for be it understood
> We left our country for our country's good !

On Monday, October 12th, 1801, this race-course was the scene of an extraordinary tumult. "The intended battle between Belcher and Burke, which was to have taken place this day in Enfield-marsh, was prevented by

the very proper interposition of Mr. Ford,\* who issued his
warrant against them, and on Sunday night Belcher was
taken into custody by Townsend, the Bow-street officer.
At an early hour on the day appointed, the road to Enfield
was crowded with horses and carriages of every description—hackney coaches, loaded within and without, and
pedestrians without number, but more particularly the
refuse of London, many of them armed with bludgeons,
and by one o'clock it was supposed that no fewer than
twenty thousand had assembled. Several magistrates of
the neighbourhood attended with volunteer associations,
and the yeomanry cavalry of Hertfordshire, with their
*field-pieces*, who presently separated the crowd. The
scene of action was then shifted into Waltham-marsh, in
Essex, the spectators being conveyed over the Lea, where
they waited in vain, and then began to disperse."—
*Gentleman's Magazine, p.* 952.

A fair or meeting for gambols and rustic sports is
mentioned by Dr. Robinson as held at Easter and Whit-
suntide (but now long discontinued), at "Bull-beggars
Hole," near the Rose and Crown at Clay-hill. "Bull-
beggar" is explained by Skinner as "larva manducus,"
(*i.e.* hobgoblin). Scot, in his " Discoverie of Witchcraft,"
says, "They have so fraide us with *bull-beggars*, spirits,
witches, &c., that we were afraide of our owne shadowes."

---

\* Afterwards Sir Richard Ford, M.P., the father of "Spanish
Ford," well known as an author and contributor to the Quarterly
Review, as well as for his fine gallery of old masters, and his
unrivalled collection of majolica and rare porcelain.

## THE MAGISTRACY AND POLICE.

The Petty Sessions are held weekly, on Friday, at eleven o'clock, a.m., at the Court-house, in Enfield. The Bench consists of the following Justices, any two of whom, acting together, have jurisdiction as a Police Magistrate, under the Metropolitan Police Acts:—

JAMES MEYER, ESQ.

EDWARD FORD, ESQ.

COLONEL ALFRED P. F. C. SOMERSET, Dep.-Lieut.

JAMES W. BOSANQUET, ESQ.

PHILIP TWELLS, ESQ.

ROBERT C. L. BEVAN, ESQ.

HENRY C. B. BOWLES, ESQ.

The police force in Enfield consists, at the present time, of one Inspector—Inspector Robert Gould ; four Sergeants,—Sergeant 25, Joseph Appleford; Sergeant 441, Edwin Adams (Enfield Town); Sergeant 22, William Macnamara; Sergeant 32, William Coote, (Enfield Highway), and thirty-six Constables;—one sergeant and two constables being mounted.

There are two Police Stations, one at Enfield, and the other at Enfield Highway, and also one at Potter's Bar which takes some of the outlying parts of the parish towards South Mimms.

The Superintendent, Mr. Alexander Manson, resides at Kentish Town Police Station, which is the divisional office of the Y division, and with which telegraphic communication has lately been established from the Enfield Station, and messages can be sent through the Commissioners' Office, Scotland Yard, to all parts of the Metropolis within a radius of fifteen miles of Charing Cross.

A new Station is now building in the London Road, the first bricks of which were laid on the 27th March, 1873, by James Meyer, Esq., J.P., the Rev. G. H. Hodson, Vicar, Mr. John Purdey, Vestry Clerk, Inspector Gould, and Mr. Creed, Overseer.

A Divisional Detective, P.C. Nathaniel Aldridge is stationed at Enfield.

## PERAMBULATION OF THE PARISH BOUNDARIES.

The custom of perambulation is said by Spelman to have been of heathen origin, and to be an imitation of the feast called Terminalia, which was dedicated to the god Terminus as the guardian of fields and landmarks. Plutarch states that it was originally instituted by Numa Pompilius.

The perambulation of Enfield was made every seventh year (though it is doubtful if the custom is a very old one) the expenses, including "refreshments," being paid out of the Church Rates. The last perambulation took place in January, 1858, and after being so long in abeyance, it may be hoped that the practice will not be renewed. The publication of the large Ordnance Map—which is legal evidence of the boundaries—has entirely superseded any real benefit which may once have attached to this custom, too often resulting in drunkenness and serious disturbance of the peace.

It was usual here, as in other parishes, to "bump" adults and to whip boys at different stations to make them remember the line of boundary. In 1830, the performers in an adjoining parish bumped an unlucky angler whom they found on the banks of the Lea, for which, however, he brought an action, and obtained £50 damages. In Chelsea the authorities seem to have been more considerate, the churchwardens' books (1679) containing the entry, "Given to the boys that were whipt 4s."

The following details are taken from the plan in the possession of Mr. Purdey, the Vestry Clerk.

1.—Beginning at the bridge, near the nine-mile stone, in the London Road called the red bridge:

2.—From the red bridge over the pales in a bevel line to the cross in Mr. Moorat's garden wall over the same, from thence through the garden over the second wall, and continue along the second garden to

3.—An oak with a cross at the edge of the New River; cross the river, and in a bevel line along Grove field to

4.—The oak, with a cross adjoining to the stile leading from the grove to the river; from thence along the hedge of Mr. Carr's field and little orchard, and in front of Mr. Ford's house through the long pond to

5.—An old horn-beam stump, with a cross along the hedge of the wood to the brook; cross the same, and along the bank to

6—A cross in the ground, where a beech tree with a cross formerly stood; then westward to a small oak in the hedge with a cross: continue along the hedge to a sallow;

7.—Then southward to a cross in a small oak in the brook: along the brook to

8.—Green Dragon-lane; along Old Park hedge to

9.—Filcap's gate, a cross in the gate-post: continue along the hedge of the Old Park to

10.—The corner of Mr. Clayton's allotment of thirty acres: along south-west hedge to

11.—The Edmonton fence, dividing the Enfield and Edmonton commons: along the fence to

12.—Cross the road to

13.—The gate and rails parting the two commons; along the Enfield fence to

H

14.—The corner of the tythe allotment in a straight line to

15.—Part of South-lodge allotment, being the cow-house, yard, &c.; cross the road in a straight line to •

16.—A cross in South-lodge fence; along the north-east fence to

17.—The end of the old inclosure; along the fence of the new inclosure to (a cross in post the corner of fence) at

18.—From thence to the corner; at

19.—And from thence to the old inclosure (a cross in an oak and a cross in post the corner of fence); to

20.—Along the old fence to

21.—The beginning of the other new intake directly opposite the Sheep's-head, Temple; along the new fence, and across gravel-pit-pond to

22.—From thence along the fence until you come opposite to

23.—The corner of tythe allotment; cross the road to No. 23. (By this means the whole of the South-lodge and inclosures are perambulated); along the tythe fence to

24—About four feet on the outside of Mr. Bevan's park pales; continue in a straight line westward along Russel's riding to

25.—From thence southward along the fence joining to Edmonton common, in a south direction to

26.—And from thence along the fence to

27.—The old Chase hedge; along same to a cross in gate post by the side of the road leading from Southgate to Potter's-bar; cross the road into Lord Feversham's shrubbery; across same to a cross in an oak over the garden pales, to a cross in post of the fence over the same wall in a straight line to the opposite fence; over same, and over the brick walls into the kitchen garden to a post E. P. 28; then cross through the kitchen garden door to an elm, and over the centre of the grass plat in front of Lord Feversham's house; along the fence of Lord Feversham's garden to a cross in the post at the end of the fence; over the pales across the field in a bevil line to a cross in the post at the corner E P; along the pale fence to

28.—A bend in Mr. Barne's pales over the same in a straight line to the north-east corner of his house, and over the lawn to a post E. P.

29.—Cross over the pales, and the road to

30.—From thence in a straight line across Mr. Alexander's field to post E. P.

31.—Over the pales and wall, and through

32.—His south-west corner window of his house, and out at the opposite one ; then in a straight line to

33.—A cross in a post No. 33 in the field ; along the field to the ditch ; along the same to

34.—A cross in post No. 34, from thence in a straight line over the hedge to No. 35 ; through the pond and yard of Mr. Wragg's to the garden fence and post 36 ; by a pale fence across the garden over the wall into the yard ; through the same, over the wall into the garden, across the lawn, to a cross in the plate and through Mr. Frank's offices, towards a cross in a stone in the garden wall ; along the back front of the house over the late Mr. Idle's fences to

37.—A cross on a post by the barn in the front of the house ; over the same, and across his yards to

38.—A cross on the shed belonging to the Cock ; over same, to a post No. 39 ; cross the yard, take in part of the pond, then by the side of Nixon's cottage fence ; along Mr. Parker's field to No. 40 ; to an ash tree in the corner of the garden ; along the field fence to a post No. 41 ; continue round the field to a post No. 42 ; cross over the road in a line northward to a cross in the ground by the stile near to Mr. Cater's park (by which you take in a piece of ground which lays open to Hadley common, which is also claimed by that parish); along the fence westward to the bend

43.—Then over Mr. Cater's park pales, in a bevil line, to a stake by the corner of the pond

44.—Across the great pond north-westward to the grip

45.—Then in the contrary direction to a post in a hedge to

46.—The park pales; continuing along the same to the point

47.—Then by the gate to

48.—Adjoining the north of Camlot way (part of Enfield is surrounded by Mimms and Hadley parishes); from 48 continue along the east part of the south fence of the allotment to the Minister of Hadley (which is in Hadley parish), to the south-east corner of Mount-pleasant inclosures at

49.—Here the parish of Enfield begins again.

From thence to 50, 51, and 52, which are the different angles of the fences belonging to Mount-pleasant inclosures, the whole of which are in the parish of Enfield. You now go along the west part of the south fence of the allotment to the Minister of Hadley (which is in Hadley parish), till you come to

53.—The east corner of the south fence of the late Mr. Nutting's field; along the garden, from thence to a post; then to

54.—The pond; cross the same, and in a straight line to

55.—The drain along the hedge through the late Mr. Nutting's second garden, the late Rev. Mr. Garrow's, and Colonel Dury's fields to

56.—The garden wall of the late Colonel Dury; over the same, and in a bevil line to

57.—The north wall of the garden; over the same to

58.—Cross the line to a barn (now nearly down), cross the garden where the mill formerly stood, to the corner of the garden at

59.—Along the footpath in the front of the Windmill and Two Brewers alehouses to

60.—The corner of the old fence now adjoining to the allotment for Old Fold Manor; along the fence to

61.—Round the corner to the angle at

62.—Then along the fence adjoining to an allotment to

63.—The end of that allotment; round the fence adjoining to the Minister of Hadley's allotment to No. 53 (where you begun); this and Dr. Green's are all that are in the parish of Enfield, and are wholly surrounded by the parishes of Hadley and South Mimms. From 53 you come to 52, along the south fence to Mount-pleasant, back to 48, the north corner of the gate of Camlet way, across the field northward to

64.—Along the fence to

65.—And from thence along the fence to the road leading to Gannick corner, at

66.—Along the fence adjoining the road to the gate.

67.—Cross at the gate to a cross in an oak tree.

68.—Along the bevil fence to

69.—Then in a straight direction to

70.—In the road from Cattle-gate ; cross the road eastward to the angle at

71.—From thence along the north side of the road by

72.—Near Cooper's-lane to 73, to the late Mr. Hammond's, Potter's-bar ; from

73.—The small garden, cross the yard and garden to a cross in his pales

74.—Then to the corner of the field at

75.—An old oak pollard tree in the county ditch along the ditch to Cooper's-lane gate ; cross the road and down the ditch to 71 ; from thence along the ditch to

76.—Cattle-gate.

A cross in Cattle-gate, over the hedge and across the pond ; along the shire ditch to a post under the window of Mr. Millard's stable, through same, over a shed, through the second shed, along the fence to a post E. P., into a field along the same.

A cross in an oak, then across a little pond, a post E. P., to the lane leading to Mr. Pulley's fields, to

A cross in an oak along Shire-ditch to the straight lane to

A cross in Mr. Pulley's wall by the front door ; in at the door, and out at the opposite door, over the corner of the wall to

A cross on an elm tree stump at the bottom of Mr. Pulley's field, a post No. 57 to

A cross in an ash pollard, to a post E. P.,

A cross in an horn-beam over the hedge ; continue along same to a post, and

A cross in an oak ; from thence in a bevil line across the field to a post in the hedge, and a cross in an oak pollard over the same hedge ; across the lane to a cross on an elm tree in fence, into Mr. Gray's first field in a straight line to a post at the bottom thereof, by a small ash over the hedge across the meadow to

, A cross on a small oak post over the fence ; along the fence to a cross in the oak pollard in the fence to

A cross on a small oak in late Sloman's field, to a post.

A cross in a small oak in the straight row to

A cross in the same row to a mark on an oak pollard going into the lane ; cross the lane over the hedge to

A cross in an oak to

A cross in a post, and along in a straight line to an oak in late Mr. Goring's first field, to

A cross in post, in second field, to

A cross in post in the said field, at the corner, over- the hedge in a bevil line to a post in the field, by the gate at the bottom of the lane leading from White-webbs to Mr. Goring's.

A cross in the gate-post ; cross the lane to a post in the opposite field to

A cross in an horn-beam in a nook, to

A cross in the post at the end of the field over the hedge, to

A cross in the post ; cross the field in a bevil line to

A cross in the post, and at a cross in an oak pollard ; then turn to the right about ten yards, and then turn to the left, continue along the south side of the fence of the field to

A cross in a post ; then along the fence to a post at the corner of the field over the hedge, along the fence to

A cross in the ground to a post.

Along the fence to a cross in an oak pollard in the fence ; along the same to

A cross in an oak pollard, and

A cross in post at the corner of the field over the hedge, along the fence to

A cross in an elm tree over the little pond to

. A cross in post in the next field, along the fence to

A cross in an elm tree in the corner.

A cross in the pales in Hullock's lane near by the stile, up the ditch across the river to the sluice, along the county drain, the middle of the shire ditch field, or Rushey meadow to

A cross in the post by the waste gate near a bridge, dividing Mr. Prescott's and Mr. English's fields, to a post with

A cross, then to

A cross in a post, to

A cross in a post over the hedge, and along the fence to

A cross in an oak pollard ; continue along the fence to

A cross in an ash, along the ditch to

A cross in an elm near the corner of the house to

A cross on the wall of the farm buildings of the late Richard Dyson, south of and near to the Waltham-cross turnpike gate.

A cross in a post in the road near the garden pales ; cross the road through the late Mr. Plume's premises to corner of the house and garden to a post E. P.,

A cross in an elm tree in the fence, along the same to a cross on a tree in the second field ; along the fence to a cross in an oak pollard over the hedge ; along county ditch to a dyke ; cross over the same ; along shire ditch to Cheshunt boundary post by the side of Cheshunt mill river ; over river into Ramney-marsh, then northward along the eastern bank of the said river to the north fence of the late Mr. Johnson's allotment adjoining Cheshunt parish ; along the said fence eastward to the new cut ; cross over same into Little Ramney

Marsh, and round the same to the entrance of the new cut into the river Lea ; across the new cut, along the western bank of the river Lea in a southward direction to the union of the Cheshunt and Enfield mill rivers with the river Lea ; cross same and continue along the western bank of the river Lea to the Government foundery of small arms ; through the same in the direction of the Old Barge-river, by the back part of Mr. Gunner's residence, and continue along the said river, taking in a small island, No. 1422, to a house formerly the King's Head, now belonging to Mr. Beckett, continuing southerly along the said river to the south boundary fence of the marsh, dividing Chingford-marsh from the allotment to Trinity College in South marsh ; along the said fence westwardly and south-westwardly to Mar Dyke ; along Mar Dyke (which is taken into the parish), to the Mill river over the same ; along the fence of land late belonging to Mrs. Nash to the lock of the new cut over the same ; along the fence of the allotments of the late Mrs. Nash and the late Matthew Robinson, and the old inclosure of Mr. William Allington, into the turnpike-road from London to Ware (which fence from the Mill river to the said turnpike-road is bounded on the south by Edmonton), cross the turnpike-road, along the fences of the allot-ments of the late William Mellish, Esq., in west field and Haydon's field to the old inclosure of the late Mr. Mellish, called Bradley Moor ; along the fence of the same to the allotment of the late Mr. Mellish in Joan Potter's field ; along the fence into the park of the late Mr. Mellish ; cross the great pond ; then to the red bridge in the London-road.

## ANTIQUITIES, TRADITIONS, &c.

There are fewer antiquities and traditions of interest connected with Enfield than might have been expected in a place of such ancient repute, whose annals record so many distinguished and historical names.

In addition to those given in the general history, the following may be briefly mentioned.

On the south side of Nag's Head-lane, near Ponder's-end, is a deep well, probably the brick conduit noted in Ogilby's roads 1698, and known by the name of Tim Ringer's Well—(King's Ring Well, 2076 in the ordnance map),—which was formerly considered infallible as a remedy for inflammation of the eyes. Dr. Robinson alludes to a tradition that a convent or old religious house once stood here, but he was unable to obtain any accurate information.

There is a small square moat—(1876 in the ordnance map)—surrounding a mound covered with trees, about half-an-acre in extent, to the south-west of the town, near Old Park Farm, but its history is unknown. A coin of Antoninus Pius was found here.

In September, 1820, an earthern vessel containing about seventy silver and brass coins of different Roman emperors, was ploughed up in Carterhatch-lane. In a gravel pit in Broomfield, human bones, nails, coins, and small earthenware vessels, have been frequently found, and in 1816 several Roman urns and skeletons were discovered. The fragments of a Roman As, a fibula or buckle, and some nondescript pieces of bronze, were dug up about twenty years ago in cutting a drain through the fosse of the old encampment at Old Park, and at the same time a broken " quern," or handmill for grinding corn, made of a fine breccia, or "pudding stone."

In Windmill Field large painted tiles have at different times been turned up by the plough, and also some sepulchral urns, in one of which were found three gold coins.

In 1755 Sir P. Thompson sent to the Society of Antiquaries a supposed Pyx* for the Host, curiously enamelled, which was found in digging a pond. A few years ago a beautiful and very perfect bottle of Roman glass was found at Forty Hill, in making some excavations in the grounds of David Henry, Esq.

THE STORY OF CANNING AND THE GYPSY.

Above a century ago a very mysterious affair happened in that part of Enfield known as the Wash, which caused great excitement in the country. The circumstances are here briefly stated :—Elizabeth Canning, a servant girl, had been on a visit to her uncle, and on

---

* Possibly the "pyxt" mentioned in the subsequent inventory of Church goods.

THE SEAT OF DAVID HENRY, ESQ, FORTY-HILL.

her return in the evening was attacked, in Moorfields, by two men, who robbed her, and gave her a blow which made her insensible ; they afterwards dragged her along the high road until they came to the house of one Mother Wells, at Enfield-wash, where, she said, one Mary Squires, an ugly old gypsy, confined her in a room after being shut up there twenty-eight days, and fed upon nothing but bread and water, she at length effected her escape. On arriving in London she told her tale to two gentlemen, with whom she had lived as servant; she made a deposition before a magistrate, but omitted many circumstances she had mentioned before, and added many others, stating that she had been robbed in Wells's house by a travelling gypsy, and that Virtue Hall, a young girl, stood by while her stays were cut off.

In consequence of these charges, Squires, Wells, and Hall were apprehended. Hall was discharged, but Squires was committed for the robbery, and Wells for aiding and abetting. Hall was again apprehended on a warrant obtained from Mr. Justice Fielding, who, after six hours' examination, not giving credit to her story, was about to commit her, when she begged to be heard, and said she would tell the whole truth, the substance of which was that Canning had been robbed at Wells's house, as she declared. On this Squires and Wells were brought to trial at the Old Bailey, and convicted on the evidence of Hall. Wells was sentenced to be burned in the hand and imprisoned, and Squires to be hanged.

Canning's story was considered so extraordinary and inconsistent in so many points, that many persons were of opinion that it was an imposition altogether. After the trial, new matter of suspicion arose, and in the course of further inquiries, before the Lord Mayor, ample evidence was obtained of the innocence of Squires, and the guilt of Canning for perjury. The result of these enquiries was laid before the King, who referred the whole matter to the Attorney and Solicitor-General (Sir Dudley Ryder and the Earl of Mansfield, then William Murray, Esq.) and, from the weight of evidence adduced, they obtained His Majesty's pardon for Squires, and Wells was discharged. Canning was then arraigned at the Old Bailey, and took her trial on a charge of wilful and corrupt perjury, which lasted seven days, when the *alibi* of Squires was proved by one of the most extraordinary chains of evidence ever brought before a court of justice. Canning was found guilty and sentenced to one month's imprisonment and seven years' transportation.

Such is the summary of a story which divided the country into two parties, called the Egyptians and the Canningites. Canning's was, however, the popular party, and the mob was zealously attached to her interest ; violent outrages occurred ; the Lord Mayor, Sir Thomas Rawlinson, was insulted, and his windows broken, and even his life threatened. Several hundred pounds were subscribed by the friends and partisans of Canning previously to her leaving for America, whither she was

allowed to transport herself, which enabled her to form a
very advantageous matrimonial alliance with a planter
there ; she died about the year 1773.

The proceedings in this extraordinary trial lasted from
January 2, 1753, to May 30, 1754, and such was the
public interest excited, that upwards of 40 volumes and
pamphlets were published on the subject.

It is singular that there should have been no haunted-
house in the parish. " Formerly (says Bourne in his
antiquities) almost every place had one.  If a house was
built in a melancholy situation, or in some old romantic
manner, or if any particular accident had happened in it,
a murder or a sudden death, or such like, to be sure that
house had a mark set on it, and it was afterwards
esteemed the habitation of a ghost."  The most diligent
enquiry has been unsuccessful in tracing the vestige of
one here, though the Chase was formerly notorious as
the residence of witches.

The Witch of Edmonton, in the fine drama of Ford
and Dekker, was a true story, and the unfortunate old
woman, who was condemned and executed for witchcraft
in 1622, was a denizen of the Chase.

It is a pity that the name of the sensible and kind-
hearted magistrate* who endeavoured to save her, and
whose better judgment puts the good Sir Matthew
Hale to shame, should not have been preserved.

---

* Perhaps " Mr. Justice Clark," who took bail for the "conjurer."

In the year 1590 a gang seems to have been discovered
"squatting" on the south borders of the Chase, when they
were dislodged by a hue and cry. The constable having
"commaunded" the servants of Sir Humphrey Weld
(afterwards Lord Mayor, and the father of Sir John
Weld, of Arno's-grove, who built and endowed the
Church at Southgate), and being accompanied
with bloodhounds, "and many moe, made serche
"for certen men which were about the arte of
"witchcrafte or conjuringe." The descriptive catalogue
of their apparatus is too curious to be omitted. Having
succeeded in capturing one of them, " with certen lattyn
"bookes aboute him, which are to be sene, and he being
"carried to the constable's house and there kept, we, with
"divers others, retorned to their cabbyn, which they had
"made under a great tree, with certen cirkells on the
"ground within the said cabbin, and one of the said
"cirkells was laid about with parchment written uppon
"with crosses, and by the said cabbyn we found a stoole
"with divers pottes by the same stoole, and a redd cock
"beinge dead by it, and againste the said stoole a fayre
"cristall-stone with this word (**Sathan**) written on yt.
"Also a parchment writinge with three or four seales of
"yellowe waxe at the same. We founde also in the same
"cabbyn a cope, a sirpler, a crowne, a scepter gilt, and a
"fair broad sword ready drawen, being set upp against
"the tree, and diverse other bookes and writinges, and a
"pece of brasse gilded, with diverse letters graven uppon
"it, and powders and rattes-bane, whiche the partie that

" fled strawed in the waye, disappointinge thereby our
" bloudd-hounde.  And the partie which we tooke, had
" about him the picture of Christe on the Crosse,
" hanginge behinde his back under his doublet, and on
" the same stringe before him, the picture of serpentes or
" such like.  And the said partie was brought by the
" constable before Mr. Justice Clark, to be examined, and
" we understand that the said conjurer is let goe, uppon
" suerties to answere the same at the next Sessions."

[" Information taken touchinge certeine conjurers.
" Septem. 21, 1590." From the Domestic Series, State
Paper Office.]

The following inventory of Church goods is taken from
the Public Records in the Augmentation Office.

[Church Goods, Middlesex, Miscellaneous Book,
No. 498.  Hundred de Ossulstone.]

The certificate and presentment of the jury of all the
goods, plate, ornaments, Juells and Bells, belonging and
appteyning to the Churche of Enfylde, w'hin the Countie
of Middx, as well conteyned w'hin the Inventory taken
by the King's Maties Comyssyoners, as also other ·goods
belongyng to the same Churche at this present third daye
of August in the vj$^{th}$ yere of the reigne of o$^r$ sovereigne
Lorde King Edward the vj$^{th}$ by the grace of God King
of England ffraunce and Ireland, defender of the faith,
and in erthe of the Churche of England and also of
Ireland the Supreme head.

Enfylde.—

Imprimis one Crosse of sylver and gilte p'sell of berall, conteyning in weyght liiij. ouncs.

Item, in other platte as chalessis, sensers, a pyxt and a paxe, conteyning in weight viij owncs and v. } the number of chalisses and censers uncerteine.

Item, a vestment deacon and subdeacon w^th the cope of tynsall coller yellow, the forest of imagery worke wrote w^th the nedle with sylke and gold.

Item, a vestment decon and subdeacon w^th the cope of crymsen velvet the offerace* of blewe velvet.

Item, a vestment of blacke velvet the deacon and subdeacon of blacke sylke w^th blewe bokelyd gartyers.

Item, a vestment of blewe damaske, wrought w^t tynsall, and a cope of blewe damaske, the offeras redd velvet.

Item, a cope of sade yellowe sylke, full of ymagery worke of golde.

Item, a vestment of redde sylke and one deacon w^th twoo copes of the same full of flowers.

Item, a cope of white sylke and a vestment of the same w^thout any abbe, stoll or phanell.†

Item, a blewe velvet vestment.

Item, a cope of blewe velvet.

Item, a cope of blewe satten of Bryghes w^h flowers.

Item, a vestment of blacke chamlett.

---

* Orfrays, gold embroidery (Chaucer).

† Fannel—a maniple,—a scarf worn about the left arm of a priest,—[*Phillips,—World of Words.*]

Item, twoo vestments of whyte bustyen.

Item, a vestement of deacon and sub-deacon of sylke of dyvers colors, the offeras of redde velvet.

Item, a vestment deacon and subdeacon of sylke and dyvers colors, the offeras of grene, redde, and whyte velvet w^th barrys of gold.

Item, a vestement of blewe chaungeable sylke the offeras of redd satten of Bridgs.

Item, a clothe to hange before the Aulter of satten of Brigs collo^r grene and rede.

Item, a nother hanging of whyte damaske w^h paynes of tysull.

Item, two Corperasis casis of tynsull and velvet.

Item, a crosse clothe of redde sylke w^h ymagery worke.

Item, a *payer of orgonse*, and foure bells in th steple.

Item, the weyght of the fyrst bell by estymacion, eight hundred, the second bell xii hundred, the third bell xvj hundred, the iiijth xxij hundred.

Item, a cloke streking on the greate bell.

Item, a sawnce* bell of twoo hundred weight.

Item, vj pounds of redye money in the churche box of Enfeld."

---

For the two following curious documents we are indebted to the courtesy of Arthur Sawyer, Esq.

---

* " It is, perhaps, that *sauncing* bell
That tolls all in to heaven or hell."

*Sir Walter Raleigh.*

I

*Copy of William Aylward's Will of* 1582, *by which he leaves* 20 *pence to the parish of Enfield to buy a Bible.*

"In the name of god amen anno dom — primo de mensis decembris. I william aylward of Endfield in ye counte of midde, maltman, being sike in bodie but in mynde perfect and in good reaymembrance—Thanks be given to god for yt. Doe ordaine and make this my laste will and testamente in manner and forme followinge thereto. I doe comitte my soulle into the hands of Allmightie god the Father and to Jesus Christe his sonne and my redemer, by whome I doe acknowledge all my synnes to be foregeven and pardoned,—and my bodie I doe give unto the yerthe at the tyme appointed, and as for those worldlie goodes which god hath lente me I doe in this manner of wise bestow them, (viz) I doe geve unto the cherche of Endfelld to the byinge of a Bible xxd. Itm I doe geve unto Agnes Redlington one litle Featherbed, one cheste, and two pewter platters, and also I doe geve her xxd. Item I doe geve unto Alice Sansome one Featherebedd. The residue of all my goodes and chattells as well moveable as unmoveable whatsoever, I do geve unto margerette my wife, whom I dooe orddane constitute and make my only lawfull and sole executrice of this my laste will and testamente, and she to retreave and take as well all mye debts as are owyinge unto me, otherwise all those debts as I doe owe, and to se my ffunceralles dischardged acordinge to the true meaninge therein expressed, in witness whereof I have sette my hand the daie and yeare

above written—william aylward his marke—witness myself
(leonard Thickedimy minister.")

*Presentation of Endowments and Church Expenses
(about A.D. 1500).*

We, Willm. Bull, Robert Curtes, John Hodge, and John
Cordell, Gardians and Churchwards of the parish Churche
of Enefelde in the Countie of Midd. Doe present and
certifie what Chauntreys, Hospitals, Colleges, Free
Chapells, fraternities, Brother hodds, gwyldes, and
stipendary prcestes be within the said Churche and by
what name they and any of them are known or called as
hereafter p'ticulerlry shall appear.

First we the said gardians doe present and certifie that
there is within the said churche a Brotherhood founded
by the pa'ssh'es of the said parish called ye lady Brotherhood, of the mere devosion of the said [ . . . ] to
the intent to maynteyne the [ . . . ] of God w't'n
the said C [ . . . ] to kepe a preest there to syng the
[ . . . . ] of God to the glorye of him and other the
holy company of heaven, towerds which maynteyning
there is given to the said Churche as hereunder ensueth.

Item we present that there is given to the said brotherhood by John Ford late of the said parish yeoman, one
close three acres of groune, as by the deade by the said
John Forde bearing date the — daye of November in
the second year of King Richard the thirde, appears—
the yerely extent whereof extendeth to ~~xxxiij.~~ xjs.

Further there is given to the said Brotherhed by Maude
Hamond late of the same par'he Widowe, one tenement
situate in South Strete in the said par'he, as by her last
will and testament more planyly apperethe, the yerely
extente wherof amounteth to vijs.

Item there is also given by one Walter Forde late of
the same par'he yoman, one tenement, to the intent to
kepe one obit for ever...... for the same Walter, as by the
last will and testament of the same Walter, bearing Date
the xij of September in the iiij year of the reigne of King
Edward iiij appereth,—the yerely extent whereof extendeth to xiiij.iiij.

Item there is given by one—Rotherhm of the same
pa'h deceased one tenement . . . . . "*to kepe an*

---

NOTE.—"Chanteries consisted of salaries allowed to one or more
priests to say daily masse for the soules of their deceased founders
and their friends; these were adjectives not able to staud of themselves, and, therefore, united to some parochial, collegiate, or
cathedral church.

" Free chappells, though for the same use and service, were of a
more substantiall and firm constitution, as independent of themselves.

"Colledges were of the same nature but more considerable in
bignesse, building, number of priests, and endowments."

These were all abolished by Act of Parliament, 1 Ed. VI. cap. 14,
"that the said lands might be altered for better uses—viz, erecting
grammar-schools, &c., &c.,—the Parliament bestowed them on the
King by his councell to dispose of the same accordingly."

*Fuller's Church History, &c., p.* 350.

*obitt*," (this passage obliterated and inserted in another hand), the yerely extent whereof is xs.

Item, there is also given by one Thomas Aylward late of the said par'he maltman, 4 acres and [. . .] of meade as obytt, as by his last will more plainly appereth, the yearly extent whereof extendeth to vs.

Ther is given by John Forde to the said brotherhedd, one tenement with a gardén, which one Robert Brown hathe taken from same brotherhed, about iiij yeres last past, the yerely extent wherof can not [ . . . . ]

Item, ther is given to the said by one Mystres Wheler late of London, widdowe, one maser w<sup>th</sup> a band of silver and gilt, worth vis. viijd.

Item, there is purchased by the Prsshns of the said Par'he, one hous called the churche hous w<sup>th</sup> a croft behynd the same, the yearly extent wherof is xv. [. . .]

There is given by Hugh Forde ij croftes of lande and 1 acre of land, the yerely extent amounteth to iiijs.

SUMMA iijl. xiijs.

Deductions and paymente going oute of the said fundes and rente, as hereafter ensueth.

First there is paid and going oute of the said one close and iij acres of grounde, for quite rent to the chief lorde by the year ijs.

Item, paid for an obyte to be kept for the said Walter Forde every year ijs. id.

Item, paid for an obyte to be kept for the said [. . .] rotherum by yere ijs. id.

Item, paid for an obite to be kept for the said Thomas Aylward by year ijs. id.

Item, paid for an obyte to be kept for the said Hugh Forde by year ijs. id.

Item, paid to John Obredyman prest, for his wages by yere vil. xiiis. iiijd.

Item, paid to Edmond Godesman for his wages, synging for the said brotherhood by yere vil. xiiis. iiijd.

*last chantry at*

So remayneth, De claro towards the repátions of the said Church and maynteyneing of Devyne service.   .   .

Item, as touching other londs, tents, juelle, plate, or ornamente other than these before expressed we have none.

So that the said pr'sshen's pay and disburse of their devocon over and above the said iijL xiijs.   .   .   .

[N.B.—The Chantrey lands above-mentioned appear to have been sold after the Reformation to John Hulson and Bartholomew Broxey, and the lands and tenements for obits to John Hulson and William Pendrede.]—*(Sale of Chantrey lands, Augmentation Office.)*

---

" A Book of Surveys of Enfield," among the records at Hadley, gives some interesting particulars of the "Survey of thé Manor and Chace of Enfield," 26 March, 2 Chas I (1635), and again 8 Oct., 1 Jas. 11 (1685).

It is stated in the first of these that there was " no perfect and exact survey now extant,"—and from the presentments it would appear that Charles I. suffered much loss from the malfaisance of his officers and tenants, every

one seeming disposed to help himself to the Royal
property, as if he scented the "grim feature" of the
coming rebellion,

"Sagacious of his quarry from afar."

"John Withering, Esq., hath a grant from His Majesty
"of a water mill in His Majesty's Chace of Enfield, at
"New Pond, for which he payeth, *or ought to pay*, per
"annum xxvs. . . . . And there is two windmills
" . . . . whereof the one . . . . at Bacon's-
"hill is pulled down and carried away by one Michael
"Grigg, of Hadley, Esq., and that there is *or ought to be*
"*paid* to His Majesty for the same twenty shillings per
"annum."—The fences which "*ought to be repaired*" by
sundry tenants, are "in much decay," and "Charles
"Crosby, deputy to John West, Esq., keeper of ye West
"Bailey walk, doth use to fell and sell all ye wood
"within ye new rails, for his own benefit, contrary to ye
"lease, to ye great prejudice of His Majesty's tenants
"there."

It is also presented,—that besides the King's Majesty's
tenants and the inhabitants of Enfield, various interlopers
"there commoned and so still do, but by what right we
"do not justly know," and it is recommended that "their
"pretended rights of common be examined in ye Duchy
"Court."

The boundaries of that part of the Chase, now annexed
to the parishes of Edmonton and Hadley, are thus
described:—"From thence to High Wood Gate als

Winchmore Hill Gate, and so by ye ring ditch to a
tenement of Sir John Moore's, Kt., in ye occupation of
Charles Tanner,* then to a tenement of Sir Lewis Palmer,*
Kt., and so to a new brick tenement of ye said Sir John
Moore's, then to a tenement of Basil Firebrace, . . . .
by the ring ditch to Southgate, and from thence taking in
ye cottage in ye occupation of John Petts . . . . to
ye ash tree where the three parishes meet at ye lane end,
and so along ye ring ditch to ye lane leading to East
Barnet, where a gate formerly stood leading into ye
Chace, taking in ye *Bush Fair* house and four more
tenements, by the house of Wm. Peck, Esq., . : . .
ye house of Robert Norris, . . . . by the hedge of
East Barnet, to a cottage formerly Sir Roger Wilbraham's,
parcel of Ludgraves, in Hadley parish, . . . thence
to the Blew House, . . . . the New Pond Head,
. . . . by the hedge of Hadley unto ye house of
Will. Nicholls, called Capon's House, . . . and so
to Hadley Church-yard, and so north and west to ye
Windmill, belonging to ye Lordship of Enfield, and so
by ye Highway to Summer Pool, als Sugar Well, from
thence along a great bank to Gannick Corner." ,

---

* Probably "Tanner's-end" and "Palmer's-green."

## NATURAL HISTORY.

The neighbourhood of Enfield is richer in its ornithology and botany than might have been expected, from its close vicinity to the metropolis. The following lists have been compiled from actual observation, and may be depended upon for accuracy.

## BIRDS.

" The ousel-cock, so black of hue,
  With orange-tawney bill,
The throstle with his note so true,
  The wren with little quill;
The finch, the sparrow, and the lark,
  The plain-song cuckoo gray."

*Midsummer Night's Dream.*

---

### FALCONIDÆ.

*Falco haliaëtus.*—Osprey. In 1865, a pair of Ospreys were seen almost daily for many weeks, at Forty-hill. These birds frequented, at the time, the lake in the grounds of J. D. Taylor, Esq., at Southgate, where they were often seen to catch fish, which they carried to the mast-head of the pleasure boat, and devoured. Another specimen was seen at White Webbs, in September, 1867, and about the same time at Forty-hill.

*Falco peregrinus.*—Peregrine Falcon. A fine female was shot at Trent-park, in the autumn of 1871, and is in the possession of Wilfred Bevan, Esq;—this is the true falcon of falconry. The male, or "tercel," is much smaller.

*Falco tinnunculus.*—Kestrel. Of not uncommon occurrence, and breeds in the district.

*Falco nisus.*—Sparrow-hawk. Still occasionally seen, and rarely breeds.

### STRIGIDÆ.

*Strix Otus.*—Long Eared Owl. Very rare. A specimen was obtained a few years since, by W. S. Parker, Esq.

*Strix flammea.*—Barn, or White Owl. Breeds in several places.

*Strix aluco.*—Tawney Owl.

### LANIADÆ.

*Lanius Collurio.*—Redbacked Shrike. A common summer visitant.

### MUSCICAPIDÆ.

*Muscicapa grisola.*—Spotted flycatcher. The last to arrive of our summer visitors. An egg of the cuckoo was found in the nest of this bird some years since, by J. W. Ford, Esq. Its occurrence in the nest of this species has not hitherto been recorded.

### MERULIDÆ.

*Turdus viscivorus.*—Missel Thrush.

*Muscicapa pilaris.*—Fieldfare. The Fieldfare, or Redwing, roosts in very large flocks in some of our young plantations during the winter months.

*Turdus musicus.*—Throstle, or Mavis; Song thrush.

  „  *iliacus.*—Redwing.

  „  *merula.*—Blackbird, or Ouzel.

  „  *torquatus.*—Ring Ouzel.  An occasional autumn visitant.

### SYLVIADÆ.

*Accentor modularis.*—Hedge Sparrow.

*Sylvia rubecula.*—Robin Redbreast.

  „  *cinerea.*—White-throat.

  „  *curruca.*—Lesser White-throat.

  „  *phœnicurus.*—Redstart.

  „  *locustella.*—Grasshopper Warbler.  Not very numerous, and from its retiring habits, rarely observed. A specimen was noticed in the grounds of Alderman Challis, Sep., 1870.

*Sylvia phragmitis.*—Sedge Warbler.

  „  *arundinacea.*—Reed Warbler.

  „  *luscinia.*—Nightingale.  This bird was until lately so common that one of the lodges on the Chase,— taken for the season by a well-known M.P.,—was given up after a few weeks' tenancy, on the ground that his family could get no sleep "for the singing of the nightingales."

*Sylvia atricapilla.*—Blackcap.

  „  *hortensis.*—Garden Warbler.  More plentiful in some seasons than others.

*Sylvia sibilatrix.*—Wood Wren.  Of rare occurrence in the woods.

*Sylvia trochilus.*—Willow Warbler.

„   *rufa.*—Chiff Chaff.

*Saxicola rubicola.*—Stonechat.

„   *rubetra.*—Whinchat.   The nest of this species is occasionally found.

*Saxicola œnanthe.*—Wheatear.

*Regulus cristatus.*—Golden Crested Wren.

### PARIDÆ.

*Parus major.*—Great Tit, or Titmouse.

„   *cæruleus.*—Blue Tit, or Tomtit.

„   *ater.*—Cole Tit.

„   *palustris.*—Marsh Tit.

„   *caudatus.*—Longtailed Tit.

### AMPELIDÆ.

*Bombycilla garrula*—Bohemian Waxwing.   A very rare winter visitant.   A specimen was shot at Cockfosters, Dec. 29th, 1866, in which season several flights of this bird were recorded.

### MOTACILLIDÆ.

*Motacilla yarrellii.*—Red Wagtail.

„   *boarula*—Grey Wagtail.   A winter visitor.

„   *campestris.* — Ray's Wagtail, or Yellow Wagtail.

### ANTHIDÆ.

*Anthus Arboreus.*—Tree Pipit.

„   *pratensis.*—Meadow Pipit, or Titlark.

ALAUDIDÆ.

*Alauda arvensis.*—Skylark.

   „    *arborea.*—Woodlark.   Far from common.

EMBERIZIDÆ.

*Emberiza miliaria.*—Common Bunting.   The rarest of these species.

*Emberiza schœniclus.*—Blackheaded Bunting.

   „    *citrinella.*—Yellow Bunting, or Yellow-hammer.

FRINGILLIDÆ.

*Fringilla cœlebs.*—Chaffinch.

   „    *montifringilla.*—Brambling.   In autumn and winter,—one occurred at Enfield-lock, in 1871.

*Fringilla montana.*—Tree Sparrow.   A casual straggler.

   „    *domestica.*—House Sparrow.

   „    *chloris.*—Greenfinch.

   „    *coccothraustes.*—Hawfinch,   or   Grosbeak. This species is perceptibly on the increase.   Though one of the shyest of British birds, it has three times built in yew trees on the lawn at Old-park, within twenty yards of the house.   The nests were composed of dry maple twigs, or roots, with a few stray fragments of white lichen in the lower part, and so open and loose in construction that the eggs could be seen through from below, yet so firmly were the materials inter-woven, that a nest, in sawing off the branch, received no injury.

*Fringilla carduelis.*—Goldfinch.   Much rarer than formerly.

*Fringilla spinus.*—Siskin, or Aberdevine.

     „    *cannabina.*—Linnet.

     „    *linaria.*—Lesser Redpole.   An autumn and winter visitor, coming in small flocks.

*Fringilla montium.*—Twite.  Of rare occurrence.

*Pyrrhula vulgaris.*—Bullfinch.  Not uncommon.

*Loxia curvirostra.*—Crossbill.  A rare and uncertain visitor, always occurring in flocks.  Five were seen at Clay-hill, October, 1868.

### STURNIDÆ.

*Sturnus vulgaris.*—Common Starling.

### CORVIDÆ.

*Corvus corax.*—Raven, or Corbie.  Bred for many years,—before 1840,—in the " Raven Elm," at Bush-hill Park, and subsequently in one of the group of Elms called " The Sisters," on the banks of the New River, below Old-park,—being the latest record of the bird's nesting in Middlesex.

*Corvus corone.*—Carrion Crow.

     „    *cornix.*—Hooded, or Grey Crow.   An occasional winter visitor.

*Corvus frugilegus.*—Rook.

     „    *monedula.*—Jackdaw.

     „    *pica.*—Magpie.

     „    *glandarius.*—Jay.

### PICIDÆ.

*Picus viridis.*—Green Woodpecker.  The "laugh" of of this beautiful bird may still occasionally, though very rarely, be heard.

*Picus major.*—Great spotted Woodpecker. Very rare.

„ *minor.*—Lesser spotted Woodpecker. Very rare.

*Yunx torquilla.*—Wryneck.

### CERTHIADÆ.

*Certhia familiaris.*—Common Creeper. Tolerably common, though seldom observed.

*Troglodytes vulgaris*—Wren.

*Upupa epops.*—Hoopoe. A single bird was observed and shot from the window, at Forty-hall, by Mr. Meyer, in the year 1841.

*Sitta Europea.*—Nuthatch. Somewhat rare.

### CUCULIDÆ.

*Cuculus canorus.*—Cuckoo, or Gowk.

### HALCYONIDÆ.

*Alcedo ispida.*—Kingfisher. Resident and breeds, but it is not desirable to indicate the locality.

### HIRUNDINIDÆ.

*Hirundo rustica.*—Swallow.

„ *urbica.*—Martin.

„ *riparia.*—Sandmartin.

*Cypselus apus.*—Swift.

### CAPRIMULGIDÆ.

*Caprimulgus europæus.*—Nightjar, Goat-sucker, or Fern Owl. Formerly common on the Chase. The reversible hind claw of this bird, and the serrated or toothed structure of the middle claw, have been supposed to enable them to carry off their eggs when disturbed. "Some naturalists (says Bishop Stanley) assert that they have such a power, and have been seen in the act of flight with eggs in their claws,—but the fact has been denied by others." The writer, however, saw one of these birds (in the year 1845) fly up from a tuft of grass at his feet, carrying two eggs in her claws. These she dropped within about a dozen yards of the spot where she rose, and they are now in the collection of J. W. Ford, Esq.

### COLUMBIDÆ.

*Columba palumbus.*—Ring-dove, or Wood-pigeon.

„ *œnas.*—Stock-dove.

„ *turtur.*—Turtle-dove. Breeds in the woods. One was picked up at Old-park with the head completely severed from the body by a hailstone, whilst sitting on her nest, after the destructive storm of July, 1859.

### PHASIANIDÆ.

*Phasianus colchicus*—Pheasant.

### TETRAONIDÆ.

*Syrrhaptes paradoxus.*—Pallas's Sandgrouse. During the summer of 1863, great interest was excited by the appearance of considerable numbers of this rare wanderer from the Steppes of Tartary. A specimen was shot on the borders of this parish near South Mimms, being the only one obtained in Middlesex.

*Perdrix cinerea.*—Partridge.

„ *rubra.*—Red-legged Partridge. Breeds on the Chase.

*Perdrix coturnix.*—Quail. Of very rare occurrence.

*Charadrius pluvialis.*—Golden Plover. Occasionally in autumn.

*Vanellus cristatus.*—Lapwing, or Peewit. On the Chase.

### ARDEIDÆ.

*Ardea cinerea.*—Heron. Occasionally frequents all the larger sheets of water.

### SCOLOPACIDÆ.

*Totanus hypoleucos.*—Common Sandpiper, or Summer Snipe. On the borders of the brooks. One was observed for ten days on the New River, at Chase-park, 1869. Never remains to breed.

*Scolopax rusticola.*—Woodcock. Formerly common. A few still come every season to Trent-park. Seven were bagged on one day during the late winter.

*Scolopax gallinago.*—Common Snipe. Tolerably common in autumn and winter.

*Scolopax gallinula.*—Jack Snipe.

### RALLIDÆ.

*Gallinula Crex.*—Landrail, or Corncrake.

    ,,    *porzana.*—Spotted Crake. A specimen of this very shy bird was shot June, 1869.

*Gallinula chloropus.*—Moorhen.

*Rallus aquaticus.*—Water Rail. Very occasional.

### LOBIPEDIDÆ.

*Fulica atra.*—Coot. Very rare.

K

## ANATIDÆ.

*Anser ferus.*—Greylag Goose, or Wild Goose. A "skein" of wild geese may occasionally be seen passing over in winter, but there is no record of a bird being killed.

*Anser segetum.*—Bean Goose.

*Anas acuta.*—Pintail.

  ,,  *boschas.*—Wild Duck. Breeds in several places.

  ,,  *crecca.*—Teal.

  ,,  *penelope.*—Widgeon.

## COLYMBIDÆ.

*Podiceps cornutus.*—Sclavonian Grebe. Graves, in his "History of British Birds," records a female of this grebe, as killed on the New River, at Clay-hill, in 1822.

*Podiceps minor.*—Little Grebe. Breeds occasionally at Bush-hill Park. Occurred on the water at Chase-park, in 1871.

## LARIDÆ.

*Larus tridactylus.*—Kittiwake. An immature specimen,. or "Tarrock," was picked up dead on the banks of the New River, in the autumn of 1871.

## BOTANY.

" Behold O man, that toilesome paines dost take,
   The flowers, the fields, and all that pleasant grows,
They spring, they bud, they blossome fresh and faire
   And decke the world with their rich pompous showes ;
Yet no man for them taketh paines or care,
Yet ne man can to them his carefull paines compare."

FAERIE QUEENE.

In the following list of phænogamous plants, those only are inserted which are thought rare or beautiful, or interesting. The localities are purposely omitted. The Latin names are those adopted by Sir J. E. Smith, and used in Sowerby's "English Botany."* It was found hopeless for unlearned writers to attempt to grapple with the restless changes of modern science, and its " barbarous binomials."

| | | |
|---|---|---|
| *Adoxa moschatellina* | - - | Tuberous moschatel. |
| *Anagallis tenella* | - - | Creeping pimpernel. |

* Sir J. E. Smith's preface to the 4th Vol. of " English Botany " is dated Nov. 1st, 1795. The *Times* of this day (May 13th, 1873), records,—" Yesterday, at Lowestoft, the *hundredth birthday* of Lady Smith, widow of Sir James Edward Smith, once President of the Linnæan Society, was celebrated by a dinner to 100 of the oldest people of both sexes."

| | | |
|---|---|---|
| *Angelica sylvestris* | - | - Wild Angelica. |
| *Anemone nemorosa* | - | - Wood anemone. |
| *Antirrhinum majus* | - | - Great Snapdragon. |
| *Aristolochia clematitis* | - | - Birth-wort. |
| *Asperula odorata* | - | - Woodruff. |
| *Atropa belladonna* | - | - Deadly Nightshade. |
| *Butomus umbellatus* | - | - Flowering-rush. |
| *Caltha palustris* - | - | - Marsh Marigold. |
| *Campanula rotundifolia* | | - Blue-bell. |
| „ *rapunculus* | | - Rampion. |
| *Carex pendula* - | - | - Great Sedge. |
| *Cheiranthus fruticulosus* | | - Wallflower. |
| *Clematis vitalba* - | - | - Wild Clematis. |
| *Colchicum autumnale* - | | - Meadow Saffron. |
| *Convallaria majalis* | - | - Lily of the Valley. |
| *Convallaria multiflora* | | - Solomon's Seal. |
| *Cuscuta epithymum* | - | - Small Dodder. |
| *Daphne laureola* | - | - Spurge Laurel. |
| *Digitalis purpurea* | - | - Foxglove. |
| *Dipsacus sylvestris* | - | - Teazel. |
| *Epilobium angustifolium* | | - Rose-bay Willow-herb. |
| *Epipactis latifolia* | - | - Broad-leaved Helleborine. |
| *Euphrasia odontitis* | - | - Eye-bright. |
| *Fritillaria meleagris* | - | - Dead-man's-bell. |
| *Fumaria capreolata* | - | - Ramping Fumitory. |
| „ *officinalis* | - | - Common Fumitory. |
| *Habenaria bifolia* | - | - Butterfly Orchis. |

*Hieracium murorum* - -. (Obtained by Dr. Uvedale
from the North of England, and naturalised
here where it still flourishes.)

| | |
|---|---|
| *Humulus lupulus* - - | Hop. |
| *Hyacinthus non-scriptus* - | Hare-bells. |
| *Hyoscyamus niger* - - | Henbane. |
| *Hypericum androsæmum* - | Tutsan. |
| „ *hirsutum* - | Hairy St. John's-wort. |
| „ *pulchrum* - | Upright St. John's-wort. |
| *Inula Helenium* - - | Elecampane. |
| *Iris fœtidissima* - - | Stinking Iris. |
| „ *pseudacorus* - -. | Flower-de-luce. |
| *Lamium amplexicaule* - - | Henbit. |
| *Lathyrus aphaca* - - | Yellow vetchling. |
| „ *nissolia* - - | Crimson Grass-vetch. |
| *Lonicera caprifolium* - - | Yellow Honeysuckle. |
| „ *periclymenum* - - | Woodbine. |
| *Lilium martagon* - - | Turn-cap Lily. |
| *Lithospermum arvense* - - | Corn Gromwell. |
| *Lysimachia nummularia* - | Money-wort. |
| *Menyanthes trifoliata* - - | Buckbean. |
| *Myosurus minimus* - - | Mouse-tail. |
| *Narcissus pseudonarcissus*, - | Common Daffodil. |
| *Nuphar lutea* - - - | Yellow Water-lily. |
| *Nymphæa alba* - - - | White Water-lily. |
| *Ophioglossum vulgatum* - | Adder's Tongue. |
| *Orchis mascula* - - - | Early Purple Orchis. |

| | | |
|---|---|---|
| *Ophrys monorchis* | - - | Musk Orchis. |
| „ *nidus avis* | - - | Bird's-nest Ophrys. |
| „ *spiralis* - | - - | Lady's Traces. |
| *Orobanche elatior* | - - | Tall Broom Rape* |
| *Oxalis acetosella* - | - - | Wood Sorrel. |
| *Reseda lutea* - | - - | Wild Mignonette. |
| „ *luteola* | - - | Dyer's Weed. |
| *Ruscus aculeatus* | - - | Butcher's Broom. |
| *Sagittaria sagittifolia* - | - - | Arrow-head. |
| *Scutellaria galericulata* | - | Common Skull-cap. |
| *Senecio jacobæa* - | - - | Large Ragwort. |
| *Solanum dulcamara* | - - | Bitter Sweet. |
| „ *nigrum* | - - | Black Nightshade. |
| *Solidago virgaurea* | - - | Golden-rod. |
| *Spartium Scoparium* | - - | Common Broom. |
| *Stratiotes aloides* | - - | Water Soldier. |
| *Symphytum officinale* - | - | Comfrey. |
| *Tanacetum vulgare* | - - | Tansey. |
| *Typha Latifolia* | - - | Great Cat's-tail. |
| *Valeriana dioica* | - - | Valerian. |
| *Verbascum thapsus* | - - | Great Mullein. |
| *Vinca major* | - - | Large Periwinkle. |
| „ *minor* | - - | Small Periwinkle. |
| *Viola odorata* | - - | Sweet Violet. |

* This singular plant has been found in great abundance for several years, growing upon brooms on a gravelly hill, at Old-park, now cut away to obtain ballast for the Great Northern Railway.

The Lavender plant (Lavandula spica) was formerly grown here in large quantities as an article of commerce, principally in fields by the side of New-lane and " Lavender-hill."

Rhubarb (Rheum palmatum) was also cultivated with great success for medicinal purposes, soon after its first introduction into this country. Mr. Thomas Jones, of Fish-street-hill, received the gold medal of the Society of Arts, in 1793, for 420 plants grown at Forty-hill, and again in 1797, for 935 plants; and in the following year he obtained a premium from the society of thirty guineas, for raising and growing 3040 plants, and giving a full account of his method of culture.

Enfield was long ago celebrated for its gardens, an interesting account of which "upon a view of them in 1691," was communicated to the Society of Antiquaries, by the Rev. Dr. Hamilton, vice-president, from an original M.S. in his possession, and printed in their Archæologia, vol. xii. p. 181.

" Dr. Uvedale, of Enfield, is a great lover of plants, and having an extraordinary art in managing them, is become master of the greatest and choicest collection of exotic 'greens' that is perhaps any where in this land. His 'greens' take up six or seven houses or roomsteads. His orange trees and largest myrtles fill up his biggest house, and another house is filled with myrtles of a less size, and those more nice and curious plants that need closer keeping are in warmer rooms, and some of them stoved when he thinks fit. His flowers are choice, his stock numerous, and his culture of them very methodical and . curious; but to speak of the garden, in the whole, it does not lie fine, to please the eye, his delight and care lying more in the ordering particular plants, than in the pleasing view and form of his garden."

" Dr. Tillotson's garden near Enfield is a pleasurable place for walks, and some good walks there are too; but the tall aspen trees, and the many ponds in the heart of it are not so agreeable. He has two houses for 'greens,' but has few in them, all the best being removed to Lambeth. The house is moated about."

" Mr. Raynton's garden at Enfield is observable for nothing but his greenhouse, which he has had for many years. His orange, lemon, and myrtle trees, are as full and furnished as any in cases. He has a myrtle *cut in shape of a chair*, that is at least six feet high from the case, but the lower part is thin of leaves. The rest of the garden is very ordinary, and on the outside of his garden he has a warren which makes the ground about his seat lye rudely, and sometimes the coneys work under the wall into the garden."

" Mr. Richardson, at East Barnet, has a pretty garden with fine walks and good flowers, but the garden not being walled about, they have less summer fruit, yet are therefore the more industrious in managing the peach and apricot dwarf standards, which they say supply them plentifully with very good fruit. There is a good fish

pond in the middle of it, from which a broad gravel
walk leads to the highway, where a fair pair of broad
gates, with a narrower on either side, open at the top to
look through small bars, well wrought and well painted,
are a great ornament to the garden. They have orange
and lemon trees, but the wife and son being the managers
of the garden (the husband being gouty and not minding
it) *they cannot prevail for a house for them other than a
barn end.*"

"Mr. Watt's house and garden made near Enfield are
new, but the garden, for the time, is very fine, and large
and regularly laid out, with a fair fish pond in the middle.
He built a green-house * this summer, with three rooms
(somewhat like the Archbishop of Canterbury's) the
middle with a stove under it, and a sky-light above, and
both of them of glass on the foreside, with shutters within,
and the roof finely covered with Irish slate. But this
fine house is under this fault, they built it in summer and
thought not of winter; the dwelling house on the south
side interposing betwixt the sun and it, now when its
beams should refresh the plants."

---

* "Greenhouses,—houses built in gardens, and necessary for
many choice *greens* that will not bear the winter's cold."—
*(Philips's World of Words.)*

[The derivation, which seems to have escaped our lexicographers,
is noteworthy.]

## FERNS AND FUNGUSES.

The district produces but few ferns, and those of the commonest kinds, but it abounds in fungi, many of them of great beauty, and some of rare occurrence. Among the most remarkable of these is one figured by Bulliard (pl. 499)—as "Tremella violacea." This is not, as suggested, the "ferruginea" of Sowerby and Sir J. E. Smith; nor the "sarcoides" or "amythystea" of Berkeley, and it has perhaps never been figured or described in this country. A specimen was found some years ago in the neighbourhood of Northaw, and another in the wood at Old-park. It was of a rich violet purple, and resembled a bunch of puckered or "gauffered" velvet. The larger specimen measured above six inches by five, and nearly two inches in height, the surface finely pubescent and glossy, and giving out a rich purple tinge when steeped in water, as mentioned by Bulliard. It was sent to one of our learned societies for examination, where it fell a prey to scientific "acquisitiveness," but a careful drawing of it has been preserved.

The beautiful "Peziza Aurantia"* may be frequently

---

* The "Peziza Epidendra" of Sowerby (coccinea of Berkeley), with its brilliant carmine cup (the most elegant, says Sir J. E. Smith, of the whole tribe of fungi), has never been seen in Enfield by the writer, but it may be interesting to some botanists to hear that after various attempts during twenty years he has succeeded in

found on the shady banks of hedges, generally on the
northern side.   It is sometimes as much as three inches
across; variously cup-shaped or convoluted; whitish
externally, and of a rich orange within.   When mature,
·the slightest vibration of the air or ground, in attempting
to gather it, will frequently cause it to explode with a
slight report, in a cloud of smoke.

Amongst others may be shortly mentioned, —Byssus
phosphorea,˙ covering decayed posts or rails, with a
velvety surface of deep ultramarine blue, sometimes edged
with white; the disgusting Phallus Impudicus, with its
sickening smell of carrion; Agaricus Cantharellus, richly
fragrant of apricots,˙ and, according to Dr. Badham, one
of the most delicious of funguses,—though the secret has
been confined to the Freemason's Tavern, where they
have been ˙used for years on state occasions, and are
always highly paid for; Agaricus Oreades, the little buff
coloured "champignon," which produces the "fairy
rings" on pastures, and which gives an exquisite flavour
to soups and gravies; Lycoperdon Epidendron, some-

---

raising a young colony of them.   The parent plants were sent by a
friend from the neighbourhood of Selborne last autumn, and were
placed in moss under a bell-glass, in a greenhouse, where the little
scarlet cups are now springing up in profusion.   Last year a similar
experiment had been made, but on lifting up the glass to exhibit the
funguses to a visitor, they blew up like an alchemist's crucible, and ˉ
the hopes of the year were dispersed in empty air.—(*Nov.* 1872).

times covering half the stump of a dead tree with its clusters of vermilion balls; Xylostroma Giganteum, which in a few years will spread its ravages through the largest oak; Agaricus picaceus, singularly beautiful both in form and colour, a delicate grey, flecked with white; and the various species of Clavaria, like branches of coral, white,—shaded with every tint of yellow, red, green, and violet.

The common puff-ball, so abundant everywhere, is compared by Dr. Badham, to sweetbreads, for the delicacy of its unassisted flavour,—the agaricus deliciosus to tender lamb kidneys, and the agaricus heterophyllus to crawfish, when grilled.

So strong is the prejudice in this country against fungi, that hardly any of them are eaten, except the common *mushroom*, which, strange to say, is the only one prohibited from being brought into Rome, where any basket containing a single mushroom is condemned by the inspector, and sent under escort to be thrown into the Tiber.*

The fact is, that the great majority of fungi are both wholesome and excellent. The Rev. J. M. Berkeley mentions a friend, who, being a détenu in Poland, made a large "hortus siccus" of the fungi to which he had access; and one day found, to his great surprise, that his whole collection had been devoured by his guard, including many which he had considered of the most dangerous nature.

---

* Regulations of the " Congregazione Speciale di Sanita."

# ENTOMOLOGY.

"Things are not now quite so bad, as when Lady Glanville's will
was attempted to be set aside on the ground of lunacy,
evinced by no other act than her fondness for collecting
insects, and Ray had to appear at Exeter on the trial as a
witness of her sanity."

**HARRIS'S AURELIAN.**

- A short summary of the entomology of Enfield must
necessarily be confined to the Lepidoptera, omitting such
as are of universal occurrence.

The following tabular statement may be interesting as
showing the relative numbers of species found in Enfield,
and in England generally:—

| | Total number known. | Inserted in following List. | Omitted as of general occurrence | Total in Enfield. |
|---|---|---|---|---|
| Diurni ...................... | 65 | 9 | 13 | 22 |
| Nocturni ................... | 107 | 26 | 18 | 44 |
| Geometræ ............... | 275 | 32 | 39 | 71 |
| Drepanulæ ............... | 6 | — | 1 | 1 |
| Pseudo-bombyces........ | 27 | 5 | 4 | 9 |
| Noctuæ ................... | 308 | 73 | 63 | 136 |
| Deltoides.................. | 14 | 1 | 2 | 3 |
| Aventiæ ................... | 1 | 1 | 0 | 1 |
| Pyralides ................. | 69 | 3 | 11 | 14 |
| . | 872 | 150 | 151 | 301 |

158*

LEPIDOPTERA FOUND IN ENFIELD.

## DIURNI.

GONEPTERYX, RHAMNI.—*Brimstone Butterfly.*
COLIAS, EDUSA.—*Clouded Yellow.*
VANESSA, POLYCHLOROS.—*Large Tortoiseshell.*
,,     ANTIOPA.—*Camberwell Beauty.*＊
‘,,     CARDUI.—*Painted Lady.*
SATYRUS, TITHONUS.—*Large Heath.*
LYCÆNA, ALSUS.—*Small Blue.*
,,     ARGIOLUS.—*Azure Blue.*
HESPERIA, LINEA.—*Small Skipper.*

## NOCTURNI.

SMERINTHUS, OCELLATUS.................*Eyed Hawk Moth.*
,,     POPULI.—*Poplar*     ,,
,,     TILIÆ.—*Lime*     ,,
ACHERONTIA, ATROPOS.—*Death's Head*     ,,
SPHINX, CONVOLVULI.—*Convolvulus*     ,,
,,     LIGUSTRI.—*Privet*     ,,
DEILEPHILA, GALII.—*Bedstraw*     ,,
CHÆROCAMPA, PORCELLUS.—*Small Elephant*     ,,
,,     ELPENOR.—*Elephant*     ,,
MACROGLOSSA, STELLATARUM.—*Humming Bird*     ,,
SESIA, MYOPÆFORMIS.—*Red Belted Clearwing.*
,,     TIPULIFORMIS.—*Currant*     ,,
,,     APIFORMIS.—*Hornet*     ,,
ZEUZERA, ÆSCULI.—*Wood Leopard.*
HEPIALUS, HECTUS.—*Gold Swift.*
LIMACODES, ASELLUS.—*Triangle.*

---

＊ In 1872, this butterfly made its periodical appearance in many parts of the kingdom, and a specimen was seen by J. C. Catling, Esq., in his garden.

LITHOSIA, Complanula.—*Scarce Footman.*
,,      Stramineola.—*Pale Footman.*
ARCTIA, Fuliginosa.—*Ruby Tiger.*
,,      Urticæ.—*Water Ermine.*
LIPARIS, Chrysorrhæa.—*Brown Tail.*
,,      Salicis.—*Satin.*
ORGYIA, Fascelina.—*Dark Tussock.*
PŒCILOCAMPA, Populi.—*December Moth.*
ERIOGASTER, Lanestris.—*Small Eggar.*
LASIOCAMPA, Quercifolia.—*Lappet.*

## GEOMETRÆ.

METROCAMPA, Margaritata.—*Light Emerald.*
PERICALLIA, Syringaria.—*Lilac Beauty.*
ENNOMOS, Tiliaria.—*Canary Shouldered Thorn.*
,,      Angularia.—*August Thorn.*
HIMERA, Pennaria.—*Feathered Thorn.*
PHIGALIA, Pilosaria.—*Pale Brindled Beauty.*
BISTON, Hirtaria.—*Brindled Beauty.*
AMPHYDASIS, Prodromaria.—*Oak Beauty.*
,,      Betularia.—*Peppered Moth.*
HEMEROPHILA, Abruptaria.—*Waved Umber.*
BOARMIA, Consortaria.—*Pale Oak Beauty.*
NEMORIA, Viridata.—*Small Grass Emerald.*
EPHYRA, Porata.—*False Mocha.*
ACIDALIA, Scutulata.—*Single Dotted Wave.*
,,      Imitaria.—*Small Blood Vein.*
,,      Emarginata.—*Small Scallop.*
TIMANDRA, Amataria.—*Blood Vein.*
CORYCIA, Temerata.—*Clouded Silver.*
FIDONIA, Atomaria.—*Common Heath.*
EMMELESIA, Albulata.—*Grass Rivulet.*
,,      Blandiata.—*Pretty Pinion.*

EUPITHECIA, Venosata.—*Netted Pug.*

„ Linariata.—*Toadflax Pug.*

LOBOPHORA, Hexapterata.—*The Seraphim.*

„ Minutata.—*Ling Pug.*  .

PHIBALAPTERYX, Tersata.—*The Fern.*

SCOTOSIA, Dubitata.—*The Tissue.*

CIDARIA, Miata.—*Autumn Green Carpet.*

„ Dotata.—*The Spinach.*

EUBOLIA, Cervinaria.—*The Mallow.*

„ Bipunctaria.—*Chalk Carpet.*

ANAITIS, Plagiata.—*Treble Bar.*

## PSEUDO-BOMBYCES.

DICRANURA, Bifida.—*Poplar Kitten.*

PETASIA, Cassinea.—*The Sprawler.*

PTILODONTIS, Palpina.—*Pale Prominent.*

NOTODONTA, Dictæa.—*Swallow Prominent.*

„ Dictæoides.—*Little Swallow Prominent.*

## NOCTUÆ.

THYATIRA, Derasa.—*Buff Arches.*

„ Batis.—*Peach Blossom.*

CYMATOPHORA, Duplaris.—*Lesser Satin Moth.*

„ Diluta. —*Lesser Lutestring.*

BRYOPHILA, Glandifera.—*Marbled Green.*

ACRONYCTA, Tridens.—*Dark Dagger.*

„ Leporina.—*The Miller.*

„ Aceris. —*The Sycamore.*

„ Ligustri. —*The Coronet.*

SIMYRA, Venosa.—*Powdered Wainscot.*

LEUCANIA, Pudorina—*Striped Wainscot.*

„ Comma.—*Shoulder-striped Wainscot.*

GORTYNA, Flavago.—*Frosted Orange.*

HYDRÆCIA, Nictitans. *Ear Moth.*
„ Micacea.—*Rosy Rustic.*
AXYLIA, Putris.—*The Flame.*
XYLOPHASIA, Sublustris.—*Reddish Light Arches.*
„ Hepatica.—*Clouded Brindle.*
NEURIA, Saponariæ.—*Bordered Gothic.*
HELIOPHOBUS, Popularis.—*Feathered Gothic.*
CERIGO, Cytherea.—*Straw Underwing.*
MAMESTRA, Furva.—*The Confused.*
„ Persicariæ.—*The Dot.*
MIANA, Fasciuncula.—*Middle-barred Minor.*
„ Literosa.—*Rosy Minor.*
CADRARINA, Alsines.—*The Uncertain.*
„ Blanda.—*The Rustic.*
RUSINA, Tenebrosa.—*Brown Rustic.*
AGROTIS, Puta.—*Shuttle-shaped Dart.*
„ Tritici.—*White-line* „
„ Aquilina.—*Streaked* „
„ Saucia.—*Pearly Underwing.*
„ Corticea.—*Heart and Club.*
TRIPHÆNA, Fimbria.—*Broad-bordered Yellow Underwing.*
„ Interjecta.—*Least Yellow Underwing.*
NOCTUA, Triangulum.—*Double-spotted Square-spot.*
„ Umbrosa.—*Six-striped Rustic.*
TRACHEA, Piniperda.—*Pine Beauty.*
TÆNIOCAMPA, Rubicosa.—*Red Chestnut.*
„ Populeti.—*Lead-coloured Drab.*
„ Gracilis.—*Powdered Quaker.*
„ Munda.—*Twin-spotted Quaker.*
ANCHOCELIS, Rufina.—*Flounced Chestnut.*
„ Lunosa.—*Lunar Underwing.*
„ Litura.—*Brown-spot Pinion.*
HOPORINA, Croceago.—*Orange Upperwing.*

L

XANTHIA, ʻCERÁGO.— *The Sallow.*

    ,,       CITRAGO.—*Orange Sallow.*

    ,,       SILAGO.—*Pink-barred Sallow.*

COSMIA, DIFFINIS.—*White-spotted Pinion.*

    ,,    AFFINIS.—*Lesser* ,, ,,

DIANTHÆCIA, CARPOPHAGA.-- *Tawny Sheers.*

    ,,     CUCUBALI.—*The Campion.*

HECATERA, DYSODEA.—*Small Ranunculus.*

    ,,     SERENA.—*Broad-barred White.*

POLIA, FLAVOCINCTA.—*Large Ranunculus.*

APLECTA, TINCTA.—*Silvery Arches.*

    ,,     ADVENA.— *Pale Shining Brown.*

HADENA, CHENOPODII.—*The Nutmeg.*

CALOCAMPA, VETUSTA.—*Red Sword Grass.*

XYLINA, RHIZOLITHA.—*Gray Shoulder Knot.*

CUCULLIA, VERBASCI. —*The Mullein.*

    ,,     UMBRATICA.—*The Shark.*

HELIOTHIS,* ARMIGERA.—*Scarce Bordered Straw.*

HELIODES, ARBUTI.—*Small Yellow Underwing.*

BREPHOS, PARTHENIAS.—*Orange Underwing.*

    ,,     NOTHA.—*Light Orange Underwing.*

ABROSTOLA, URTICÆ.—*Light Spectacle.*

    ,,     TRIPLASIA.—*Dark Spectacle.*

PLUSIA, IOTA.—*Plain Golden Y.*

    ,,     Y. AUREUM.—*Beautiful Golden Y.*

AMPHIPYRA, PYRAMIDEA.—*Copper Underwing.*

CATOCALA, NUPTA.—*Red Underwing.*

## DELTOIDES.

HYPENA, ROSTRALIS.—*Buttoned Snout.*

---

* The wings of this rare moth were found by Mr. Wilson in a summer-house at Clay-hill.

## AVENTIÆ.

AVENTIA, Flexula.—*Beautiful Hook-tip.*

## PYRALIDES.

PYRALIS, Fimbrialis.—*Gold Fringe.*
SCOPULA, Ferrugalis.—*Rusty Dot.*
SCOPARIA, Cratægalis.—*Whitethorn Bar.*

———

## METEOROLOGY.

The following table shows the *mean* rainfall for each month in the year at Enfield, from observations of sixteen years, viz., 1849—1864 inclusive, made at the Vicarage-house, by the Rev. J. M. Heath:—

|  | INCHES. |
|---|---|
| January, | 1·90 |
| February, | 1·15 |
| March, | 1·64 |
| April, | 1·55 |
| May, | 2·26 |
| June, | 2·04 |
| July, | 2·36 |
| August, | 1·95 |
| September, | 2·42 |
| October, | 2·51 |
| November, | 1·87 |
| December, | 1·55 |
| Whole year ... | 23·20. |

The year 1854 was the driest, and 1860 the wettest, within this period, giving respectively 16·46 and 34·57 inches in twelve months.

The *mean* rainfall for ten years, 1863 to 1872, both inclusive, as taken at Old-park, by Alfred L. Ford, Esq., was as follows:—

| | INCHES. |
|---|---|
| January, | 2·75 |
| February, | 1·62 |
| March, | 1·68 |
| April, | 1·32 |
| May, | 1·99 |
| June, | 1·92 |
| July, | 1·86 |
| August, | 2·17 |
| September, | 2·86 |
| October, | 2·76 |
| November, | 1·71 |
| December, | 2·54 |
| Whole year, | 25·18. |

The driest year during this period was 1864, and the wettest, 1872, when the respective rainfall was 16·38 inches, and 35·90 inches.

The average given in the last ten years corresponds very exactly with the observations taken at Tottenham by the late Luke Howard, during a period of thirty-three years, from 1797 to 1830, giving an average of 25·13 inches, that at Old-park being an average of 25·18 inches. The great discrepancy between these results and those observed by Mr. Heath, arises from the rain-gauge at the Vicarage being placed at the top of the house, whilst those at Old-park and at Tottenham were on the ground. It is a well-known and curious fact that the elevation of a gauge will diminish the amount of rain* collected, and the currents of air on a roof materially affect the accuracy of the register.

The mean temperature at Old-park for ten years, from 1863 to 1872, was,

| | |
|---|---|
| January, | 34°05 |
| February, | 38°05 |
| March, | 40°55 |
| April, | 48°45 |
| May, | 52°85 |
| June, | 59°65 |
| July, | 62°45 |
| August, | 60°20 |
| September, | 56°00 |
| October, | 46°95 |
| November, | 48°20 |
| December, | 35°95 |

The highest temperature during this period being 93° July 21st, and July 22nd, 1868, and the lowest, 2° Jan. 3rd, 1867.

---

.

* Dr. Dalton found that the rain in a gauge fifty yards above the ground was in summer only two-thirds, and in winter only *one-half* of that in a gauge on the surface.

## TREES

Worthy of record for their antiquity, magnitude, or beauty.

(BY J. W. F.)

---

"Much can they praise the trees so straight and hy,
  The sapling pine, the cedar proud and talle,
  The vine-propp elme,—the poplar, never dry ;
  The builder oake, sole king of forests all ;
  The eugh, obedient to the bender's will,
  The birch for shafts, the sallow for the mill ;
  The warlike beech ; the ash for nothing ill.

*The Faerie Queene, Canto* I.

---

There being many "old patrician trees" in the parish of Enfield which are, perhaps, without their equals in the county, a notice of them may be interesting for the purpose of future comparison, or as a record of such as may soon disappear. The measurements have all been made personally by the writer, and are in each case taken where they most fairly represent the size of the tree.

### ACACIA.—*Robinia Pseud-acacia.*

There are two magnificent specimens at the Rectory, and a third at Bohun Lodge, possibly the oldest in the country. No trees of such size are recorded by Loudon. The respective measurements are at 3 feet from ground. Girth, 16-ft. 8-in., spread of branches, 69-ft.; girth, 14-ft. 2-in., spread, 66-ft. At ground, 18-ft. 4-in.; at three feet, 13-ft. 11-in. Height, 70-ft.

The acacia was one of the first North American trees introduced into Europe. The oldest, which is in the Jardin des Plantes, was planted in 1635, and destroyed in the late revolution. It was raised from seed sent over to Jean Robin, the professor of botany, from whom the tree takes its generic name. It was introduced into England in 1640.

### ASH.—*Fraxinus Excelsior.*

A grand old shell in the park at Forty Hall may well have been a sturdy tree when Elizabeth lived here at Elsynge Hall. It still supports a few vigorous branches. Measurement at ground, girth, 26-ft. 10-in. At 3 feet, 18-ft.

Another tree in the wood measures at 5-ft., 11-ft. 6-in., and has a clean stem to the first branch of more than 40-ft.; the height close on 100-ft.

"The leaves of this tree," says Gerard, "are of such virtue against serpents as that they dare not so much as touch the morning and evening shadowes of the tree, but shun them afar off." "*We write,*" says he, "*upon experience.*"

### BEECH.—*Fagus Sylvatica.*

Many noble beeches still remain in Trent Park, the lingering relics of the ancient Chase of Enfield. The finest specimens are not far from Camlet-moat, to the right and left of the drive, soon after entering

by the lodge on the Camlet way. The following are particularly worthy of notice. To the right of drive, a tree
with seat round it—At 1-ft. 6-in., girth 20-ft. 9-in.;
at 4-ft., 15-ft. 3-in.; at 14-ft., 12-ft. 3-in. Height,
102-ft. The stem is estimated to contain 211-ft. of
timber.

To the left of drive a magnificent tree—At 1-ft. 6-in.,
girth, 19-ft. 8-in.; at 4-ft., 15-ft. 10-in. Height, 98-ft.
The stem is estimated to contain 168-ft. of timber, and
the top 180-ft.

This tree at 12-ft. from the ground divides into five
mighty stems, the branches from which weep to the ground
on every side, and cover an area of 107-ft. diameter.

Many splendid beeches in this park have of late years
been, unhappily, felled. Especially worthy of record was
one near the Camlet-road, which rose for 40-ft. without a
branch, and with a bole as large as the foregoing.

COPPER BEECH.—*Fagus Purpurea.*

There are three copper beeches in the grounds at Capel
House, which, from their great size, must have been
among the earliest planted in this country, and may vie
with those at Enville and Sion as the largest and loftiest
in England. 1.—At 3-ft., girth 8-ft. 1-in.; spread of
branches, 81-ft. 2.—At ground, 20-ft.; at 3-ft., 9-ft.
10-in. 3.—At 3-ft., 10-ft. 8-in.

The original tree from which all the others in Europe are
derived was discovered in a wood in Germany, in the
middle of the last century.

### BIRCH.—*Betula Alba.*

A very fine one at South Lodge is unapproached in size by any hitherto recorded, or probably existing in the neighbourhood of London. At ground, girth, 16-ft. 7-in.; at 7-ft., 7-ft. 8-in. The spread of branches is 77-ft.; the height 65-ft.

### CEDAR.—*Cedrus Libani.*

The oldest cedar in England is undoubtedly that still flourishing in the Palace Garden of Enfield, which was planted by Dr. Uvedale between 1662 and 1670. The next in age were those planted in the Chelsea Physic Garden by Sir Hans Sloane, which, when measured by Sir Joseph Banks in 1784, were fast going to decay, and were then far behind the Enfield cedar in size and beauty. The largest was blown down in the autumn of 1853, when the interior was found to be almost entirely perished.

One other besides the Palace cedar was traditionally reported to have been planted by Queen Elizabeth. This stood in the grounds at Hendon-place, and was blown down in 1770. Its spread of branches was 100-ft., and it was then considered to be the finest tree in England.

"The great cedar," at Combe Bank, near Sevenoaks, measures, at 6-in. from the ground, 19-ft. 6-in.; at 6-ft., 17-ft. 5-in. We give the measurements of nine trees in the parish, all of which are of exceptional size, and as the cedar at the Palace has increased in girth several feet in the course of fifty years, these statistics ˉmay hereafter be of interest.

1.—The Palace Cedar. Measurement at ground, in 1821, 19-ft. 9-in.; in 1873, 25-ft. 3-in.; at 1-ft. 6-in., in 1821, 16-ft. 1-in.; in 1873, 19-ft. 7-in.; at 3-ft., in 1821, 13-ft. 6-in.; in 1873, 16-ft. 2-in.

A seedling from the above, planted by the writer at Old Park in 1846, measures 5-ft. 7-in. in circumference. Another planted there in 1851, is now 33-ft. high.

2.—At Bohun Lodge. Measurement at 1-ft. 6-in., 18-ft. 6-in.

3.—At East Lodge. Measurement at ground, 18-ft.; at 3-ft. 6-in., 11-ft. 9-in. This, the larger of two sister trees, is remarkable for its height, which is upwards of 90-ft.

4.—At South Lodge, 1, measurement at 3-ft. 6-in., 14-ft. 10-in.; spread of branches, 84-ft. 2, the companion tree, at 3-ft. 6-in., 14-ft. 8-in.

5.—At the Mount, Hadley. Measurement at 3-ft. 6-in., 14-ft. It is remarkable that this fine old house and grounds are in the parish of Enfield, although entirely surrounded by that of Hadley.

6.—At Belmont. Measurement at ground, 14-ft. 7-in; at 3-ft. 6-in., 11-ft. 10-in. This, the finer of two trees, is 75-ft. high.

7.—At Forty Hall. 1, Measurement at 1-ft. 6-in., 15-ft. at 4-ft.; 13-ft. 8-in. Diameter of spread of branches, 92-ft. 2, Measurement at 1-ft. 6-in., 15-ft. 7-in.; at 4-ft., 15-ft.

Diameter of spread of branches, 100-ft. There are three other fine specimens on the lawn, one of which is remarkable for preserving a timber-like stem for upwards of 60-ft.

The following measurements are worth recording, as the date of planting can, in each case, be fixed with certainty.

1.—The father of Mr. Taylor, of Grovelands, Southgate, planted a cedar there in the year 1770, the measurements of which, as now taken, are:—At ground, 16-ft. 6-in.; at 1-ft. 6-in., 13-ft. 8-in.; at 4-ft., 12-ft. 4-in. Diameter of spread of branches, 77-ft.

2.—Peter Collinson, the well-known botanist, and friend of Linnæus, planted with his own hand, in 1768, on the estate of Osgood Hanbury, Esq., at Coggeshall, two cedars.

Memorandum:—

" In token of the love and friendship which has for so
" many years subsisted between myself and my dear
" friend John Hanbury and his family, and as a lasting
" memorial of that friendship, I desire that one guinea
" may be given to my sincere friend Osgood Hanbury to
" purchase of Gordon, two cedars of Lebanon to be
" planted in two places of the new part of the park last
" taken in. Let the occasion of the said cedars and of
" their ages be registered in the great Bible at Coggeshall,
" that succeeding generations may know our friendship,
" and the antiquity of these trees. To my worthy friend

" Osgood Hanbury and his son I recommend their care
" and protection."—*P. Collinson.*

For the present dimensions of the larger of these trees
we are indebted to the courtesy of O. Hanbury, jun., Esq.
Measurement at ground, 18-ft. 10-in.; at 1-ft. 6-in.,
15-ft. 3-in.; at 3-ft., 15-ft. The largest branch extends
65-ft. from the main stem.

The data here given show that, with one or two
exceptions, the cedar of Lebanon is more rapid in its
growth than any tree in cultivation.

A short note may be added respecting the far-famed
cedars on Lebanon.

Miller, in his dictionary, gives the spread of the
largest tree then remaining as 111-ft. The girth of the
largest, according to Maundrell, was, in 1696, 36-ft. 6-in.

The original trees are constantly decreasing in number.
In 1550, 28 were counted ; in 1575, Ranwolff saw 24
sound trees ; in 1600, there were but 23 ; in 1696,
Maundrell found only 16 remaining ; in 1810, Burckhardt
counted 11 or 12 ; in 1818, Dr. Richardson found that
" the old cedars, the glory of Lebanon, were no more than
seven in number." And a friend, who visited the district
in 1872, saw three of these lying on the ground. Four
trees only remain of the mighty forest which once
employed eighty thousand hewers.*

---

* 1 Kings, v. 15.

The Maronites have a curious tradition that no sooner do the snows begin to fall than these cedars change their figure. The branches, which before spread themselves, rise insensibly, gathering together, and turn their points upwards towards heaven, forming a pyramid. Nature, they say, inspires this movement, without which they could never sustain the immense weight of snow remaining for so long a time.

> " It was a cedar tree ;
> Its bróad round-spreading branches, when they felt
> The snow, rose upwards in a point to heaven,
> And standing in their strength erect,
> Defied the baffled storm."—*Thalaba.*

" The Gentiles were wont to make their divels or images of this kind of wood that they might last the longer."—*Gerard.*

### CHESTNUT (HORSE).—*Æsculus Hippocastanum.*

A very fine tree near the entrance lodge at Forty Hall. Measurement at ground, 18-ft. 1-in.; at 4-ft. 6-in., 10-ft. 10-in. Greatest spread of single branch, 42-ft.; height, 80-ft. This tree was selected by Loudon, and figured in his Arboretum as a magnificent specimen of a chestnut in its prime.

A remarkably picturesque chestnut at Chase Park has no main trunk, but immediately throws out branches, which resting on the ground cover an area, the diameter of which is 81-ft.

Loudon records a tree in Enfield 100-ft. high, but this we have been unable to trace. Mr. St. Hilaire states that the chestnut was brought to England from the mountains of Thibet in 1550. It was not known in England before 1615. The chestnut was brought from the mountains of Thibet to Constantinople, in 1850, and thence obtained by Clusius from the Imperial Ambassador at the Porte in 1576. It is first mentioned in this country by Parkinson in 1629, who placed it in his orchard as a fruit tree, and describes the nut as superior to the ordinary sort.

### CHESTNUT (SPANISH).—*Castanea Vesca.*

An old tree at South Lodge measures at 5-ft., 15-ft. 7-in. Another in the wood at Forty Hall, upwards of 90-ft. high; measures at ground, 17-ft. 7-in.; at 5-ft., 11-ft. The stem is timber for upwards of 70-ft., below which height it throws out no important branches.

### CORNELIAN CHERRY.—*Cornus Mas.*

A very old example of the Cornelian Cherry, which rarely reaches the dignity of a tree, died at Old Park a few years since. The tree was upwards of 4-ft. in circumference, and was by estimation larger than the famous trees in the castle at Heidelberg, long noted as the most remarkable in Europe. The tree was introduced into England in 1596, and is the only English grown wood which, from its weight, will sink in water. Pliny speaks of it as nearly equal to iron in hardness, and as such " fit for making wedges."

CRAB.—*Pyrus Malus Acerbus.*

An extraordinary crab tree in White Webb's Park, measures at 1-ft., 8-ft. 2-in., and is 149-ft. in circumference, covering upwards of a quarter of an acre of ground with its dense circular head. This is, as far as can be ascertained, unequalled by any other known specimen.

DECIDUOUS CYPRESS.—*Taxodium Distichum.*

There are two exceptionally fine trees on the banks of the lake at South Lodge. 1.—Measures at ground, 16-ft. 7-in.; at 5-ft., 10-ft. 4-in. Height, upwards of 70-ft. 2.—Measures at 5-ft., 8-ft. 4-in. This tree was introduced from America before 1740. In damp places the roots throw up remarkable conical protuberances, from 1 to 2-ft. high, and as much as 4-ft. thick, always hollow. Michaux says, "They are cut off, and made use of by the negroes for beehives."

ELM.— *Ulmus Campestris.*

Of the well-known specimens on Forty-hill, the largest unfortunately lost its head in a great storm in 1863. This tree measures at the ground, 26-ft.; and at 4-ft., 18-ft. 6-in. A fine engraving of these trees, now very scarce, was published August 10th, 1818, by J. C. Lewis, the author of "The Rivers of England," and engraver of Claude's Liber Studiorum.

The keel of "The British Queen" was cut from an elm tree felled at Forty Hall. She was the largest vessel that had then been built, being 35-ft. longer than any ship in the navy. At the time of the Crimean war the central portions of five keels, upwards of 40-ft. long, were cut here for dispatch-boats.

An extraordinary elm, known for generations as "The Raven Elm," was cut down in Bush Hill Park, in 1839. This tree was so thick that the largest cross-cut-saw in the district was found too short for the purpose, and three extra feet were joined on to it, making the saw 12-ft. long. Two planks, each 32-ft. long, 7-ft. wide, and 12-in. thick through their entire length, were cut out of it, and were made into a dining-table for an old baronial hall. The trunk contained 13 loads, or 650 cubic feet of timber.

On Hadley Common—the portion of the Chase allotted to that parish under the Enclosure Act—are two gigantic and interesting relics. The one known as "Latimer's Elm," and so marked on the Ordnance Map, measures at ground, 36-ft. 9-in.; at 4-ft., 20-ft. 4-in. Under this tree tradition hands down that Latimer once preached, and from its venerable age it was probably a stately tree even in his time. Its situation is on a level with the dome of St. Paul's, and on a clear summer's day the spectator at its foot may watch the ships gliding down the distant Thames.

The other tree, or rather barkless shell, stands on the verge of the common opposite to Hadley Church. It measures at the ground, 30-ft.; at 5-ft., 20-ft. From a limb of this "gaunt and lifeless tree," Lord Lytton, in the

M

concluding chapter of the last of the Barons—the closing scene of the Battle of Barnet—hangs the wizard Adam Warner.

### EVERGREEN OAK.—*Quercus Ilex.*

A beautiful tree at Old Park rests its branches on the ground in every direction, and has a spread of upwards of 70-ft. diameter.

Two lofty examples at Capel House measure at 3-ft., 9-ft. 7-in., and 9-ft. 9-in. respectively.

The first notice of the evergreen oak in this country is of one growing " in the king's privie garden at Whitehall," where it was observed by Clusius in 1581. Evelyn, referring to the same specimen in 1678, speaks of it as a " sickly imp of more than fourscore years growth."

### FIR, SILVER.—*Picea Pectinata.*

A remarkably fine tree for this county, 98-ft. high, formerly stood in the grounds at South Lodge. It was struck by lightning in the summer of 1868, and a large piece, several feet long and a foot in width, torn out of the main stem at 75-ft. from the ground, at which height daylight was distinctly perceptible through the trunk.

The loftiest trees recorded by Loudon in the neighbourhood of London were, one at Whitton, 97-ft., and another at Sion, 92-ft. high.

### HAWTHORN.—*Cratægus Oxycantha.*

A tree at Trent Park measures at 1-ft. 6-in., 7-ft. 10-in. A picturesque old thorn at Old Park measures 8-ft. 8-in.

### HOLLY.—*Ilex Aquifolium.*

There are many fine hollies in the rough, uncleared Chase at Trent Park, measuring from 6 to 7-ft. in circumference, and 40-ft. in height ; one now little more than a vast ivy bush, is at 5-ft., 7-ft. 9-in. in girth. There is a very large tree at Gough Park, and another in Bush Hill Park, remarkable for its clear stem and wide-spreading head and branches.

Cole, in his Paradise of Plants, states that he knew a tree which the owner " cut down, and caused to be sawed " into boards, and made himself thereof a coffin ; and, if I " mistake not, left enough to make his wife one also. " Both the parties were very corpulent, and, therefore, you " may imagine the tree could not be small."—*Sylva Florifera*, I., *p.* 283.

### HORNBEAM.—*Carpinus Betulus.*

Two at Trent Park are of great size and spread. 1, measures at 1-ft. 6-in., 13-ft.; at 4-ft., 10-ft. 6-in. 2, measures at 1-ft. 6-in., 14-ft. 6-in. One at Old Park measures at 3-ft., 6-ft. 6½-in.

### LARCH.—*Larix Europœa.*

Two died at Old Park of extreme old age before 1850. The girth at 1-ft. from the ground was 9-ft., and 8-ft. 3-in. respectively. It was difficult to trace the rings of the section, but the trees could hardly be much less than 200 years old. The timber, which was of great beauty, was sawn into boards, and used in fitting-up a billiard-room.

The larch is first mentioned in Parkinson's Paradisus, 1629, as "rare, and nursed up but with a few, and those only lovers of variety."

Those at Dunkeld are supposed to be the oldest now living in the country; the largest measured in 1825 was at 3-ft., 15-ft. in circumference. Referring to these, Headrick, in his Survey of Forfarshire, says, " They were brought by the celebrated Lockhart of Lee (who had been Ambassador from Cromwell to France), about 1660. After Cromwell's death, thinking himself unsafe on account of having served a usurper, he retired for some time into the territories of Venice ; he there observed the great use the Venetians made of larches, and when he returned home he brought a number of plants in pots. He nursed them in hothouses and in a greenhouse until they all died, except three ; these, in desperation, he planted in the warmest and best sheltered part of his garden, where they now stand." The wood of the larch is perhaps the most durable known. The piles upon which Venice is built are, after upwards of a thousand years, as sound as when first driven, and hard and black as ebony. It is not liable to become worm-eaten, as may be seen in many of Raphael's pictures, which are painted on this wood.

### LAUREL, PORTUGAL. —*Cerasus Lusitanica.*

At Old Park, one 30-ft. high, and 105-ft. diameter. Loudon records the largest known trees in England, but

mentions none of this size. It was introduced about
1648, being first grown at Highgate by Mr. James Cole,
who, as Parkinson informs us, used to cover it in winter
with a blanket.

### LIME.— *Tilia Europæa.*

There are four magnificent limes in Bush Hill Park.
1, measures at ground, 26-ft. 9-in.; at 3-ft., 15-ft. 1-in.
2, measures at ground, 26-ft. 3, measures at ground,
25-ft. 4, measures at ground, 23-ft. 6-in.; and at
5-ft. 8-in., 14-ft. 8-in., at which height it throws out three
remarkable limbs at right angles to the main stem;
the largest measures 6-ft. 11-in. in girth. This tree is
106-ft. high.

The noble double avenue at Forty Hall was probably
planted by Sir Nicholas Raynton in the time of Charles I.
when the fashion of so planting this tree was introduced
by Le Notre, in accordance with the prevailing custom in
France.

### MULBERRY.— *Morus Nigra.*

There are two very ancient trees in the parish. One
at Owl's Hall measures at 1-ft. 6-in., 6-ft. 8-in.; at 4-ft.,
6ft. 10-in. The other in the old garden of the house said
to have been the birthplace of Isaac D'Israeli, measures
at 1-ft. 6-in., 7-ft. 2-in.; at 4-ft., 7-ft. 7-in. It is
believed that the mulberry was brought to this country by
Cardinal Pole in 1555, when he planted it at Lambeth
Palace.

Its frequent occurrence in many old gardens is due to the attempt made by James I., in 1609, to introduce the cultivation of the silkworm, when the King, by letters to the Lords Lieutenant of the several shires gave order for the planting of ten thousand mulberry trees in each shire.

It is curious that the trees of the above date are all black mulberries, whereas of the white kind *(morus alba)*, the true food of the silkworm, very few exist.

However promising or early the season, the mulberry never bursts its buds until all danger of frost is over.

" *Cum germinare videris morum, injuriam postea frigoris timere nolito.*"—PLINY.

### OAK.—*Quercus Robur.*

The following are selected from among the many trees for which Enfield has long been noted.

A venerable pollard at Trent Park swells out into a vast stool at the base, where it measures 45-ft. 8-in. in circumference.

A noble tree by the drive of the house is 106-ft. high, and 29-ft. to the first branch. Measurement at 2-ft., 19-ft. 11-in.; at 14½ft., 15-ft. 6-in. It is estimated to contain 527-ft. of timber, 407 in the stem, 120 in the top.

A very ancient tree at Old Park measures at 2-ft., 20-ft. 4-in.; at 4-ft., 17-ft. 1-in., and the diameter of spread of branches is 107-ft. (The spread of the Minchenden Oak at Southgate which covers the largest extent of ground of any tree in England is now 126-ft., having increased 8-ft. since 1820. This, however, is a pollard.)

Another tree at Old Park, in full vigour, which Sir Samuel Cunard pronounced to be the finest grown tree he had seen in this country, measures at 3-ft., 14-ft., and has a spread of 110-ft.

A tree in the Warren Field at Forty Hall, measures at 1-ft. 6-in., 20-ft.; at 4-ft., 16-ft. 4-in., and the diameter of spread of branches is 102-ft.

The well-known weeping oak in front of Dr. Collyer's house measures at 4-ft. from the ground, 15-ft. 1-in.,—which will give the reader a scale of comparison for the size of the foregoing.

### POPLAR, BLACK.—*Populus Nigra*.

A large tree with a noble head at South Lodge measures at 4-ft., 13-ft. 10-in.

A row of fine Lombardy poplars—*populus dilatata*—(the last of which was blown down about three years ago) formerly stood in the grounds in front of Col. Somerset's house. "The poplar never dry," is the most incombustible wood known, on which account it is in great request for the floors and wood-work of engine-rooms. As it is a tree of rapid growth and thrives well in this neighbourhood, it would be found a profitable investment to the planter.

### TULIP TREE.—*Liriodendron Tulipifera*.

There are two very old trees at Capel House. 1, measures at 3-ft., 9-ft. 1-in., and is fast dying from age. 2, measures at 3-ft., 10ft. 2-in. Other fine specimens are growing at Enfield Court, Gough Park, and D'Acre Lodge. The tree was introduced about 1660. The original still survives in the grounds at Fulham Palace. Farmer, in his History of Waltham Abbey, mentions a tree there as " the largest and biggest that ever was seen."

## WILLOW.—*Salix Alba.*

There are two very fine willows growing on the banks of the New River in White Webbs Park. The finest measures at 3-ft., 15-ft. 6-in. East Lodge was formerly famous for great willows; the remains of several still survive.

A specimen of the Weeping Willow, *Salix Babylonica*, at Old Park was brought from the tomb of Napoleon at St. Helena, in 1835. Its height is a little above 40-ft.

## YEW.—*Taxus Baccata.*

There is a tree in the Vicarage garden remarkable for its great spread, upwards of 40-ft., and for the amount of timber in the stem.

The ancient yew tree in the Church-yard is noticeable as having been clipped for centuries into a pyramid, of which shape it still retains traces, although the preservation of this formal style has probably been neglected for more than a hundred years.

# BIOGRAPHY.

## SIR WALTER RALEIGH.

" He 'gan to hope of men to be received
For such as he him thought, or fain would be,—
But as in court, gay pourtance he perceived,
And gallant show to be in greatest gree,
Eftsoones to court he cast, t'advance his first degree."

*The Faery Queene.*

An old and generally accepted tradition claims for a
cottage at Chase-side, (the property of Colonel Somerset,
and situated between the Workhouse and the Gordon
Estate)—the distinction of having been formerly the
residence of Sir Walter Raleigh ;—and the authorities of
the Ordnance Survey have endorsed the popular belief
by so naming it upon their map of the parish.

It has evidently been, at one time, a house of more
pretension than its present appearance might at first
indicate, and the woodwork and the old panelling of the
rooms are indisputably of the 16th century.

Some confirmation is given to the common tradition
by the discovery, about thirty years ago, of a small recess
in the wall, near the fireplace, which was concealed by a

movable pannel, and contained a curious tobacco-pipe, apparently of Mexican design.

This pipe (which was purchased by the late James Spencer Bell, Esq., then M.P. for Guildford), was made of a close-grained fragrant wood, and mounted with a silver rim and lid;—the bowl 1½ inches in diameter, being quaintly carved with three faces—the eyes of the middle face being borrowed from its neighbours. Its whole length was about nine inches.

It is certain that Sir Walter Raleigh came up from College in hopes of obtaining promotion at Court, at the very time when Queen Elizabeth was residing in Enfield, and as he never came to court again till after the lapse of thirteen years, when he had obtained wealth, promotion, and renown,—it must have been on this occasion that the romantic incident · of the cloak occurred, to which history ascribes his first introduction to the Queen's notice, and the commencement of his brilliant career.

There seems no good reason to question the truth of the story which presents a scene so picturesque and so much in harmony with the character of both actors as to make every one reluctant to doubt its reality.

Some modern writers, indeed, suffering under the enlightened intellect of the age, have thought fit to treat the tale as apocryphal, but there is perhaps hardly any fact in English history which, as we hope to show, rests upon better evidence, or of which both the time and place can be more probably identified after the lapse of three centuries.

The original narrative is given in the " History of the Worthies of England, endeavoured by Thomas Fuller, D.D., London, 1662," and is as follows :—

" He was bred in Oriel Colledg, in Oxford, and thence "comming to Court formed some hopes of the Queen's " favours reflecting upon him ;—this made him write in " a glasse window, obvious to the Queen's eye,—

" 'Fain would I climb, yet fear to fall.'

" Her Majesty, either espying, or being shown it, did " under write,—

" ' If thy heart fails thee, climb not at all."

So far the statement of Fuller is substantiated by the
fact (which will be more fully detailed) that Raleigh
abruptly left Oriel College and came up along with his
cousin, to his relations the Dennys, who lived at Cheshunt ;—of which, as well as of Waltham-abbey, they were
the proprietors ;—his aunt, Lady Denny, was in attend-
ance on the Queen, to whom she˙was related through
the Boleyns, and who at this time was holding her court
at Enfield.

Here, however, a slight difficulty arises in the narrative
of Fuller, who proceeds to say,—" However, he at last
" climbed up the stairs of his own desert, but his intro-
" duction to the Court bare an elder date, from this
" occasion. This Captain Raleigh coming out of Ireland
" to the English court in good habit (his cloaths being
" then a considerable part of his estate) found the Queen
" walking, till meeting with a plashy place she seemed to
" scruple going thereon. Presently Raleigh cast and
" spred his new plush cloak on the ground, whereon the
" Queen trod gently, rewarding him afterwards with
" many suits for his so free and seasonable a tender of so
" fair a foot-cloath. Thus an advantageous admission
" into the first notice of a Prince is more than half a
" degree to preferment."—[*Fuller's Worthies, folio edition,
p. 262.*]

There is certainly some confusion in this statement,
which it must be remembered was written long after the
occurrence which it relates. The construction is some-

what ambiguous, but it seems to imply, and no doubt,
correctly, that the incident of the cloak occurred at an
earlier date than that of the window, and it is distinctly
said to have been Raleigh's *first introduction.* His
return from Ireland however, was thirteen years after the
exchange of rhymes on the " glasse,"—if that took place
on his first coming to court; and by this time Raleigh had
become equally distinguished for valour and ability, and
his exploits were so conspicuous as to be particularly and
circumstantially recited by the historians of the period.
He had then obtained not only his " first preferment," but
had been appointed along with his cousin, Sir Edward
Denny, to the government of Munster, a post of the
greatest importance, shortly afterwards followed by the
substantial reward of 12000 acres of the forfeited princi-
pality of the Earls of Desmond, whose rebellion he had
assisted to quell.

Some error is therefore patent in the consecutiveness
of Fuller's narrative, but as he himself says, " It is impossible for an author of a voluminous book, consisting
of several persons and circumstances, to have such
ubiquity of intelligence, as to apply the same infallibly to
every particular."

It is well known that Gibbon had proposed to write a
biography of Raleigh, which, after much research and
hesitation, he finally abandoned, from finding it hopeless
" to obtain accurate information as to the most important
" events of his public and the whole of his private life;"

and such was the destitution of biographical detail, that the old lives by Oldys (1733) and by Birch (1751) were prefixed without alteration or amendment to the edition of Raleigh's works, published in 1829, by the directors of the Clarendon press.

It must always be a matter of regret that Sir Walter Raleigh himself did not spend some of the time consumed in writing his "History of the World," on his own biography. The few allusions to his own knowledge of the scenes which he describes are touches of genius, and are full of interest. In default, however, of such a narrative, a summary of known facts and dates will be the best guide to the reader's judgment.

Sir Walter Raleigh was born at Hayes, in Devonshire, in 1552, being the second son by his father's third marriage with "Catherine, *daughter of Sir Philip Champernown, of Modbury*, and widow of Otho Gilbert, of Compton."

He was entered at Oriel College, Oxford, about his sixteenth year, but he soon left it along with his cousin Champernown, who had been his fellow-student, to join a company of volunteers, which was then enlisting under the auspices of Queen Elizabeth for the assistance of the Huguenots in France.

Sir Anthony Denny, of Cheshunt and Waltham Abbey, had married Raleigh's aunt, "Dame Joan, *daughter of Sir Philip Champernon, of Modbury;*" he had been gentleman of the bed-chamber and privy counsellor to

Henry VIII., who made him one of his executors.
"Nor (adds Fuller) was it the worst piece of service he
"performed to his master, that when all other courtiers
"declined the employment, he truly acquainted him with
"his dying condition, to dispose of his soul for another
"world."

Their second son, Sir Edward Denny (who afterwards
accompanied Raleigh to Ireland, "where, by God's
"blessing, Queen Elizabeth's bounty, and his own valour,
"he achieved a fair estate in the county of Kerry")—was
five years the senior of Raleigh, and they were both
seeking enrolment in the troop of gentlemen volunteers
which shortly afterwards joined the French expedition
under the command of *Henry Champernon*.

It is clear that during these preparations Raleigh
must have been living on the spot, and at this time Queen
Elizabeth was holding her court at Elsynge Hall, where,
as we learn from Sir William Cecil's letters, she came in
July, 1568, and it must, therefore, have been here that
the young student "comming to court from Oxford"
formed some hopes of the Queen's favours "*reflecting*
upon him," which we are told "made him write in a
glasse window" his line of budding ambition.

In the following year, 1569, he went with his company
to France, where he is said to have narrowly escaped the
massacre of St. Bartholomew. He did not return to
England till 1576, when he proceeded to the Low
Countries, where he served for a year under the Prince of

Orange, and in 1578 finding his half-brother Sir Humphrey Gilbert engaged in a design for making discoveries in North America, he embarked in it with eagerness.

On his return from this expedition in 1579, the rebellion in Ireland had broken out, and having obtained a captain's commission he joined the Queen's army there along with his old companion, Edward Denny, when they both rapidly obtained promotion and wealth,* Raleigh himself being made Governor of Cork.

· It could hardly have been at this time that a considerable part of Raleigh's estate consisted of " his new plush coat," and it certainly could not have been now that he obtained that " first notice of a prince which is more than "half a degree to preferment." If his " introduction to " the Court," and to the " first notice" of the Queen was

---

* " Sir Edward Denny was buried in Waltham Abbey, under a "curious marble monument, supported by large marble pillars "where lies the portraiture of the said Sir Edward and Dame Joan, "his wife, and underneath are six sons and four daughters kneeling. " This tomb is of a curious piece of workmanship ; the epitaph is in "gold letters on a black marble, and is thus :—

" An epitaph upon the death of the Right Worthy Sir Edward " Denny, Knight, son of the Right Hon. Sir Anthony Denny, "counsellor of estate and executor to King Henry VIII. and of *Joan* " *Chamnon*, his wife, who being of Queen Elizabeth's Privy "Chamber, and one of the Council of Munster in Ireland, was "governor of Kerry and Dismondy, there departed this life about "the 52 year of his age, the 21st Feb., 1599."

*Farmer's Hist. of Waltham*, 1735.

owing to his tender of the "fair foot-cloath," this must have been on his coming from Oriel (not Ireland) to Enfield ; and the action itself is much more like the impulsive enthusiasm of a boy than the more sober loyalty of the Governor of Cork.

In Sir Walter Scott's graphic description of these events he, with much natural probability, represents the incident of the cloak as occurring just before the inscription of the couplet ; but it need hardly be added that the time and place which he assigns to them are wholly imaginary and inconsistent with history.* Every native of Enfield may be excused if, with the evidence before him, he should with more likelihood place the scene of action on an autumnal day of 1568, in one of the forest walks of Forty Hall (then Elsynge Hall) leading along the banks of the " MAIDEN BRIDGE BROOK.". Tradition is silent as

---

* The date assumed in Kenilworth (1575) is some six years after Raleigh embarked for France, and six years before he returned from his campaign in Ireland. Perhaps no work of Sir W. Scott's is so full of anachronisms, arising probably from a wish to introduce all the celebrated characters of the age into his brilliant picture. Lord Southampton is addressed by Queen Elizabeth as the patron of Shakespeare, when that nobleman was not two years old, and the poet was acquiring his small Latin and less Greek in the grammar-school at Stratford. The "Tempest" is quoted, which was not written till a quarter of a century later, after the Queen's death ; and Raleigh himself receives the honour of knighthood in July, 1575, which was not conferred till 1584, after his return from Virginia.

N

to the origin of this name, but in the earliest survey of
the Chase the stream has the less romantic appellation
of " OLD POND GUTTER." In one of the Forty Hall
deeds (temp. James I.) the bridge which crosses it is
called " Cole's Bridge, otherwise Maiden's Bridge."

### THE EVIDENCE OF FULLER.

" Right well I wote
" That all this famous antique history
" By some the abondance of an ydle braine
" Will judged be, and painted forgery ;
" Rather than matter of just memory."

*The Faery Queene.*

One by one, the most picturesque incidents in English
history, to which tale and song have conceded renown,
have been consigned by " modern progress" to the limbo
of myths ; and the latest biographer of Raleigh, Mr.
Edwards, pronounces Fuller's anecdotes to be too well
known and too apocryphal to need repetition,—giving,
however, no better reason than that Raleigh died whilst
Fuller was a schoolboy.

It may be worth while then to inquire from what
sources Fuller is likely to have obtained his information,
and what probable reliance he could place upon his
authorities. His own truthfulness has never been
questioned, and his memory is well known to have been
wonderful. As to his fitness to weigh evidence, he shall
speak for himself :—

"The causes of books being farced with fauxities are
(he says) :—

" 1. Want of honest hearts, which betrayed their pen
" to untruths.

" 2. Want of able heads to distinguish reports from
" records—not choosing but gathering ; or rather not
" gathering, but scraping what could come to their hands.

" 3. Want of true matter to furnish out those lives in
" any proportion—as cooks are sometimes fain to lard
" lean meat, which otherwise would hardly be eatable for
" the drynesse thereof.

" For my own part I had rather my reader should arise
" hungry from my book,—rather uninformed than misin-
" formed thereby—rather ignorant than having a falsehood,
" or at best a conjecture for a truth obtruded upon him."

He tells us further on—" to give the particulars whence
" I have derived my information—first, printed books ;
" secondly, records in public offices ; third, manuscripts in
" the possession of private gentlemen ; fourth, instructions
" received from the *nearest relations to those whose lives
" we have presented."*

" Now let us see how far Fuller had access to Raleigh's
near relations.   In 1634 he was collated to the rectory of
Broad Windsor, in Dorset.   Here he was on the most intimate terms with the family of the Drakes ; Henry Drake,
who is called in his life of Sir Francis Drake "his dear and
" worthy parishioner," was married to "Amy, widow of
*Sir Arthur Champernoun."* In 1648 (Newcourt dates the

preferment 1640), he was presented to the perpetual
curacy of Waltham Abbey, within four miles of Elsynge
Hall. Here he was the intimate friend of Sir Henry
Wrothe, to whom he dedicated one of the books of his
Church History, and a visitor at his house at Durants,
which was only two miles distant.

The Dennys were still the proprietors of Waltham ;
the magnificent tomb of Sir Edward Denny, Raleigh's old
friend and relation, had lately been erected in the Abbey
directly before Fuller's eye as he officiated at the communion table. Sir Edward Denny's son (Baron of
Waltham and afterwards Earl of Norwich), had " settled
" upon the curate of Waltham, to whom a bare stipend of but
" eight pounds a year did belong, one hundred pounds per
" annum, with some other considerable obligations, without
" which the minister thereof must have kept more fasting
" days than ever were placed in the Roman calendar."

It is certain then that Fuller had the opportunity of
obtaining his information direct from Raleigh's relations,
as well as from those living on the spot, and of whose
evidence we know that he availed himself in other
matters. One old servant of the Dennys, whom he elsewhere quotes as his authority, may have brushed the very
cloak of Raleigh when he was a boy.

If " the most honest and laborious author of the 17th
century" had the means of obtaining " true matter to
" furnish out " any of his lives he must have had them
here ; and if the events recorded ever happened at all,

they must have happened when Raleigh first left Oriel
with his cousin to come to Court, which was at that time
at Enfield.

One difficulty still remains to be considered—the
evident confusion as to the dates and order of the two
events. The wonderful tenacity of Fuller's memory has
been mentioned above ;—but it was a memory of a very
peculiar kind—it was one more of isolated facts than of
logical sequence.

It is said that he could repeat a series of five hundred
strange and unconnected words after hearing them twice,
and that, on one occasion, after walking from Temple Bar
to the conduit at the end of Cheapside, he could repeat
the sign of every shop on both sides of the street, either
backwards or forwards.

Equally singular was Fuller's method of composition.
We are told that "he wrote near the margin the first
"words of every line down to the foot of the paper, after-
"wards filling up the lines and connecting the beginning
"and ends." He also "left blank spaces for the dates,
"or sometimes filled them up conjecturally, without any
"supposed need of nice method, as he designed to be
"more exact upon better opportunity." "A stranger to
"my method," he himself tells us, "would hardly rally
"my scattered and posthumous notes."

Now this contingency is exactly what occurred:—
Fuller died Aug. 15, 1661, and his Worthies of England
was not published till the following year. A part of the

work was in the printer's hands at the time of his death, the
remainder, *including the Worthies of Devonshire*, among
whom Raleigh is placed, being edited by his son John,
(then a young student at Cambridge), from his father's
"scattered and posthumous notes," and under circumstances which added still further to the chances of acci-
dental error. "The *discounting of sheets* (concludes the
"original preface), to expedite the work at severall presses,
"hath occasioned the often mistake of the folios.
"Whatever faults else occur in this impression, it is my
"request that thou would'st score them on my want of
"care or skill in correcting the same, that they may not
"in the least reflect on the credit of my dead father."—
JOHN FULLER.

The easily-made mistake of a transcriber or printer in
substituting "Ireland" for "Oriel," or a very slight confusion
of memory, or of posthumous papers, would account for
the discrepancy of dates which certainly exists.

There is just the error that might arise from a voluminous collection of notes imperfectly posted up or assorted ;
but the mistake of a bookbinder in misplacing a page of
a work does not affect the credit of the author.

> "I have given you my tale and my tale-master."
> "I have it
> "Upon his own report, and I believe it ;
> "He looks like sooth."
>
> (WINTER'S TALE.)

### WILLIAM WICKHAM.

William Wickham was born in the Manor House of Honeylands or Pentriches, of which his father was lessee, in the reign of Henry VIII. He was educated at King's College, Cambridge, was made Dean of Lincoln, in 1571, Bishop of Lincoln, 1584, and was translated to Winchester, in 1595, where, says Fuller, "he may be termed William Wickham, junior, in distinction of his namesake and predecessor; one equal to any of his order in piety and painfulnesse." He preached the funeral sermon for Mary Queen of Scots, at Peterborough, 1587, and died at his house, in Southwark, in 1596.

He married Antonine, daughter of William Barlow, Bishop of Chichester. She had four sisters married to four Bishops,—viz., Margaret to William Overton, Bishop of Coventry and Lichfield ; Anne to Herbert Westphaling, Bishop of Hereford; Elizabeth to William Day who succeeded Wickham, at Winchester; Frances, married first to Matthew Parker, son of the Archbishop of Canterbury, and secondly to Matthew, Archbishop of York. Thus her father was a Bishop and her father-in-law an Archbishop, she had four Bishops her brothers and an archbishop her husband. She died May 10th, 1629, æt 78. (Epitaph on Agatha, wife of William Barlow, Bishop of St. David's and of Chichester).

It is to this Bishop that the dilapidation of the once magnificent Cathedral, College, and Palace of St. David's is attributed. It is said that his "lady longed for the gay

"world, and wanting more than all the revenues of the
"see for himself and his family, he first raised the wind
" by selling off the lead from the roof of the buildings,
"and then obtained permission to remove from the palace
"on the plea that it was not watertight." In consequence
of this sacrilege the aisles of the cathedral are roofless,
and the cloisters are mere heaps of ruins. The palace,
built by Bishop Gower, in the 14th century, formed a quad-
rangle 120-ft. square, of which only parts of two sides
remain. Of St. Mary's College, founded by John of
Gaunt in 1365, the only relic is a chapel,—bare like the
rest, and rapidly hastening to decay.

### ROBERT UVEDALE.

He was born in 1642, and was a Fellow of Trinity
College, Cambridge, where he was a competitor with Sir
Isaac Newton for the law fellowship. Barrow gave his
decision in favour of Uvedale as being the senior in age
and equal in attainments. About 1660 Dr. Uvedale,
who was then Master of the Enfield Grammar School,
took a lease of the Palace for educating private pupils.
He was considered one of the first botanists in Europe,
and after his death his *hortus siccus* was purchased for a
large sum by· Sir Robert Walpole, and is now in the
British Museum. He married the grand-daughter of Sir
Matthew Hale, and died in 1722. He was the lineal
descendant of Peter de Uvedale, of Wykeham, in Hamp-
shire, a peer of the realm, 6-8-9. Edward III., by whom

he was summoned to Parliament as baron. Nicholas
Uvedale, his son, was the first great benefactor of the
celebrated William of Wykenham, having in 1334 placed
him at school at Winchester, as is recorded by a tablet
placed conspicuously in the front of the chapel at
Winchester, inscribed,"UVEDALLUS WYKEHAMI PATRONUS."
Some interesting letters of Dr. Uvedale's are printed by
Nichols in his Lit. Hist. of the eighteenth century, in
which he complains bitterly of the irregularity of the
Enfield Post-office, and desires his correspondents to
direct his letters " to be left at the Bull, in Bishopsgate,
" without mentioning Enfield, for our post letters are re-
" turned to the general post; from London to a post-office
" set up here, and frequently stay three or four days and
" sometimes longer before we receive them, which yet the
" gentlemen of the neighbourhood can get no redress for."
(May 29, 1701.)  This grievance seems to be unabated
in 1710, when he again writes :—" The post-house in
" Enfield is near two miles from me, so they think good
" to send them when they have enough to make a
" perquisite of; and our complaints either to them or
" their masters signify not, for we cannot help ourselves."
In August, 1700, he writes to a correspondent:—" I am
" now to thank you heartily for your kind present of
" heathcocks (grouse).   The pye came very well,
" undamaged in the least, but the fowl, by the length of
" the journey, were injured ; we could taste by the flesh
" on the breasts that they must certainly be very delicate,

" wholly new to us in these parts, and will be here wished
" for again,"—and the worthy doctor proceeds to state how
they might be preserved by judicious potting, " as I have
" had woodcocks from a great distance a standing cold
" dish in the family a month after received." The receipt,
he states, he had " from the learned in the kitchen, and
"they tell me it is authentical."

### ROBERT UVEDALE,

Of Trin. Coll., Camb., B.A. 1662, M.A. 1666, L.L.D.
1682, was the son of the above ; Vicar of Enfield
from 1721 to 1731. He was born May 25, 1642, and
educated at Westminster under Dr. Busby. He assisted
Dryden in his translation of Plutarch, for which he wrote
the Life of Dion. His son, Robert Uvedale, D.D.,
married the daughter of Bennet Langton, and became
Rector of Langton and Vicar of Swinehead, co. Lincoln.

### ISAAC D'ISRAELI.

Isaac D'Israeli was descended from one of those
Sephardim-Hebrew families who had been long
settled in Spain, where they had become almost an order
in the State. " Prosperous and wealthy (says Milman)
" they were cultivators and possessors of the soil, not
" seldom ministers of finance, and the most enlightened
" class in the kingdom, which· they had fertilized with
" their industry, enriched with their commerce, and
" adorned with their learning." Above 600,000 of the

race were expelled from the country towards the close of the fifteenth century, at the dictates of Torquemada ; and the ancestors of Isaac D'Israeli took refuge in the more tolerant territories of the Venetian Republic. Here " they dropped their Gothic surname," and assumed that of Disraeli (a name never borne before or since by any other family), and here, under the protection of the lion of St. Mark, they flourished as merchants and bankers for more than two centuries, when Benjamin Disraeli, the younger of two brothers, migrated to this country, and became a denizen of England in 1748, and having acquired a competence in the midway of life, he settled in Enfield, where his only child Isaac was born May, 1766. " Here," says his grandson, " he formed an Italian garden, " entertained his friends, played whist with Sir Horace " Mann, who had known his brother at Venice as a " banker ; ate maccaroni which was dressed by the " Venetian Consul,* and lived till he was nearly ninety," leaving an only child, Isaac Disraeli.

Conflicting traditions assign more than one house in Enfield as having been his residence, but the probabilities are in favour of that used as the Great Eastern Railway Station, which, with its beautiful façade and tracery work

---

* The allusion here is to the late John Charles Lucena, Esq., who was for thirty years agent of affairs and Consul General from the Court of " Portugal," and who died June 2nd, 1813, aged 61.— *Gent. Magazine, p.* 286.

of carved brick (probably unrivalled in England), is doomed to destruction by the march of mechanics.

Such a garden as that alluded to was certainly attached to this house at the end of the last century, and many of the statues with which it was adorned,* some of them of great beauty, were for many years to be seen standing in the stonemason's yard adjoining. The only vestige now remaining is a part of the boundary wall and iron palisading behind the National Schools.

The identity of the house is further supported by Mr. Disraeli's statement, that his father was sent to a school in the neighbourhood kept by a Scotchman, one Peter Morison, " but his delicate health was an excuse for con-" verting him into a day-scholar, and finally the solitary "walk home through Mr. Mellish's park was found "dangerous to his sensibilities."

The school alluded to was near Ponder's-end, to which the footpath through Mr. Mellish's park led, and there was some cause for the boy's nervousness, as Mrs. Mellish was stopped and robbed by foot-pads in this very walk through her own park.

It would be difficult to point out any other house to which the above details would apply.

Isaac Disraeli remained here till his 38th year, when he married Maria, daughter of George Basevi, of Brighton,

---

* Several of these are now in the grounds of David Henry, Esq., by whom a beautiful young Bacchus was given to the writer.

THE OLD RAILWAY-STATION, FROM A SKETCH IN 1848.

Esq., a member, like himself, of a Sephardim-Jewish family,—his celebrated eldest son being born in 1805, shortly after which he settled at Bradenham, in Bucks., where he resided till his death in 1848, and was buried there in the vault of the chancel amongst the descendants of the Hampdens and the Pyes.

The Jewish Chronicle, writing in April, 1868, says, " There seems to be a singular mistake as to the relation " of the Premier to Judaism. Some Jews censure him as " an apostate, some Christians scoff at him as a Jew, with " a singular disregard of all they owe to the Hebrew race. " Now, the fact is that Disraeli is neither an apostate nor " a Jew. Benjamin Disraeli was admitted into the com- " munion of Israel, but his father, thinking fit to quarrel " with his synagogue, failed to teach his child Judaism. " One day Rogers, the celebrated banker-poet, happening " to visit at Isaac Disraeli's house when Benjamin was " about five or six years old, and regretting to find so " intelligent a youth without religious instruction, took " him to Hackney Church. From this event dates his " absolute and complete severance from the Jewish com- " munion—he became a Christian, and a great genius " was lost to us."

The accompanying illustration has been engraved from a drawing made in 1848, and verified by a photograph lately taken by Mr. Farr. Since the above account was written, the building has been cleared away to make room for the new station of the Great Eastern Railway, and the central part of the façade has been purchased for the sum of £50 of Messrs. Patman by the Directors of the South Kensington Museum, where it has been erected as a screen in the structural division. It was taken down brick by brick, with the greatest care, all being numbered and packed in boxes of sawdust for carriage. Nothing could exceed the beauty of the workmanship, the bricks having been ground down to a perfect face, and joined with bees-wax and rosin, no mortar or lime being used. In this manner the whole front had been first built in a solid block, the circular-headed niches, with their carved cherubs and festoons of fruit and foliage, being afterwards cut out with the chisel. The arches were built without *voussoirs*, the lines of the brickwork running straight across the work, with the joints so fine as scarcely to be perceptible to the nicest scrutiny. The date of the building is about the end of Charles II.'s reign, and it bears all the characteristics of Sir Christopher Wren's design. The similarity of its elevation to that of Temple Bar cannot but strike the most inattentive observer, and the arched recesses and their enrichments recall the beautiful blank windows towards the western end of St. Paul's Cathedral.

### LORD GEORGE GORDON.

The notorious Lord George Gordon was the third son of Cosmo Duke of Gordon, who resided in Enfield at a house on Chase-side, known as Gordon House, and afterwards the residence of Sir Thomas Halifax. He was born

December 19th, 1750, and represented the borough of
Ludgershall during several sessions. In 1780 he was
committed to the Tower for his complicity in the riots.
Some years after, he was convicted of a libel on Marie
Antoïnette and the Empress of Russia, when, to avoid
punishment, he fled the country, but was shortly afterwards discovered at Birmingham in the garb of a Jew, when
he was committed to Newgate, pursuant to his sentence
for the term of five years. Here he continued to profess
the Jewish religion, having (says Walpole) undergone its
extreme rites, and died November 28, 1793. His last
moments were embittered by the refusal of the Jews to
allow his interment in their burial-ground, and it
accordingly took place in a vault at St. James's, Hamp-
stead-road. The mob, at the time of the Gordon riots,
having threatened to destroy the wooden aqueduct at
Bush Hill, with the intention of burning London, the
proprietors of the New River made an application to
Government for its protection, in consequence of which
the 62nd regiment of foot was sent down and quartered
in Enfield till the danger was over.

### RICHARD GOUGH.

At the upper end of Baker-street stands a handsome
red-brick house formerly the residence of Harry Gough,
Esq., M.P. for Bramber, who purchased it in the year
1723. After the death of his widow in 1774 it descended
to his son Richard Gough, well known as the editor of

Camden, and the author of sepulchral monuments and
other archeological works. Mr. Gough improved the
estate by the purchase of some adjoining property, and
also made considerable additions to the house, the
eastern wing being built for the reception of his curious
and extensive library, the whole of which was sold
by auction in 1810, with the exception of his
collection of British topography and his MSS., which he
bequeathed to the Bodleian Library. Mr. Gough resided
in Enfield* till his death, February 20, 1809, and was
buried in the churchyard of Wormley, in Hertfordshire.
A Latin epitaph, written by himself more than fifteen
years before his decease, was inscribed pursuant to his
instructions on a plain marble tablet on the south side of
the chancel near the communion table. After the death
of Mr. Gough's widow, August 18, 1833, æt 93, the estate
was purchased by Mr. Rees Price, and is now the
property and residence of Miss Child. At the time of
the alteration of the course of the New River, the iron
gates and skreen, which stood close to the house, were
removed to their present position, where they form a
characteristic example of the beautiful old iron-work,

* "Where," he says, "he can with pleasure, from his earliest
"life, review many pleasing hours of retirement and antiquarian
"research spent in this parish, so happily situated as a centre of
"many curious monuments in the adjacent counties."—*Gough's
Camden*, v. 2, p. 107.

GOUGH-PARK, THE SEAT OF MISS CHILD.

which is so striking a feature of Enfield and its neighbourhood.

A curious fragment has been preserved of the
"Diary of Master R. Gough: 1752—April 17, I went
"to school for last time; we came to Enfield.   April 22,
"The red cow calved.  May 5, A man killed at Bushill.
"May 20, A court held by Mr. Bowles; went to it and
"to Mr. Bridgen's.  June 1, Mrs. Breton and her sister
"came; I played at cricket. July 8, Job at Jervis's
"married the woman at the Goat."

### MAJOR CARTWRIGHT.

Major Cartwright, a noted politician and writer, was
for many years an inhabitant of Enfield.   He was born
on the 17th September, 1740, at Marnham, in Nottinghamshire.  He was descended from a family who had been
long established in the county, and who had suffered
great loss of property by their adherence to the cause of
Charles I. during the civil wars.*   He was an elder

---

* A curious note in the Cartwright pedigree relates the manner in
which their estates came into the possession of the family.   "Hee
"(Edmund Cartwright) was a scholer and Master of Artes of Jesus'
"College, Cambridge, where hee was intimately acquainted with
"Thomas Cranmer, son of Thomas Cranmer of Aslacton, whose
"only daughter Cartwright married,—which Cranmer, becoming
"afterwards Archbishop of Canterbury, tooke his brother Cartwright
"and sister into his house, and at the dissolution of the abbeys
"provided for him the Abbey of Mauling, in Kent; Rowney, in Bed-
"fordshire; and Ossington, in Nottinghamshire,—which are worth

O

brother of the Rev. Edmund Cartwright, D.D., the
inventor of the power-loom. Though somewhat
impracticable and extreme in his opinions, he was a
man, said Fox, " whose enlightened mind and profound
" constitutional knowledge placed him in the highest
" rank ·of public characters, and whose purity ·of prin.
" ciple and consistency of conduct through life com-
" manded the most respectful attention." He died at
the advanced age of 85, and was buried at Finchley,
September, 1824.

### REV. DANIEL CRESSWELL, D.D.

The Rev. Daniel Cresswell, D.D., was vicar of Enfield
from March 6, 1823, till his death, 21 March, 1844,
æt 68. He was well known both as an accomplished classical scholar, and a profound mathematician, and for nearly
twenty years a most efficient magistrate and chairman of
the Enfield Bench. He was tutor at Trinity College to
Dr. Blomfield, the late Bishop of London, with whom in
after life there existed some mutual antagonism which led
to frequent contests, in which the vicar always came off
victorious. Dr. Cresswell was a great valetudinarian, and

---

" three thousand a-year ; and married his heir, Hugh, to one of the
" Lord Cobham's daughters." " It is lamentable to observe,
(says Miss Cartwright, in quoting this passage), that Archbishop
" Cranmer should have made the spiritual reforms he laboured to
" establish subservient to the interests of his own connexions."

very punctilious as to his meals, particularly his dinner, which was invariably at three o'clock. On the occasion of the consecration of St. James's Chapel, at Enfield Highway ~~(July 9, 1835),~~ he wrote to the Bishop of London, particularly begging him to be punctual, so that he might not be detained beyond his usual dinner-hour. The Bishop, however, was not disposed to be accommodating, and came provokingly late, when Dr. Cresswell, instead of reading the morning service, began the shorter form for evening prayer. The Bishop, after several ineffectual attempts to call his attention, sent his chaplain to stop him, when the Doctor, quietly taking out his well-known accurate chronometer, bowed to his lordship, and proceeded with the evening service, on the conclusion of which the Bishop made a full apology for the unseemly interruption. The last "Essay of Elia" (written only a month before Lamb's death), "Thoughts on presents of game," was suggested by the attentive kindness of "the worthy Vicar of Enfield," from whom "he acknowledges a tithe contribution of extraordinary sapor." The essay appeared in the Athenæum, Nov. 30, 1834. Dr. Cresswell was buried in Enfield Churchyard, where his epitaph, written by himself, is alike beautiful for its pure Latinity and its exposition of Christian faith.

Hoc sepulchrum
sua ossa recepturum condi voluit
Daniel Cresswell, S.T.P.*

---

* Sacræ Theologiæ Professor—*i.e.*, Doctor of Divinity.

Coll. S.S. Trin. apud Cant. olim socius
Ecclesiæ de Enfield inde vicarius
Qui quanquam ad bonas literas incubuerat
Ad bonos mores animam intenderat
Ad sapientiæ Christianæ fontem accesserat
Optatum tamen ac propositum
(Tantum interest inter velle et posse, scire et facere)
Longe abfuit ut assequeretur
Nec nisi in Dei clementia
Jesu Christi morte conciliata
Spem ullam salutis habuit
Laudes ergo ~~inerftas~~ quas hæres aut amicus
Nimia facilitate mortuis largiri solet
detrectans
Ipse sibi hunc lapidem inscripsit
Tu vero lector
Nam quæ de alio hic narruntur
Ad te fortim spectant
Nosce teipsum
Sancti spiritus ope tui victor evade
Christo te committe
Pectore et vita triunum Deum venerare
Obiit xxi Martii die A.D. MDCCCLIV.
Ætatis suæ LXIX.

*hamentos*

---

The classical and mathematical tastes of Dr. Cresswell
led him, when a young man, to cultivate the acquaintance
of the celebrated Porson, with whom he was in the
habit of interchanging riddles. Some of these, copied
thirty years ago, from the originals, in Porson's hand-
writing, are of great beauty and will probably be new to
most readers.

## 213

### I.

Totum pone, fluit;—caput aufer, splendet in armis;—
Caudam deme, volat;—viscera tolle, dolet.

---

### II.

Te primum, incauto nimium propriusque tuenti
    Laura,—mihi furtim surripuisse queror.
Non tamen hoc furtum tibi condonare recusem,
    Si pretium tali solvere merce velis.
Sed quo plus candoris habent tibi colla secundo,
    Hoc tibi plus primum frigoris intus habet.
Sœpe sinistra cavâ cantavit ab ilice totum
    Omina, et audaces spes vetat esse ratas.

---

### III.

My first, though the emblem of chastity reckoned,
All her character lost in becoming my second;
And yet I rejoiced,—for her ruin gave room
For my whole mid the desert of nature to bloom,
Who forth from her covert with modesty burst,
And in exquisite purity rivalled my first.

---

### IV.

My first, though your house from the thief it defends,
    You scurvily treat as a wretch you despise,
My second,—I speak it with grief,—comprehends
    All the great,— all the good,— all the learn'd,— all the wise.
Of my whole—I have little or nothing to say,
Except that it marks the departure of day.

### JOHN ABERNETHY.

John Abernethy was born in London, in the parish of St. Stephen, Coleman-street, on the 3rd of April, 1764. He received his first education at a day school in Lothbury, kept by a Mr. Fuller,* afterwards a well-known banker, but was sent, while very young, to the Grammar School at Wolverhampton, of which he became the head before he was fifteen; when (in 1779) he was apprenticed to Sir Charles Blicke, surgeon to St. Bartholomew's Hospital. On the resignation of Mr. Pott, he became assistant surgeon to the institution, and afterwards succeeded that gentleman as lecturer on anatomy and surgery. Soon after he appeared as an author, and published lectures and a Hunterian Oration, giving an account of Hunter's labours and opinions, and he also wrote the articles in Rees' Cyclopædia on anatomy, &c. His most celebrated work, which he used to recommend to his patients, was on local diseases, aneurisms, and

---

* "Died March 2nd, 1800, at his house on Scotland Green, Enfield, in his ninety-fifth year, William Fuller, Esq., banker of Lombard-street,—he was son of William Fuller who kept an academy in Founders' Court, Lothbury,—to which, on his death, his son succeeded, and having (by qualifying in writing and accounts many now eminent merchants of London, besides many others who served the East India Co., both at home and abroad), accumulated the sum of £30,000, he engaged in a banking house about the year 1756, but continued his employment of teaching for some years after he commenced banker."—*Gent. Magazine.*

disorders of the digestive organs. His practice and reputation now rapidly advanced, and on the death of Sir C. Blicke, he was elected surgeon to the hospital which was considered the first in the metropolis. Mr. Abernethy was said to be frequently abrupt in his manner, and impatient to a complaining sufferer; and pages might be filled with anecdotes which have been told of his ec. centric behaviour. Many of these, however, were greatly exaggerated, and he often offended by saying what were very salutary though very unpleasant truths. His roughness was only on the surface, and he was invariably and unaffectedly kind to the hospital patients, whilst his generosity was as unbounded as it was delicate. He has been known to return his fees to a poor officer's widow with a cheque of £50, to enable her to give her child a daily ride. A young officer in the army having been thrown from his horse, received a fracture of the skull and other severe injuries. Abernethy, being the nearest surgeon, was sent for, and attended him daily for some months, at the end of which the poor patient enquired what he was indebted to him for his professional care. Abernethy enquired, with a smile, who the young woman was who had nursed him so tenderly. " She is my wife." "What is your rank in the army?" " I am a half-pay lieutenant." " Oh, very well, come and see me when you are a general; and we'll talk about it."

Feeling the wear and tear of his laborious life, Abernethy took a house in Enfield,* to which he used to

---

* Now the residence of Mr. Alderman Challis.

go down on Wednesdays and Saturdays. Here he might be seen in drab kerseymeres and top boots, riding his favourite mare, "Jenny," which he had for five-and-twenty years. In the spring of 1831, he gradually grew weaker, and died on the 20th of April, in that year. He was buried in Enfield Church, where a plain tablet is placed on the wall over his vault.

### CHARLES BABBAGE.

Charles Babbage was born December 26th, 1792, and was educated by the Rev. Stephen Freeman, whose school was at the red brick house, at the upper end of Baker-street, in Enfield, "He was much loved," says a fellow pupil, " by dear old Freeman who first taught him mathematics." Here he and a studious schoolfellow were in the habit of getting up in the morning at three o'clock, lighting a fire in the schoolroom, and studying surreptitiously until five or half-past five. Frederick Marryat proposed to join them, not so much from a desire to study as for the sake of doing what was forbidden. So, at least, Babbage interpreted the request, and he refused to let Marryat join them. One night, in trying to open the door of his bedroom, Babbage found that Marryat's bed had been pulled up against it. He gently pushed it back, without waking the future captain, and pursued his way to the schoolroom. This happened on several successive nights; but at length Marryat improved the plan by fastening a string from his hand to the door lock

Babbage detected the trick, and untied the knot. A few nights later, so stout a cord was used that he could only free the lock by cutting it. Presently a chain took the place of the cord, and for one night Babbage was kept from his studies; however, the end of the matter was that Marryat was allowed to prevail, when the consequences predicted by Babbage presently followed. Others joined them, play took the place of work, fireworks were let off, and of course the delinquents were discovered.

From Enfield he was transferred to Peterhouse, Cambridge, and aimed at the senior Wranglership, but Herschel being in the year, he would not contend with him, but abandoned all honours, coming out as Captain of the Poll. Babbage was originally destined for the law, which he studied under the late Mr. Brodie (brother of Sir Benjamin), but making no progress in so uncongenial a pursuit he turned his attention to science, by the advice of his fellow student, the late John Walker, Esq., Q.C., and in 1828, his mathematical eminence obtäined his election to the chair of Newton as Lucasian Professor in his university. This he held for ten or eleven years, though, it is said, he never lectured. His chief celebrity, however, he owes to his project of a calculating engine for the computation of tables,* founded upon the method of differences and

---

* Mr. Babbage was the first to introduce the use of "toned paper" in printing his tables of logarithms, having found by a series of careful experiments that it gave greater distinctness to the type.

essentially the same in principle as that of Pascal. The invention was considered of such importance that the Government, under the advice of the Royal Society and a committee of the most eminent mathematicians, determined upon constructing a machine at the expense of the country, and Mr. Babbage was engaged to superintend the work. It was accordingly commenced in 1821, when it was supposed that two or three years would be sufficient for its completion. Nothing could be more certain in theory, or more perfect in workmanship than this wonderful engine,—by which mathematics were reduced to mechanism. But after twelve years had been spent in its construction, the complication of details became so great that the work was suspended and the workmen dismissed; a quarrel also ensued with the engineer, who withdrew his tools,—and it remains to this day unfinished. It should be added that though the Treasury paid the whole of the expenses, Mr. Babbage himself derived no advantage, either direct or indirect, from the invention. Mr. Babbage took an active part for many years in scientific institutions; he was one of the oldest Fellows of the Royal Society, and one of the founders of the Royal Astronomical Society, and of the Statistical Society, of which he was considered the father. He died on the 20th of October, 1871.

THE RIGHT REV. CONNOP THIRLWALL, D.D.,

*(Bishop of St. David's).*

This distinguished scholar and theologian was the son of the Rev. T. Thirlwall, Rector of Bowers Gifford, Essex, who was formerly a resident in this parish. He was born in 1797, and educated at the Charter House. In 1814 he entered at Trinity College, Cambridge, where the next year he obtained the Bell and Craven University Scholarships. In 1818 he was Senior Optime and Senior Chancellor's Medallist; elected Fellow of Trinity, 1819; M.A., 1821. He was called to the Bar, at Lincoln's Inn, in 1823, but afterwards took Holy Orders, and became assistant tutor of his college. He was formerly one of the Examiners of candidates for degrees at the London University. In 1840 he was presented by the Lord Chancellor to the living of Kirby Underdale, in Yorkshire, and the same year was consecrated Bishop of St. David's, where he acquired the Welsh language with extraordinary rapidity. In 1825 he translated, in conjunction with Julius Hare, Niebuhr's History of Rome, and between 1835-40 published his History of Greece, in eight volumes. Since that time he has written many sermons, charges, and controversial pamphlets.

A volume of compositions in prose and verse, some of them written at the age of eight years, was published by his father in 1809. It is now extremely rare. " Primitiæ, or Essays and Poems, on various subjects, by C. T., eleven years of age. The preface by his father, 1809."

### CAPTAIN MARRYAT.

Captain Marryat, the naval novelist, was born in 1792, the second son of Mr. Joseph Marryat, of Wimbledon House, M.P. for Horsham and Sandwich, and Chairman of the Committee of Lloyd's. Of his boyhood there is little to tell, except that, like most children of precocious minds and strong passions, he was very troublesome. He learnt easily and forgot quickly, preferred play to lessons, and was constantly flogged for idleness and inattention. His school days were passed in company with Babbage, under the Rev. Stephen Freeman, and furnished a record of pranks, tricks, and runnings-away, whilst his master pronounced that he would never come to any good or turn out otherwise than a dunce. It was at this school that he was one day found by his master standing on his head with a book in his hand, and when Mr. Freeman asked him why he chose so strange a posture, the answer he got was, " Well I've been trying for three hours to learn it on my feet but I couldn't." At last he took to running away from school, and when taken to task for this at home, he replied that it was all a mistake to suppose that he ran away from books and work,—it was because he did not like to wear the cast-off clothes of his eldest brother. When he was fourteen years old he was removed from Mr. Freeman's school, " having," writes one of his old schoolfellows, " run away again, and been captured in the horse-pond, at Edmonton, by a party of the boys and old Bunn, the usher." He

was now transferred to a tutor, from whom he very soon
escaped, and his father, finding it useless to oppose his
inclinations, made arrangements for his going to sea, and
he started on his first voyage in the Impérieuse, com-
manded by Lord Cochrane, for the Mediterranean.
Marryat's active service ended in 1830, after he had been
twenty-four years afloat.  Between 1839 and 1843 he
lived in London, in Duke-street, and Spanish-place,
mixing in society and writing novels.  His health now
began to fail, and in 1847, having twice broken a blood-
vessel, he removed to Hastings for a milder climate, and
when there, received the terrible news of the loss of the
Avenger, in which his eldest son perished.  After this
shock, all chance of recovery faded away; he lingered on
till August, 1848, and on the 9th of that month died
peacefully, having been heard to murmur a sentence of
the Lord's Prayer just before he breathed his last.

He was a brave, energetic spirit, and whether on sea or
land was ever foremost in the redress of wrong or
injustice.  Succeeding generations have to thank Captain
Marryat if his fictions have helped to make the
barbarities of the old service impossible; and in some of
the reforms which he worked, he served his country with
his pen as signally as with his sword.

### CHARLES LAMB.

Charles Lamb first came to Enfield in 1825, where he
says, in a letter to Southey, " we are on a half visit at a

Mrs. Leishman's." This visit was a long one of five months, and ended in Lamb and his sister leaving Islington and becoming constant residents. Writing to Patmore, he says, " we are dawdling our time away very idly and pleasantly at a Mrs. Leishman's, Chase, Enfield, where, if you come a hunting, we can give you cold meat and a tankard. Her husband is a tailor, but that, you know, does not make *her* one." In reply to an application for a subscription towards a memorial to Clarkson, to be built on the spot where he first formed the resolution to devote his life to the abolition of the slave trade, he sends a guinea, but says " the vanities of life are subjects " for trophies, not the silent thoughts arising in a good " man's mind. I sat down upon a hillock, at Forty-hill, " last night, with a thousand good speculations about " mankind. How I yearned with cheap benevolence. " I shall go and enquire of the stone-cutter, that cuts the " tomb-stones here, what a stone with a short inscription " will cost, just to say—'here C. Lamb loved his " brethren,' every body will come there to love."

In 1826, Lamb took what he described as an odd-looking gambogish-coloured house at Chase-side.* The situation (says Talfourd) was far from picturesque, for the opposite side of the road only presented some

---

* This house, which has been much altered and enlarged, was afterwards that of Mrs. Compton, and is now known as "the Manse."

middling tenements, two dissenting chapels, and a public house, but the neighbouring field-walks were pleasant, and the country, as he liked to say, as good as Westmorland. He had here a neighbour in Sergeant Wilde, afterwards Lord Truro, whom he supplied with several squibs to assist his contest for Newark.

The cares of housekeeping, however, pressed too heavily on Mary Lamb, and they removed into lodgings, he says "twenty-four inches further from town." Here, he writes to Wordsworth, in 1830, "we are settled down with an old couple: our providers are an honest pair, dame W. (Westwood) and her husband;—he, when the light of prosperity shined on them, a moderately thriving haberdasher, within Bow Bells, retired since with something under a competence, writes himself gentleman, hath borne parish offices, sings fine old sea songs at three score and ten, and has one anecdote,—upon which and about £40 a year, he seems to have retired in a green old age."

On the marriage of their adopted daughter to Moxon, the publisher, they finally moved to a Mr. Walden's, in Edmonton, where, in consequence of a fall during one of his walks, Lamb died September 27th, 1834, in his sixtieth year. Mary Lamb died May 28th, 1847, and the loving brother and sister lie together in the churchyard at Edmonton.

———

Amongst other known names connected with Enfield, may be mentioned those of Sir Ralph Abercromby, who

was educated at the same school as Isaac Disraeli, by
Peter Morison ; Mrs. Andrè, the mother of the unfortu-
nate Major Andrè, who lived at the bottom of Forty-hill;
Major Rennell, in Baker-street ; Dr. Birkbeck, at
Forty-hill; Keats, the poet, educated at Messrs. May
and Bluck's school; Frederick Joyce, the inventor of
the percussion cap, at the Rev. S. Freeman's ; Baron
Bramwell, and his brother, F. J. Bramwell, C.E ; Sir
William Grey ; Corbould, the engraver, and his brother,
the artist; at "the Palace" school under the late
Dr. May.

## THE RIVER LEE.

"And the old Lee that brags of Danish blood."
DRAYTON'S POLYOLBION.

The River Lee forms the eastern boundary of the parish. "It begynnethe (says Lambarde) near Whitchurche, and from thence passinge by Hertforde, Ware, and Waltham, openethe into the Thames at Ham, in Essex, whence this place is at this day called Lee-mouth. It hath of long tyme borne vessels from London twenty myles towards the head, for in the tyme of King Alfrede the Danes entered Leymouth, whence King Alfrede espied that the channell of the ryver might be in such sorte weakened that they should want water to returne,—he caused therefore the water to be abated by two greate trenches, and setting the Londonners upon them he made their batteil wherein they lost four of their capitaines. Not long after they were so pressed that they forsoke all and left their shippes as a prey to the Londonners ; which breakyne some and burninge other conveyed the rest to London."

In 1571, an Act passed for bringing this river to London, to supply the city with water, but this cut was never begun, and it was not till 1580 that the stream was made navigable as far as Ware, to the great discontent

P

of the malsters and farmers of Enfield, who complained that malt and grain were thus conveyed cheaper than by land.

The bank in Enfield-marsh, called "the Pimpler," was twice cut through in the night, as well as the bank at "Lothersey-gate," and at Sewardstone, and Lady Wrothe's old lock "though often repaired, was as often cut open."

When Lord Burghley wrote to Sir Thomas Wrothe on these outrages, Sir Thomas told the inhabitants of Ware that "the Lords of the Council had done them much wrong in causing them to make a passage for boats to their undoing, and rather than they shall force us to make up the breaches we will be hanged at our own gates," and he gave such encouragement to the offenders that there were more breaches cut than before.

An intelligent farmer, in a letter to the Queen, stated the true reason for all this opposition from the Enfield men was, that they could not monopolize the corn which they had been accustomed to buy up of the farmers,—but that since the navigation was opened, there was a fair open market at Queenhithe.

In 1583 the Enfield people again complained of the injury they received, and of the many carriers reduced to poverty,—when they were told, in reply, "that the navi-"gation is and ought to be as free as the highway ; that "it maintained more able-bodied men to serve the Crown

"by land and sea than could be found among all *the*
"*badgers* \* of Enfield."

In 1767 application having been made to Parliament,
upon a survey made by Smeaton, setting forth the improvements of which this navigation was capable, a sum of
money was granted for making new cuts between Hertford
and Bromley-lock, and from Bromley-lock to Limehouse,
by which seven miles were saved.

It is curious that modern tactics should have just
reversed King Alfred's plan of operations for defeating
invaders. In 1803 John Rennie was employed by
Government to survey the Lee, and to construct embankments across the lower part of the valley for the purpose
of flooding the whole extent with water, in case of an
invasion, which was then anticipated.

The old and irregular course of the river is now of
little use, having been long superseded by the new
" navigation," which has proved a great benefit to all the
districts through which it passes.

---

\* Badger,—a licensed huxter in corn and fruit.—( *Philips.* )

## THE MILL RIVER.

"Ther was hir whete and eke hir malt yground."

[*Chaucer,—The Reeve's Tale.*]

---

By the survey of 1572, it appears that Queen Elizabeth had "a watercourse or stream issuing out of the Lee, uppon which was antiently a mill belonging to the manor of Enfield ;" this was let to Sir John Wrothe, at a rent of 6d. per annum, and is called the water mill, to distinguish it from the Lock or Oil mill,—the latter being the site of the Royal Small Arms Factory, the nucleus of which was established here in 1804, apparently to utilize a small water-wheel and fall belonging to the Crown.

On the recommendation of a Committee of the House of Commons, in 1854, it was decided to organize a manufactory of small arms, to a limited extent, under the direction of the Board of Ordnance, and a sum of £150,000 was voted for the purpose.

The experiment proved so successful that the buildings and machinery were rapidly increased, and the establishment was placed on its present footing, and continued for seventeen years under the superintendence of Colonel W. M. Dixon.

It would be hopeless to attempt, in the compass of these pages, any adequate description of the marvellous mechanism which has become celebrated throughout

Europe. Admission can be obtained by the public on Mondays and Thursdays, and an intelligent guide accompanies visitors through the various departments, and explains the different operations.

----

Among other streams in Enfield, one rises from a spring near Potter's-bar, and another about three-quarters of a mile south of it, which running west through Old-pond,* crosses the bottom of Clay-hill, and passing under the New River, at "Bull-Beggar's-hole," and thence by Maiden's-bridge, runs by the side of Turkey-street to Enfield-wash, and crossing the Highway, turns due east into the marshes, and falls ultimately into the Lee.

Another stream rises near Ganna-corner, and, crossing the centre of the Chase, passes under the New River at Bush-hill, and runs thence through the parish of Edmonton.

A third rises near the same place, and, running through New-pond * and other sheets of water, quits the Chase at Cock-fosters.

----

* Both these ponds are now filled up.

## THE NEW RIVER.

" May thy brimmèd waves for this
" Their full tribute never miss,
"Summer drought or singed air
" Never scorch thy banks so fair,
" Nor wet October's torrent flood
" Thy molten crystal fill with mud ;
" May thy lofty HEAD be crowned
" With many a tower and terrace round."

*Milton's Comus.*

A History of Enfield would hardly be complete without some account of the New River, which wanders for so many miles of its devious course through the parish, and forms so important a feature and ornament of the scenery. Such, however, are the doubts and inaccuracies which pervade almost every account which has been published of " this noble aqueduct," (as Sir Christopher Wren calls it), and particularly as regards the original cost of the undertaking, that the task is one of no small difficulty.

The chief authorities, which are adopted in the following pages, are the Patent Roll of 1612, the original Charter, June 21, 1619, and Acts of Parliament,—the Minutes of Evidence taken before the Committee of the House of Commons on the Metropolitan Water Supply, Stowe's Survey, ancient documentary evidence, and the very interesting and elaborate account given by Mr. Smiles, in his " Lives of Engineers,"—from which work

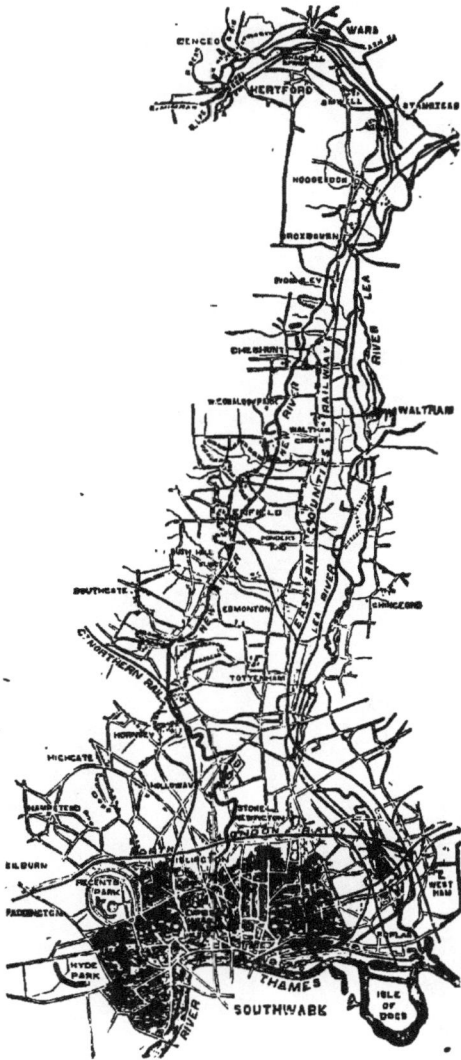

MAP OF THE NEW RIVER, FROM THE ORIGINAL BY TELFORD.

[THE DOTTED LINES SHOWING THE OLD COURSE, 'NOW SUPERSEDED.]

the following illustrative engravings have been copied by permission.

London was originally supplied with water from the Thames * and from various streams and springs, of which Walbrook, which ran through the middle of the City, the Fleet, Clerkenwell, Clement's-well, Holy-well, &c. survive in the names of the streets, which have been built over them. As London grew in size and population these sources became inadequate, and various conduits were constructed which conveyed water from James's Head, Mewsgate, Tyburn, Highbury, Hampstead, &c. There were sixteen of such conduits, the sites of which may still be traced by their names. Stowe gives an account of one of the annual inspections which were made by the authorities. " On the 18th Sept. 1562, the Lord Mayor, the Aldermen, and many worshipful persons and divers of the Masters and Wardens of the twelve Companies rode to the Conduit's head (now Conduit-street), for to see them, after the old custom,—and afore dinner they hunted the hare and killed her, and thence

---

* The Water-works, at London-bridge, were erected by Peter Moris, a Dutchman, and conveyed the water from the Thames "vp unto the north-west corner of Leadenhall, where the first maine pipe ran this yeare, 1582, on Christmasse even, and divided there into severall spouts, and ranne foure waies,—plentifullie serving to the vse of the inhabitants that will fetch the same into their howses."—*Hollingshead's Chronicle.*

to dinner at the head of the conduit. There was a good number entertained, with good cheer, by the Chamberlain, and after dinner they hunted the fox. There was a great cry for a mile, and at length the hounds killed him at the end of St. Giles's."

As the demand for water increased, there were frequent contentions at the conduit for the first turn, which sometimes grew into riots,—the water-carriers came prepared for a fight, and a proclamation was issued forbidding persons from resorting to the conduits "armed with clubs and staves." Moreover, the springs from which the conduits were supplied, gradually began to fail, whilst the growing density of the population added every year to the impurity of the river,—and the inhabitants of the lanes leading to its banks endeavoured to close the thoroughfares, and allowed no one to pass without paying toll. A large number of persons then obtained their livelihood as water-carriers, selling the water by the

OLD WATER CARRIER,

FROM TEMPEST'S CRIES.

"tankard," of about three gallons, who seem to have formed a somewhat unruly portion of the population. Some of these water-carriers were women. William Lamb, who formed the conduit where Lamb's Conduit-street now stands, gave " 120 pails to poor women, such as were willing to take paines therewith to carry and serve water."

In the year 1571 the Corporation obtained an Act of Parliament " for the bringing of the River Lee to the north side of the City of London," (13 Eliz. cap. 18), but no steps were taken to carry out the undertaking, as though the Corporation were willing to sanction it, yet they were not disposed to supply any part of the necessary capital.

Two several Acts were afterwards successively passed (3 and 4 James I.) " for the bringing in of a fresh streame of runninge water from the springs of Chadwell and Amwell, to the north partes of the Citty of London." Nothing, however, came of them,—the citizens waiting for the corporation to move, and the corporation waiting for the citizens.

" The worke (says the patent, 17 James I.) upon view was found to be very fezible, and was like to be profitable to manie,—nevertheless the said mayor, cominaltie, and citizens, weighing the great charge and expence the said worke would requyre, and doubtinge what damage and losse might fall upon the chamber of the said cittie, in case the worke should not fall out to be gainfulle, did, thereuppon, forbeare as their comon charge to undertake that worke,—soe as the same lay longe neglected and unlike to be by them performed."

It was at this juncture that " Hugh Middelton, citizen and gouldsmith, well affecting the good of our said cittie of London, and being moved with a desire and zeale to performe soe publique, necessarie, and worthie a worke, was willing to adventure, and upon his own private charge to undertake the said worke, and did, out of a pyous and commendable purpose, make offer to the Lord Mayor, Aldermen, and Comons, assembled in a comon councell, the eight and twentieth day of March, in the seaventh yeare of our raigne, to undertake the said worke at the proper costs and charges of himself and his heires."

"After long and deliberate consultacon and advisement on this offer, they declared theire verie good likeinge thereof, as a thinge of great consequence, and worthie of acceptacon for the good of the said cittie." *

Here we pause in our narrative, to give a short account of " one of the most distinguished benefactors London has ever known ;"—" a man (says Mr. Smiles) full of enter-prize and resources, an energetic and untiring worker—a great conqueror of obstacles and difficulties—an honest

---

* Patent Roll,—17 James I.

and truly noble,"—and in sad sooth must be added—
ill-requited man.

Hugh Myddelton was descended from an ancient
family in North Wales, and was born at Henllan, near
Denbigh, about 1555,* being the sixth of sixteen
children. He was entered by his father as an apprentice
to the Goldsmith's Company and embarked in that trade,
which then included that of banker and money-changer.

His "shop" was situated in Basinghall-street, and he
lived in the overhanging tenement above it, as was the
custom of city merchants in "good old days." Here,
according to long tradition, Hugh Myddelton and Sir
Walter Raleigh might be seen sitting together at the
door of the goldsmith's booth, smoking the newly-intro-
duced weed (tobacco), greatly to the amazement of the
passengers. Pennant states, on the authority of the

---

* Will of Sir Hugh Myddelton. It has generally, but erroneously,
been stated that he was born at Denbigh. The autograph of Sir
Hugh has been engraved from one in the possession of H. C. B.
Bowles, Esq., the Treasurer of the Company.

Sebright MS., that Captain William Myddelton (Hugh's brother), with Captain Price, of Plasyollin, and one Captain Koet, were the first who smoked,—or, as they called it, "drank" tobacco publicly in London, and that the Londoners flocked from all parts to see them.

Myddelton was also one of the merchant adventurers of England, and was largely concerned in the manufacture of woollen cloth, in which he employed several hundred families. In 1603 he was elected to represent Denbigh, in the first parliament of James,—of which his brothers, Thomas and Robert were also members. Among the first committees of the House on which the brothers were appointed, was one to consider of bringing a fresh stream of water from the Lee, or from Uxbridge, to the City. Thus his attention was early drawn to this subject, which his energy of character and public spirit eventually carried out with success.

The Corporation of London were only too glad to transfer to Myddelton the labour, anxiety, and expense, which they considered so gigantic. "The matter (says Stowe) had been well mentioned, though little minded,—long debated, but never concluded—till courage and resolution lovingly shook hands together in the soule of this no-way-to-be-daunted, well-minded gentleman."

On the 28th March, 1609, the Corporation formally accepted his proposal, and "a warrant" was made out on the 21st of April following, constituting him their "lawfull deputie and assigne." Of this document, how-

ever, there is no record, and it was not till two years
afterwards that " by their indenture under the comon
seale, bearinge date the eight and twentieth day of March
(1611), they fully, freely, and absolutely, conveyed, assigned, and confirmed" the undertaking to Myddelton
and his heirs.

On the 21st of April, 1609, Myddelton began the
work, and turned the first sod at Chadwell. Master
Hassall, Vicar of Amwell, who, greatly to his honour
and patriotism, gave his land for the formation of the
New River, thus describes the spring which "riseth at
the foot of a hill near Ware ;—this spring, Chadwell,* is
not more commendable in respect to the pureness of the
water, than admirable both in regard of the strangeness
of her birth, issuing out of a hole of incredible depth,
as also in respect of the richness of the current, which
of itself instantly grows into a river of about twenty feet
in breadth,—afterwards pouring her rich spoils into the
bosom of her sister Amwell, so hand in hand coming
along with her to London." *

The works were no sooner commenced, than a host of
opponents sprang up. The owners and occupiers of land
petitioned Parliament, representing that their meadows
would be turned into "bogs and quagmires," and their
arable land into "squallid ground;" that their farms

---

* St. Chad, to whom this spring was dedicated, was an early
English Bishop (Lichfield), who died of a pestilence in 673.

would be "mangled," and their fields "cut up into
quillets and small peces ;" that "the cut, which was no
better than a deep ditch," would be dangerous to cattle,
and "on soden raines" would inundate the adjoining
lands, to the utter ruin of many poor men ;—that "the
Church would be wronged in its tithe without remedy,"
and that "the highway between London and Ware would
be impassable." A Bill was, in consequence, actually
introduced and committed, for the repeal of the Act, but
happily Parliament was prorogued, and did not meet
again for four years, during which time the panic had
subsided, and the subject is not again mentioned in the
Journals of the House.

Worse than all, however, was the popular opposition
which Myddelton had to encounter. The Rev. Wilhelm
Bedwell, "pastour of the parish of Tottenham," writing
in 1631, speaks of the New River as "brought with an
ill-will from Ware to London ;" and Stowe says bitterly
"if those enemies of all good endeavours could have
prevailed, by their accursed and malevolent interposition,
either before, at the beginning, or in the least stolne
advantage of the whole prosecution, this worke of so
great worthe had never been accomplished." "The
depth of the trench (he adds) in some places descended
full thirty feet, whereas in other places it required as
spritefull art to mount it over a valley, in a troughe,
borne up by woodden arches, rising in height above 23
feet."

Myddelton's difficulties, however, did not end here, for after having adjusted all his controversies in an amicable manner, and brought the water "divers miles towards London, yet, finding the charge of the work greater and heavier than at first was expected, the success thereof doubtful, and the opposicons very strong," his own funds became exhausted, and he was compelled to apply to such relations and "other friends as were well affected toward the work, and willinge to adventure and joyne in contribution towards the charge thereof."*

Still the capital was insufficient to complete the undertaking. Joint-stock companies were not then in existence, and shares, loans, and debentures, were all unknown. In this dilemma, Myddelton again applied to the City for their assistance in this great and useful work, but only to meet with a refusal, and as a last resource he applied to the King, who had naturally become interested in the works from observing their progress through the Royal Park at Theobalds. Several interviews took place here between them, the result of which was that—
* "Wee, considering out of our royal and gracious inclination, and being willinge to give our ayde and furtherance to soe good, publique, and commodious a worke," did, "with consent of the adventurers, agree to beare and paye the one-halfe and moyetie of all the charges, disbursed and expended, and to be disbursed

* Pat. Roll,—17 James I.

and expended," &c., in return for which assistance a moiety of the interest and profits of the undertaking was made over to the King.

An amusing account is given in a letter from Mr. Joseph Meade, to Sir Martin Stuteville (9 Jan, 1622), of a narrow escape which King James had from being drowned in the river which he had helped Myddelton to complete. He had gone out one winter's day, after dinner, to ride in the park, at Theobald's, accompanied by his son, Prince Charles, when about three miles from the palace his horse stumbled, and he was thrown into the river. It was frozen over at the time, and His Majesty's body disappeared, leaving only his boots visible above the ice. Sir Richard Young rushed in to his rescue and dragged him out, when there "came much water out of his mouth and body." "His Majestie," continues the writer, "rid back to Theobalds, went into a warme bed, and as we heare, is well, which God continue. He did not, however, soon forget the accident, for when the Lord Mayor, Sir Edward Barkham, and the Recorder, Sir Heneage Finch attended him, at Greenwich, in June, 1622, to be knighted, James took occasion, in rather strong terms, to remind them of his recent mischance " in Myddelton's water."

The work at last went on without further interruption ; the water was brought within a mile of London ; the voice of derision became silent, and the King, Corporation, and Citizens, now vied with each other in doing

honour to the brave-hearted and patriotic Myddelton.
On the 29th September, 1613, the water was let into the
basin called "The New River Head," in the presence of
his brother, Sir Thomas Myddelton,—who was that day
elected Lord Mayor,—the Aldermen, and Common Council, amid a great concourse of spectators, who assembled
in large numbers to celebrate the public pageant.

"A troup of labourers (says Stowe, in his Survey) to
the number of sixty or more, well apparelled and wearing
green Monmouth caps, carried spades, shovels, and such-
like instruments of laborious imployment, marching after
drummers, twice or thrice about the cisterne." A metrical
speech, composed by Myddelton, the dramatist, was then
read, "when the flood-gate flew open, the streame rannē
gallantly into the cisterne, drummes and trumpets
sounding in a triumphall manner, and a brave peale of
*chambers* gave full issue to the entertainment."

A large print, of much artistic merit, and now extremely
rare, was published in commemoration of the event. It
is entitled "Sir Hugh Myddelton's Glory," and is dedicated, by G. Bickham, to the proprietors of the New
River. The grouping of some of the figures, and their
light and shade, are particularly fine.

The site of the New River Head had always been a
pond,—"an open, idell pool (says Hawes) commonly
called the Ducking-pond,—being now, by the master of
this work, reduced into a comely pleasant shape, and
many wayes adorned with buildings." The house ad-

R

joining was built in 1613, and was altered and new-fronted
in 1782. The fine room, built for a board-room, still
remains in its original state, with its walls lined with
panelled oak, and enriched with carving, by Gibbons,—
and a painted ceiling, having a portrait of William III.
and the arms of Myddelton and Green. There is a
very interesting and highly-finished indian-ink drawing
in the Print-room of the British Museum,—taken about
1730, by Bernard Lens, miniature painter to George II.,
which represents the New River Head, with *the Windmill*,
and Sadler's-wells adjoining, standing in the open
country, with a clear view across the fields, of St. Paul's
and Westminster Abbey, broken only by intervening
trees. A duplicate of this curious drawing, from the
collection of the late Sir Henry Ellis, is in the possession
of the writer.

One of the most difficult and expensive parts of the
undertaking still remained to be accomplished,—the
distribution of the water over the metropolis. During a
period of two centuries this was accomplished by means
of wooden pipes, principally of elm.* The only pumping

---

* The rows of lopped elms, so common in the neighbourhood of
London and the adjoining counties, owe their origin to the great
demand for long straight trees, which were bored for New River
pipes. The custom, which is noticed by Gilpin, appears to have
been restricted to the elm, which was found to be more durable for
this purpose than any other timber. The last outlay on elm pipes
was in 1816, previously to which the annual cost had been from
£5000 to £8000.

establishment was a windmill, with a horse-wheel below, so that when there was no wind, a couple of horses were put to work. The building is still in existence. The extent of these pipes, at the end of the last century, was estimated at 400 miles, of which 20 miles had to be replaced annually. The expense arising from this, and the amount of leakage (calculated at one-fourth) was very heavy, and the Company were only able to supply water to the height of six feet, every consumer having a forcing pump in his own house.

Between the years 1810 and 1816, when a severe competition existed among the different water companies, it was detemined to substitute iron pipes. Great public opposition was however made to this proposal, and among other outcries, it was gravely asserted that the consumption of the water would produce cancer.

At this time however there was a great depression in the iron trade of the country, which induced Government to support the scheme, and on the application of the governor (John Walker, Esq.), and the treasurer (Samuel Garnault, Esq.), Mr. Vansittart, then Chancellor of the Exchequer, gave a letter to the Bank of England, authorizing a loan of £100,000, on condition that the money was expended in iron from the Staffordshire foundries.

This alteration led incidentally to very beneficial results. At the time that the New River Head was constructed, the enormous growth of London had not been foreseen, indeed it had been restricted by sumptuary legislation, and Sir Hugh Myddelton had not secured a sufficient extent of ground for the necessary connexions.

Around that little centre were fifty acres of land, over which the company had obtained an easement for laying down their pipes, at a fixed rental for each line. These pipes had multiplied very rapidly, there were hundreds of them, and they covered those fifty acres like the threads of a garment.* The annual burden became so heavy that the land was ultimately purchased, and on the substitution of iron, care was taken to carry the mains on lines, in which streets could be laid out,—and the whole has now been long built over, and forms a large district of squares and streets.

At the time that the change was made, this land was let as pasture for £500,—it now produces above £4000 a year in ground rents, and it need hardly be said that when the leases fall in, the rental of this property will be very largely increased.

In the year 1822 it was determined to rebuild London Bridge. The representatives of Peter Moris held a lease from the Corporation, which had yet 260 years to run, of four arches of the old bridge, from which their water was pumped up by a series of water-wheels, turned by the tide, and the City, being anxious to arrange terms of compensation with them, came to an agreement, by which the New River paid them an annuity of £3750

---

* Mr. Mylne. Minutes of Evidence, July 29, 1851.

for the goodwill of their works, and agreed to supply
the inhabitants from their own mains,—thus giving
them high service instead of low, and enabling the
Corporation to remove the old bridge,* without any
cost to the city.

The various statements which have been made as to
·the original cost of this undertaking are strangely conflicting. Pennant· and others, misled by analogy with
"joint-stock companies," suppose the shares to have
been £100 each; thus making the whole outlay only
£7200; whilst Entick more correctly states them to
have been £7000 each, making a total of £504,000.

"In point of fact, there is no such thing as a share in
the New River Company," † in the modern sense of the

---

* Mr. Mylne. Minutes of Evidence, July 29, 1851.

† Mr. Talbot (counsel for the New River Company),—Minutes
of Evidence, 1851. This statement however now requires some
modification. By the Act 29 and 30 Vict. c. 230 (1866), it is enacted
that these parts shall be called "*original shares,*"—but they still
remain real property,—and the new £100 shares created by the same
Act "shall be called the *New River Company's New Shares,*"—
but "all such shares shall be personal estate, and 'be transmissible
as such, and shall not be of the nature of real property."

Landed·property was, till a much later period, the only "invest·
ment" known. Bishop Warburton tells us that Pope's father, who
had acquired a competence in trade, of between fifteen and twenty
thousand·pounds, retired from business into the country. Being
however a Roman Catholic, he was unable, under the existing laws

word,—a matter of some importance to state, as it has
led to more than one Chancery suit. They were
properly parts or portions "commonly called shares,"
in the King's or Adventurers' moiety, as the case might
be, and till lately were so described in legal documents,
and were always conveyed by lease and release, and by
fine and recovery, as landed property,—which was
"holden (says the Charter) of us, our heirs and successors, as of our mannor of East Greenwich, in our
countie of Kent, in free and comon socage, by fealtie
only, and not in cheife, nor by Knight's service."

Sir Hugh Myddelton originally undertook to advance
the whole capital, and commenced the work as an
individual enterprize. Afterwards King James took "a
moiety" of it, and "divers loving subjects well affecting
the said worke," made, at different times, their several
agreements with Myddelton to contribute "to the charges
for such rateable *parts and porcons* in the said worke as
was agreed between them;" they, on the other hand,
receiving in return, "rateable charges and partes out of
the profitts—rateably and *respectivelie to the proporcon*

---

either to purchase land or to place his money out on mortgage ;—
and as he was an adherent of James II., he made it a point of
conscience not to invest it in Government securities,—so he was
compelled to keep it in a chest, and to live on the principal, and
when Pope came to the succession, it was nearly all spent.

of their severall disbursements,"—which appear to have
been originally of various amounts.

Of these proprietors, called "Adventurers," there were
twenty-eight, and by the Charter of 1619 they were incorporated as "one body politique, in deed, fact, and
name, and by the name of the Governor and Company
of the New River, brought from Chadwell and Amwell
to London," with power "to purchase and possesse
mannors, lands, tenements, rents, revenues, possessions,
liberties, priviledges, rights, jurisdiccons, franchises, and
hereditaments, and to have and enjoy a comon seale,*
to seale any manner of instruments, deedes or writings,"
and appointing Sir Hugh Myddelton "to be the first and
present Governor."

It is the less surprising that there should be some
difficulty in ascertaining the original outlay, and the
amount paid by each adventurer, when we find that even
the number of these proprietors, as well as their names,
is differently stated by different authorities. Lodge, in
common with others, says, that there were twenty-seven,
and that one of them was "Ralph, son of Hugh
Myddelton." Mr. Smiles gives the number as twenty-
nine, and adds that besides "his son Hugh, who held

---

* This seal is "The hand of Providence, issuing from clouds,
and distributing water over London,"—with the motto—
"ET PLVI SVPER VNAM CIVITATEM."
(Taken from the 7th verse of the 4th chapter of Amos.)

one share, and his brother, Sir Thomas, who held another, there were *four* other shareholders of the name of Myddelton, but it does not appear that they were relatives of the goldsmith."

The Charter itself enumerates twenty-eight adventurers, amongst whom there is no "Ralph,"—but there are *five* of the name of Middelton, besides Sir Hugh, and his brother, and eldest son,—and of these five, William appears to be his second son, and Richard and Timothie his two nephews. There were also Robert Bateman, his brother-in-law, and William Bateman, his nephew,—making, with the "two shares"—which Mr. Smiles says were held by Sir Hugh—nine adventurers in the family.* This may perhaps account for the ultimate division of the moiety into *thirty-six* equal parts or shares, of which number the Myddelton family would hold just one quarter, and have a corresponding representation at the Board;—the Charter further providing that if any of the twenty-eight persons named should "departe with all or so much of the said share or part," which he then held, as that he should not "still retayne a full thirtie-sixe part or share of the moiety," he should be removed from his seat.

As the books of the Company were destroyed by fire,

---

* It would seem that these nine shares were held in trust, and that they constituted the nine shares mentioned in Sir Hugh's will, as belonging to himself or to other feoffees for his use, and which could not be sold for the payment of his debts.

which consumed the whole of the premises at Blackfriars, December 24, 1769, it is impossible to know what amount was paid upon these "partes or porcons," or what was the total expenditure upon the work. There is, however, every reason to believe that the statement of Entick, which was published before the documents of the Company were destroyed, is substantially correct. A "copy of a very old paper," in the New River Office, says : " N.B.—By the best accounts that can be gotten there appear to be expended on each share about £7000, before any dividend was made,—and notwithstanding they were made a corporation, in 1619, they were not capable of making any dividend till the year 1635, which then amounted to no more than £5 16s. 8½d. per share; 1640—£33 2s. 8½d. ; 1650—£40 18s. 8¾d."

From evidence laid before Parliament, the original cost of the river alone, *exclusive of the reservoirs and pipes*, appears to have been £428,420, being at the rate of about £6000 per share.

It is certain that Myddelton, who was a very wealthy man, was all but ruined by his outlay on this work ; and after its completion we find him a petitioner to the Corporation for a loan of £3000, which he obtained at six per cent interest (September, 1614). This was not repaid during his lifetime ; and in 1634 they remitted to Lady Myddelton £1000 of the principal, in consideration of the great benefit bestowed on the City, as well as for "the present comfort of Lady Myddelton."

Now, at the time when the Charter was granted (in 1619), Myddelton was the holder of no more than eight shares,* which, at Entick's estimate of £7000 each, would only amount to £56,000,—no very exorbitant sum to have exhausted the coffers of one of the merchant princes of London.

Mr. Smiles, in his interesting narrative, to which we are so much indebted, considers that the statements hitherto printed as to the cost of the New River have been greatly exaggerated, and he bases his calculation on the payments made from the Treasury, as they appear in the accounts of the State Paper Office. The first of these payments, however, is for the moiety of disbursements, from August 24, 1611, to December 1, 1612, and the last one entered is in April, 1616 ; making the total payments out of the Royal purse only £8609 14s. 6d., and the total expenditure only £17,219 9s. 0d. But this is a very defective balance sheet. Mr. Smiles has himself previously pointed out that Myddelton had, *before May*, 1610, expended above £3000, to which must be added a further sum of at least £4000, for the following sixteen months (previous to August 1611).

Moreover, the distribution of the water was, as stated by Mr. Mylne, " by far the most expensive part of the undertaking." We have no means of estimating the outlay on this head, except that it absorbed the whole

---

* Mr. Smiles:—A ninth share belonged to his eldest son Hugh.

receipts for a period of twenty years, and the loss of
interest alone (Myddelton was paying 6 per cent) during
this time would have more than trebled the original
cost,—independently of any calls that might have been
made. So heavy was this burden that in November,
1636, "as the concern seemed to offer no great prospect
of improvement, and a further call on the proprietors
was expected," Charles I., who required all his available
means for other purposes, finally disposed of his moiety
(now constituting the "King's shares,") to the Company,
under the great seal, in consideration of a fee-farm rent
of £500, which is now paid to the Adair family, and is
known by the name of the "King's Clogg."

If the whole real cost of this moiety had been only
£8600, Charles I. could hardly have asked or obtained
such an unreasonable equivalent for his share in a
concern which for twenty years had not paid a sixpence,
and on which an additional outlay was expected.

Lastly, there seems some reason to doubt whether
Myddelton was ever really repaid the whole amount which
he was entitled to, under the agreement with the Crown.
Fuller certainly implies that there was some injustice in
his treatment in this respect. "But oh—what an injury
was it to him, that a potent person and idle spectator
should strike in—(reader I could heartily wish it were a
falshood what I report)—and by his greatness possess a
moiety of the profit which the unwearied endeavours of

the aforesaid Knight had purchased to himself." * This
language would have been wholly inapplicable if the
stipulated payment had been fairly made, and Fuller in
no way censures the "adventurers" who had purchased
above a third of the undertaking.

Nor is Fuller the only one who alludes thus obscurely
to Myddelton having been in some way deprived of his
just claims and position. The Rev. Wilhelm Bedwell,
in his "Description of Tottenham High Cross," (London,
1631), says, "He who first chalked out the way, we
know was our English Tycho, a man so ingenious,
industrious, and learned, that I suppose there were few
things undertaken by him, if fecible, which hee would
not have effected and done,—but it seemeth, that before
the worke was altogether finished, he was put by it, and
others imployed to make an end of it."

Sir Hugh was knighted after the opening of the
New River, in 1613, and in October, 1622, he was
created a baronet. "These empty honours (says
Lodge) were the only recompense that poor Myddelton
ever received." He died, beyond all doubt, an impover-
ished man, on the 10th December, 1631,—his will being
dated the 21st November, and proved the 21st December
of that year. Though the later undertakings of his life
were prosperous, and probably lucrative, yet he seems
never to have recovered from the losses and embarass-

---

* Fuller's Worthies of England, 1662.

ments of his patriotic enterprize. His loan from the
City of London was still unpaid after the lapse of seventeen years ; he directs his land and houses to be sold for
the satisfaction of mortgages upon them, and the whole
of his pecuniary legacies amounted to only £3100, for
the payment of which, and of his debts, he directs that
his property in the Mines Royal of Wales, should be
sold, and also four of his New River shares, if the sum
realized by the sale of the mines should not be sufficient.

He leaves his "house at Bush-hill, Edmonton," and
his shares in the New River (which, however, yielded no
income) to Lady Myddelton for her life, together with
the jewels she had been "used to wear at festivals," and
the great jewel given to him by the Lord Mayor (probably
his brother) and Aldermen, and also "the deep, silver
bason, the spout pot, and maudling cup, and small
bowl, all which had been given to her."

He states that "thirteen partes or shares" in the New
River were then belonging to him, or to other feoffees
for his use, "the profits" of which he gives to his wife
for her life,—but he only devises six of them, and
appoints no residuary legatee. It would seem probable
that the four shares which he directs to be sold had been
purchased by him since the date of the Charter, and
were at his own disposal ; whilst the remaining nine
consisted of the share held by his eldest son, Hugh,
which had reverted to him on his death (and which may
be the one bequeathed to the Goldsmith's Company),

and of eight shares held by trustees for his use, with
more or less power of appointment over the reversion.
Five of these he leaves to his younger children, William,
Henry, Simon, Elizabeth, and Ann. To the poor of
Henllan (his birth-place), of Denbigh, and of Amwell, he
leaves small legacies, as well as to his clerks and others,
who had assisted him in his different enterprizes,—and he
leaves £5 to each of his men servants, "except the boy
in the kitchen," who has only forty shillings, and forty
shillings to his one "maid servant."

The title is now extinct.

---

When compared with the engineering·works of the
present day, the New River may perhaps appear a small
undertaking, but at the time of its construction, it was,
beyond all doubt, the greatest enterprize that had been
attempted in England. Myddelton had no past experience for his guide, and with only his practical good sense
and strong determination to rely upon, he had to encounter, single handed, the sneers of incredulity and the
harassing opposition of hostile interest.

The stream was originally forty-eight * miles in length,

---

* It is strange that every writer we have seen should have stated
this length to have been under forty miles. Our authority is that of
Mr. Mylne (Min. of Evid. 6 May, 1852). "2700—What is the
measured distance of the New River, as constructed?" "It was
48 miles when I was appointed, but we have taken off some of the
contours nearer London, and it is reduced to 38 miles." Since 1852
the length has been still further diminished, and it is now only about
28 miles.

and had a fall of two inches to the mile, with occasional
weirs across its bed of three or four feet in height. The
water-course was ten feet wide and four deep, and the
number of bridges 160.

The surface waters of the district were carried off,
sometimes by a culvert under the bed of the river, and
sometimes by a "flash," which consisted of a wooden
trough carried over it. One of these flashes was situated
at Clay-hill, where the name is still retained.

Amongst the most important constructions was "The
Frame," at Bush-hill, which was a wooden trunk lined
with lead, 660 feet in length and 5 feet deep. This was
supported upon eighty brick piers, beneath which was a
lofty tunnel for the passage of the Salmon-brook, and the
storm-water from Enfield-chase.

On the keystone of this arch are the arms of Sir Hugh
Myddelton,—argent, on a pile vert, three wolves' heads,

erased, of the field. Crest, out of a ducal coronet, or,—
a dexter hand, proper. The inscription round the arch
records that "this arch was rebuilt in the yeare 1652.
The Right Hon. Henry Earl of Clarendon, being
Governor." And on a marble tablet above, "the frame
and lead was raised one foot higher Ann. Dom. 1725."
Another strong timber aqueduct, similarly lined,—466
feet long and 17 feet high, known by the name of
"Myddelton's boarded river," was situated near Islington.

The continuous wear of the current for above a century
and a half had so attenuated the lead of these structures,
and the consequent leakage had become so great, that it was
decided by Mr. Mylne to remove them, and to substitute
clay embankments in their stead. The Bridgewater
canal had just been completed, and Brindley had ex-
hibited on the table of a wondering committee of the
House of Commons his manufacture of "*puddle*,"—a
word only known till then in Johnson's dictionary as
"a dirty plash."

In May, 1778, "the Frame," at Bush-hill, was taken
down, and some idea may be formed of its original cost
from the fact that the wasted remains of the old lead,
which even then weighed fifty tons, were sold for about
£1000.*

---

* A professional calculation,—based upon the prices of lead,
materials, and labour,—from the Churchwardens' accounts of some
of the London parishes, and of Battle-abbey, in the seventeenth
century,—and computing the probable original thickness of lead in
these two structures, estimates their first cost at £4000,—being more
than half of Pennant's supposed expenditure for the whole work.

THE FRAME AT BUSH-HILL.

The New River Company has, from time to time, enlarged its works, *—widening the stream to about twenty-five feet, and adding to its supplies of water from various sources, the principal of which is the River Lee, which was resorted to, to compensate for the loss of the Amwell spring, which had abandoned its source and found its way into the Lee. No opposition was at first made to this drain, but as the amount became serious, disputes arose with the Lee trustees, and finally a long course of protracted litigation was put an end to by an Act of Parliament, 18 & 19 Vict. c. 196, which enacted that, subject to the payment of a gross sum of forty-two thousand pounds, and an annual payment of three thousand five hundred pounds, for the restoration of the locks, "all the water flowing down the River Lee and the navigation thereof, should be transferred to and be absolutely vested in the New River and East London companies for ever; reserving to the trustees of the River Lee the use of such supply as was required for the purposes of the navigation. By the latest returns, taken from the "City Press," the daily supply now derived from its different resources amounts to twenty-five millions of gallons, and its yearly supply to nine

---

* The cost of these improvements and extensions varied from £20,000 to £27,000 a year, and was paid out of the income which would otherwise have been divided among the shareholders,—between the years 1810 and 1850, upwards of £920,000 was thus expended.

thousand millions, of which three hundred and fifty
millions are used by manufactories, forty-five millions for
flushing sewers, fifteen millions for extinguishing fires,
and ninety millions for watering the streets, 8,500,000,000
being used for household consumption.

The district supplied by the New River com-
prises the whole of central London, between a line
extending from the Tower to Stamford-hill, and one
drawn from Charing-cross northwards by Tottenham-
court-road to Camden-town.

To meet this demand, the old river channel stores up
117 million gallons, the Cheshunt reservoirs 75 millions,
and that at Hornsey 39 millions; while those at Stoke
Newington, constructed in 1833, for subsidence, contain
130 million gallons. Major Bolton's report of March,
1873, gives the joint area of these reservoirs as above
100 acres. The total water area amounts to 215 acres,
and will contain 467,000,000 gallons, being a quantity
sufficient to meet the whole consumption for eighteen
days.

The daily average supply to 120,000 houses, inhabited
by 800,000 individuals, is 24 million gallons, which, if
required, could be increased to 35 millions, and the
resources are practically unlimited.

The water of Loch Katrine, by which Glasgow is
supplied, has generally been considered as ·the standard
of purity, but it appears from an article in the Lancet,
giving the results of an elaborate investigation, -commu-
nicated by the London Institution, that the Loch Katrine

water, pure as it undoubtedly is, contains putrescible matter corresponding to o·13 parts of ammonia in a million gallons, being one-third more than that in New River water, which contains only o·09. The returns for the month of March last state that "the water of the New River Company was perfectly clear and colourless, when examined in bulk through a tube two feet in length ;"—the analysis gives in a million gallons o·oo1 of saline ammonia, and o·oo4 of organic ammonia, being less than half the amount contained in Loch Katrine water..

For the purpose of ensuring this high quality of purity, there are, in addition to the large reservoirs for subsidence, thirteen filtering-beds, covering altogether a sand area of more than 11¼ acres, which contain upwards of twelve million gallons. The steam engines employed for raising this immense body of water possess 1780 horse-power, besides water-wheels which work fifty-one pumps.

The length of cast iron mains, some of which are four feet in diameter, is no less than 650 miles, and extends over an area of above 17 square miles of houses. There are also about two miles of tunnelling of immense bore, now conveying the water under ground, which, for 250 years, had flowed in an open stream through Islington.

The actual cost to the Company, including working expenses and interest, is stated in the Report of the Committee of the House of Commons* to be £22 8s. 3d.

* 16th July, 1851.

per million gallons, and the charge to the public
£22 19s. 3d., leaving a profit of not more than 2½
per cent.

In small quantities, paid for in the bulk, the price is
from 6d. to 7½d. per thousand gallons, a price much
below what it would cost any one to pump it, if he had
a well at his own door. The Reform Club, in Pall-mall,
is supplied from a well, the cost of which, and of a four-
horse engine, was £1230. The expense of pumping is
£170 per annum.

When paid by water-rate, the charge, as authorized by
Parliament, is 4 per cent on rentals under £200, and
3 per cent on those above £200, but the actual charge
made by the Company is never more than half, and in
some cases not more than one-tenth of the authorized
price.

In point of fact, all the water that is consumed for all
purposes, throughout the New River Company's district,
in one week, is supplied at a charge of less than two-
pence a head, and the whole of the water used for
drinking alone, costs less than *two-pence per head per
annum,—being less than the price of half a pot of beer to
each individual.*

The average daily supply to each house is two hundred
gallons, being at the rate of thirty gallons per head of
population, and more than double the amount laid down
by the Parliamentary Commission. No other city ap-
proaches in its supply to that given to London,—to
which, says Sir William Clay, "water is furnished not

only in greater profusion than to any other city in the world, but in a degree beyond the utmost want of its inhabitants."

It was mentioned above that the early records of the Company were destroyed by fire, in the year 1769; but "a valuation of the entire works was made in the year 1765, and an account subsequently rendered to Parliament up to 1820." * From that time a continuous account of the whole expenditure on the works to the year 1852 was received and adopted by Parliament, when the capital expended was fixed by statute to have been £1,519,958,—or £21,110 per original share,—in addition to which the Company have since been authorized to raise, on bond and debenture, a further amount of one million. In 1866 it being deemed expedient to authorize a further sum of money to be raised by the creation of new shares, power was given by the 29 & 30 Vict. cap. 230, to allot shares of the nominal value of £100 to the extent of £500,000, thus raising the total amount to £3,019,958.

It is very seldom that "a share" in this magnificent property comes into the market, the last that was sold was an "Adventurer's Share," in 1864.

In 1870, there were sold at the Auction-mart, by Messrs. Fox & Bousfield, four-fifths of one King's share, and five-twelfths of one Adventurer's share, in lots chiefly

---

* Minutes of Select Committee, May 6, 1852.

of one-twentieth part. These were purchased at the rate of about forty-one thousand pounds for an Adventurer's share. The King's shares, which do not give a qualification for a seat at the Board,* and are burdened with the payment of "the King's Clogg," sold at the rate of rather less than forty thousand pounds. Some of the new £100 shares fully paid up sold at £195, and some on which only £20 had been paid, sold at £50 per share. At this time the dividend per share was only £1578 on the Adventurer's, and £1516 on the King's shares;—since that time it has been steadily rising, being now upwards of £1900,—(of which about £1820 is derived from the water, and £80 from the land, so that the present market value of a share cannot be estimated at much less than fifty thousand pounds.)†

It has been said above, that when the New River was first made, all depended upon individual enterprize and influence, and that joint stock companies and the various resources of modern finance were then not in being. But this was only a small part of the difficulty. Skill

---

* By the terms of the agreement with the King, the whole management of the Company was left in the hands of Sir Hugh Myddelton and his fellow Adventurers. The Board consists of twenty-nine members who receive a payment of about £4000 a year for their services. (Patent Roll, 10 Jas. I—A.D. 1612.)

† Whilst this was in the printer's hands, a quarter share in the King's moiety has been sold in four lots of one-sixteenth each (May 14, 1873), at the Rate of above £49,000.

SOURCE OF THE NEW RIVER AT CHADWELL.

and knowledge were wanted as well as money. Engin-
eering, levelling, surveying, and practical mechanics, were
alike wholly unknown in this country. When the water-
works at London-bridge were constructed, a Dutchman,
Peter Moris, was employed,—the great level of the Fens
was drained by Vermuyden, Canvey Island was embanked
by Coppenburgh and his company of Dutch workmen.
A Dutch engineer was engaged to construct the haven at
Yarmouth, and even when old Westminster-bridge was
built, we had to send for Labelye, a Swiss engineer.

Not a single attempt had been made to cut a canal in
all England, when Myddelton first undertook to construct
his aqueduct,

"And roll obedient rivers through the land."

Notwithstanding all that has been done by modern
science,—with the aid of steam, and of unlimited resources
of capital,—the New River still remains a wonderful
work,—and bold as the assertion may be, it is beyond
any comparison the greatest and most important that has
ever been planned and executed by a single man,—single-
handed, single-headed, and single-hearted.

The monumental pedestal represented in the accompanying engraving, bears the following inscription.

" Sacred to the memory of
SIR HUGH MYDDELTON, BARONET,
whose successful care,
assisted by the patronage of his King,
conveyed this stream to London:
an immortal work,
since man cannot more nearly
imitate the Deity
than in bestowing health."

## THE ENVOY.

There are,—as Goldsmith said,— a hundred faults in
this thing, and a hundred things might be said to prove
them beauties,—but it is needless. A book may be
amusing with numerous errors, or it may be very dull,
without a single absurdity.

Should the gentle reader meet, here and there, with
something to please or inform him, he may be assured
that it was written expressly for intelligent readers like
himself; and if he should find more that is tedious or
common place, he will tolerate it as being intended for
those of duller intellect or less refined taste.

If, perchance, there should be some,—more critical or
more learned,—whose pleasure may consist in finding
fault or detecting errors, they will no doubt have abundant
sources of amusement in these pages,—where the writer
has probably often been misinformed, without erudition
enough to set him right.

To conclude, in the words of the old grammarian,—

" Aiunt,—𝕿𝔥𝔞𝔦 𝔰𝔞𝔶𝔢,
Quid aiunt,—𝔚𝔥𝔞𝔱 𝔰𝔞𝔶𝔢 𝔱𝔥𝔞𝔦 ?
Aiant,—𝕷𝔞𝔱 𝔱𝔥𝔞𝔦𝔪 𝔰𝔞𝔶𝔢."

# PART II.

---

## THE PARISH CHURCH,

### ITS MONUMENTS, &c.,

#### WITH NOTICES OF THE

### ECCLESIASTICAL HISTORY OF THE PARISH;

#### ALSO AN ACCOUNT OF THE

### PAROCHIAL AND OTHER SCHOOLS.

r

ENFIELD. IN 1793.

## THE PARISH CHURCH.

THE church, dedicated to S. Andrew, stands within a spacious churchyard on the north side of the Market-place, just opposite the tenth mile-stone from London, and due north of S. Paul's. We know from Domesday Book that a church existed here at the time of the Conquest, as it had done in the reign of Edward the Confessor, and probably for several centuries previously. But of the original structure no vestige remains, nor of any building of the Norman period, except possibly in the basement of the tower. The most striking features of the present building, externally, are an array of battlements, and an abundant use of stucco. Internally, the church consists of a nave and chancel separated by a lofty arch, and of broad aisles, extending, without any break, the whole length both of nave and chancel, so that the church forms a parallelogram, 100 feet by 63, with a south porch and western tower. The floor of the church is now very much below the level of the ground, so that you descend several steps on entering. This is owing to the gradual accummulation of soil in the course of centuries, as may be clearly seen by comparing the level of the churchyard with that of the Bowling-green, to the west of it. There are no documents in existence, so far as can be discovered, which throw light on the architectural history of the church. The Bishop of London's registers do not go back beyond the beginning of the 14th century, and since that time there has been no consecration. We are left, therefore, to the evidence supplied by the building itself; and successive alterations and reparations, in 1771, 1789, 1810, 1824, 1853, and 1866, have effaced so many landmarks, that it is very difficult to arrive at any satisfactory conclusions; but, so far as we may conjecture, the history of the structure has been somewhat as follows :—

The church was probably rebuilt, on a larger scale, in the twelfth century, soon after its connexion with the Monastery of Walden began, and to this church the present tower belongs. It is built of flint and rubble, with stone quoins in three stages, without any buttresses, and gradually tapering. The battlements, and the walls for a few feet below them, are a more recent addition. The original windows remain in the upper stage, but those in the middle stage are mostly blocked up, and the lower ones have debased tracery and cement hood mouldings. Owing to this, and to its being cased in cement, the tower has lost much of its ancient appearance.

To the same period with the tower belongs the interior wall, to the south of the altar, pierced by a lancet window of the twelfth century, formerly blocked up, and only opened in 1866. This was originally the external wall of the chancel, which then had no aisles, and extended further to the west than it now does, as is clearly proved by the old sedilia discovered in 1852, of which a drawing is here given. This, it will be observed, shows the arch of the last seat towards the west, cut in two by the present pier.

Below the lancet window, on the south side, there is a recess in the wall, which (as may be seen in the same drawing), formerly went through the wall, and is represented as blocked up. This was, without doubt, one of those openings which have perplexed ecclesiologists, and been variously named Squints, Hagioscopes, Lychnoscopes, &c., according to the different theories propounded to explain their use. Some have supposed that they were intended for watching the altar light; others, that

they were to allow lepers and others outside the church
to witness mass and be communicated ; others, that they
were confessionals.   In this one, there is the peculiarity
that its splay is away from and not towards the altar.

Some time in the fourteenth century, the whole of the
church to which this wall belonged, from the present
altar steps to the tower, must have been pulled down or
otherwise destroyed, and another built, to which belonged
the arcade of arches with clustered columns, which extend
the whole length of the church, five being in the nave
and two in the chancel, all of the same dimensions, and
giving the same width to nave and chancel.   This church
had chancel aisles, extending as far east as the present
altar steps, and the building of them must have led to
that curtailment of the sacrarium, which affected the
sedilia, as we have seen.   These aisles were in all probability narrower than the present aisles, and had sloping
roofs.   The corbels on which the roof of the old south
aisle rested may still be observed.   Foundations of a
wall within the present south aisle were discovered in
1824.   Of this church again, externally, nothing remains
except part of the east wall, and internally, little more
than the columns and arches ; for towards the end of the
fifteenth century the walls of the nave were carried up to
form the clerestory, thereby enclosing within the church
one of the windows of the tower, now blocked up behind
the organ, which formerly opened above the roof.   We
are enabled to approximate to the date of this clerestory

from the ornaments, which may be observed carved on
square stones between the windows, a rose or rather
quatrefoil, and a wing, alternately. (Two on the south
side are gone). The same emblems occur on the tower
of Hadley Church, with the date 1494. Of these, more
will be said presently.

Probably at the same time the present north aisle was
built with the external turret staircase which then communicated with the rood loft by a raised passage or
gallery across the aisle. At the east end of this aisle
there seems to have been then a chantry chapel, that
founded by Baldwin de Radyugton in the year 1398.
About 1471 another chantry priest was endowed with
£10 per annum, charged on the estate of Poynetts, in
Essex, to say masses for the souls of Robert Blossom and
his wife at the altar of S. Mary, which may have stood in
this chapel, or in a corresponding chapel at the east end
of the south aisle. There are now no traces of an altar
in either.

Some years, probably, after the building of the north
aisle it was extended eastward so as to include the
chantry chapel, and this part was made to correspond
with the rest. The east window of the aisle seems of a
somewhat different character from those on the north,
and a stone* which was found under the plaister of the

---

* This stone is now let into the west wall of the church, by the
south gallery staircase.

wall externally above this window, with the inscription, ANNO DOMINI 1531, serves to fix the date of the completion of the work. The coat of arms in the window itself, with the date 1530, points to the same conclusion, and leads us to suppose that the alteration was connected with the building of the arch over Lady Tiptoft's tomb, as a monument to her grandson Edmund Lord Roos, who died in 1508. The arms are those of Thomas Lord Roos, created first Earl of Rutland (great nephew of Edmund), by whom, probably, the arch was erected. The initials, T. R., are on the glass. This portion of the chancel aisle was enclosed and used as a vestry till 1867, when the present vestry was built.

The south aisle did not assume its present character till 1824, when it was in great measure rebuilt, in order to correspond to the north aisle, and to be able to receive a gallery similar to one which had been built over the north aisle in 1819. At the same time the muniment room above the south porch, and the turret staircase which led to it, were pulled down, and many of the contents, unfortunately, dispersed and lost. This room above the porch may be seen in the view given of the church as it existed in 1817.

The east window of the chancel was formerly blocked up to within three feet of the top of the arch by an oak altar-piece, and the lower portion of the window was bricked or plaistered up externally, so that in an engraving of the church in 1770 no mullions are to be seen.

Large sums were expended in repairs and restorations (?) in 1771 and 1789, and it is on record that from May, 1789, to May, 1790, no Divine service was performed in the parish ! It appears from a stone tablet in the west wall that the church was again repaired and beautified in 1810. In 1853 the high square pews, which encumbered not only the nave but the chancel, were cleared away, and the nave and aisles repewed, leaving only one square pew, for which a faculty was claimed. At the same time the chancel, with the consent of the rectors, was appropriated to the choir, and the organ gallery thrown back one bay further west. But the most extensive restorations were carried out in 1866-7, at a cost of more than £4000, raised by voluntary contributions, mainly owing to the exertions of Rev. W. D. Maclagan, then curate-in-charge of the parish. It was found necessary to put entirely new roofs to nave, chancel, and aisles, and to lay down a new floor throughout the church, which, unhappily, is already (in 1873), almost destroyed by dry rot. The galleries were rebuilt, and very much was done in every way to improve the appearance and comfort of the church. The stone pulpit and brass eagle desk were presented by Colonel Somerset, of Enfield Court. The font had been given previously in 1850 by Mrs. Everett, of Chase-side House. The east window will shortly be refilled with stained glass as a memorial to the late J. J. Austin, Esq., of Juglans Lodge (who died in 1872, at the age of 92), at the expense of his family.

Allusion has been already made to the Rose and Wing which are found in the clerestory, and also on the tower of Hadley Church. They were supposed at one time (Lysons) to have formed a rebus on the name of Rose-wing, an Abbot of Walden invented for the occasion, as he had no real existence, the abbot in 1494 being Sarysfort.

There can be no doubt but that a rose and wing were borne as badges by Sir Thomas Lovell, K.G., who, on the death of Lord Roos in 1508 without issue, succeeded to the Manor of Worcesters in right of his wife Isabella, sister to Lord Roos.

In the vaulting of the choir of St. George's Chapel, Windsor, above the stall formerly assigned to Sir T. Lovell, as Knight of the Garter, there appears "a quatrefoil, gules, tied by a cord, or, to a bird's wing erased, sable." Willement, in his account of the S. George's Chapel, says, in a note, "A wing sable, the bone embrued, is given as the badge of Lovell in the Harleian MS. 4632."

Pennant mentions in his Itinerary that in his time the same emblems, a rose and a wing, were to be seen on a wall which formerly belonged to Holiwell Nunnery in Shoreditch, to which Sir Thomas Lovell was a great benefactor, and where he was buried in 1524, after his body had been laid in state in Enfield Church, on the way from Elsynge Hall to London.

A full account of the ceremonies observed on this occasion is preserved in the Herald's College.

Though Sir Thomas Lovell did not come into possession of the Manor of Worcesters till the death of Edmund
Lord Roos in 1508, yet previously, by an Act of Parliament passed in 1492, "the guidance and governance of
Edmund Lord Roos and his estates" had been vested in
him, "the said Edmund not being of sufficient discretion
to guide himself and his livelihood." So that he had a
connexion with the neighbourhood before the year 1494,
the date found at Hadley.

It is possible, however, that Sir Thomas may have
adopted a device or badge belonging to his wife's family,
the Rooses or Tiptofts,* as we know that the de
Bohun badge, the swan, was adopted by Thomas of Woodstock and Henry Bolingbroke, who married the heiresses of
that family.

In one of the gallery windows of the north aisle
there are some remains of stained glass, in which may
be traced two groups, of four women each, on each side of
an arch, over which is *a wing*. The women are in a
praying posture, and apparently in a religious dress.
There are also a few letters of an inscription, and some
flowers resembling wild hyacinths, but the whole is in a
fragmentary and confused state, and nearly effaced.

---

* Fuller mentions that on the mantel-piece of the Old House
at Durants was a bat's wing. It may be merely a coincidence
that Roos of Lyme Regis, Dorsetshire, has for crest—a rose gules,
between two wings expanded.

This was, probably, a memorial of Sir Thomas Lovell. We are told that on several of the windows of Holywell Chapel was the inscription :—

> " All ye nunnes of Holywell,
> Pray ye both day and night
> For the soule of Sir Thomas Lovell,
> Whom Henry the 7th made knight."

### THE BELLS.

The upper stage of the tower is the bell chamber. In this are hung nine bells. Their present framework was put up in A.D. 1809, and can all be taken apart. The eight bells constituting the peal are hung on the same level. The remaining bell, known by the name of Ting Tang, and employed as a five minutes' bell before the services, is elevated above the rest, and is of an earlier date ; it bears this inscription on its collar, in two circles and in raised capitals.

RICHARD IOSEPH    WILLIAM HVNSDVN    HENRY HODGE
RICHARD WRIGIIT, CHVRCHWARDENS    W    W    J680

No 1, or the treble bell of the peal, has this inscription in three circles round the collar, in large and small capitals, the colons indicating the completion of a circle, and the latter part of the last line forming the third circle, with the name of the founder :—

DOES BATTLE RAGE DO SANGUINE FOES CONTEND
WE HAIL THE VICTOR IF HIS : BRITAINS FRIEND
MAY GEORGE LONG REIGN WHO NOW THE SCEPTRE SWAYS
AND : BRITISH VALOUR EVER RULE THE SEAS :

T. MEARS & SON OF LONDON, FECIT 1808 :

No. 2 has the following inscription on the collar, in cut letters :—

Rᵀ· Dews, Esqʀ· Rᴰ· Langford, Esqʀ· Joseph Bell, Esqʀ· Cʜ. wardens, 1808.

and in raised letters below it :—

Thomas·Mears of London, Fecit.

Nos. 3, 4, 5, 6, and 7 have all of them this inscription on their collars in raised letters, with small fleurs-de-lys between the words :—

R. PHELPS, FECIT 1724.

Of these, No. 4 is cracked about 10 inches from the top down the cannon, and requires re-casting; No. 7 is said to contain some silver, which idea, no doubt, arises from its being the clearest-toned bell in the belfry.

No. 8, or the tenor bell, weighs about a ton; its note is E; round its collar is this inscription, in large and small capitals :—

Richard Phelps Made me, 1724 * Mʀ· Rob : Udall, d : d : vic : In Bridges Matw· Atwood Wm· Kirby, Cʜ : wardens.

In the chamber below is the clock which strikes the hours on the tenor bell. On the correcting dial is the name of the maker, *sic*, Willᵐ· Rout, Enfield, 1764.

Below this again is the chamber where the ringing now takes place. The floor was erected in A.D. 1870, on four strong oak posts, for the convenience of the ringers, who formerly stood on the ground floor, which is now only used as a lumber-room, but which, it is hoped, may before long be put into a better state.

THE ORGAN.

The organ stands in the west gallery. An inscription, in gilt letters, on its front, sets forth that it "was the sole gift of Mrs. Mary Nickells, late of this parish, and was erected by her executors in the year of our Lord 1752." She left by will May 2, 1751, £900, of which £500 was laid out in the purchase of an organ, and the remainder invested to provide for the organist's salary. Gibbs was the builder, and it was re-built and enlarged by Gray and Davidson in 1867. On the great organ are 7 stops, on the choir 5, on the swell 8, and on the pedals 1 stop, and there are also 5 couplers.

MONUMENTS.

The oldest and by far the most interesting monument in the church is that of Lady Tiptoft, who died 1446. An altar tomb occupies the easternmost arch on the north side of the chancel, over which is a stone canopy of a later date. The original tomb has four panels on each side, each containing a shield, and is covered by a slab of grey Purbeck marble, inlaid with a very fine brass in good preservation. Under a triple canopy richly adorned with finials and crockets, is a full-length figure of a lady, with the hands raised in prayer. On three circles

---

NOTE.—The illustrations of Lady Tiptoft's brass are taken from a paper in the Transactions of the London and Middlesex Archæological Society, by Rev. C. Boutell, kindly placed at my disposal, and I have largely availed myself of the paper itself.—ED.

BRASS TO LADY TIPTOFT IN ENFIELD CHURCH. A.D. 1446.

within the spandrils of the canopy are respectively
the words—Mercy, Jhu, Ignosce. From the pillars which
support the canopy hang six shields. Round the edge
of the slab on a brass fillet, at the corners of which were
the four evangelistic symbols, (though only one, that of

EMBLEM OF S. MATTHEW.

S. Matthew, now remains), is the following inscription in
old English letters, with birds, beasts, leaves, and various
other devices between each word.

D'na Jocosa quondam filia et una hered' Caroli D'ni
Powes ac etiam filia et una hered' Honorabilissimo
D'nc Marchie, et uxon famosissimo militi ; [Johanni
Typtoft, que obiit xx]ii die Septe'bn', A°.D'ni mccccxlvi,
cujus anime, et omniu' fideliu' defuncton', J'h's,
pro sua sacnatissima passione, misereat'

The portions within brackets are concealed by the arch above.

Translation :—(Here lies) the Lady Jocosa, formerly daughter and co-heiress of Charlton Lord Powes, and also daughter and co-heiress of the most honourable Lady March, and wife to the most famous soldier, John Tiptoft. She died on the 22nd day of September, A.D. 1446, on whose soul, and that of all the faithful departed, may Jesus, for his most holy passion's sake, have mercy.

The costume of the effigy consists of a long and flowing robe, deeply bordered with ermine ; over this

HEAD OF EFFIGY.

appears a sleeveless jacket, also enriched with ermine; and, above all, an heraldic mantle secured by a tasselled cordon, richly jewelled. The coiffure is an elaborate composition of the horned form, bordered with jewels, surmounted by a coronet, and with a cover-chef completely conceals the hair. A rich necklace supports a pendant jewel. There are narrow bracelets about the wrists, and on the third finger of the right hand is a large ring.

The uppermost shield, on the right-hand side, bears the arms of her father—*Powys*. Or, a lion rampant, gules. The lowest, the arms of *Tiptoft*. Argent, a saltire engrailed, gules. That in the centre, *Tiptoft* impaling *Powys*, which is itself impaled by the arms of *Holland*. Gules, three lions of England, within a bordure argent. On the left side of the canopy, the uppermost shield bears *Tiptoft* impaling *Powys*; that in the centre, *Powys* and *Holland*, quarterly; and the lowest, *Powys*.

On the mantle may be seen the lions of Powys and Holland.

This Jocosa, or Joyce, was the daughter of Edward, fourth Baron Charlton de Powys, who died in 1422, leaving two daughters, between whom his barony fell into abeyance. He married Alianore, widow of the celebrated Roger Mortimer, fourth Earl of March, and daughter of Thomas Holland, Earl of Kent, whose grandmother, Joan Plantagenet, was sister and sole heir of John, son of Edmund of Woodstock, younger son of Edward I., created by him in 1321 Earl of Kent. She married John de Tiptoft or

U

Tibetort, who was summoned to Parliament as Baron
Tiptoft in 1426, and filled many high offices of State
during the reigns of Henry IV., Henry V., and Henry VI.,
till his decease in 1443. His father, Sir Pain de Tiptoft,
married Agnes, sister to Sir John Wroth, who had married
Maud, daughter and heiress of Sir Thomas Durant, of
Durants, and in this way the Tiptofts became connected
with Enfield.

Jocosa, Lady Tiptoft, left at her death one son and
four daughters. The son was created Earl of Worcester
in 1449. He was one of the most accomplished scholars
and travellers of the day, and was made by Edward IV.
Chancellor of Ireland and Constable of England. But
his adhesion to the House of York proved fatal to him.
During the few months of Henry VI.'s restoration in 1470
he was beheaded on Tower-hill, and his honours were
forfeited. His son was restored by Edward IV., but died
unmarried in 1485, when the earldom of Worcester
became extinct, and the barony of Tiptoft fell into
abeyance.

The estates passed to Thomas, tenth Baron de Ros or
Roos of Hamlake, who had married Philippa, the eldest
daughter of Lady Tiptoft, and who died under attainder
in 1461. His son Edmund obtained the reversal of his
father's attainder in 1485, but was of weak intellect, and
died unmarried in 1508, and was succeeded by his sister
Isabel, wife of Sir Thomas Lovell, K.G., under whose
guardianship he had been placed by Act of Parliament in

1492. She also died without issue, and the barony which had been in abeyance, devolved on George, son of her sister Eleanor, who had married Sir Thomas Manners.

This George, Lord Roos, died in 1513, and was succeeded by his son Thomas, who in 1525 was created by Henry VIII. Earl of Rutland and K.G., and died in 1543. His arms appear, as has been already mentioned, in the east window of the north chancel aisle, with the initials, T. R., and the date 1530, enclosed in a garter. On another shield in the same window are his arms impaling those of *Paston*, his second wife.

It was very possibly by this Earl of Rutland that the arch or canopy above Lady Tiptoft's tomb was erected in memory of Edmund Lord Roos, or, more probably, as we may infer from the armorial bearings, as a memorial at the same time of his sister Isabel, Lady Lovel.

A depressed four-centred arch, with a horizontal cornice, surmounted by a crest of Tudor flower, is built up so as to fill the opening of the pier arch. The masonry stands on the east and west extremities of the tomb, so as to cover portions of the inscription on the brass fillet. Over the point of the arch, on each face of the tomb, under a helmet, on which is a wreath surmounted by a crest, a peacock in his pride, hangs in a sloping position, a shield, quarterly, 1 and 4, gules, three water bougets argent, for *Roos*. 2 and 3, Argent, a fess between two bars gemelles, gules, for *Badlesmere*. (Both Rooses and Tiptofts were descended from heiresses of the

Badlesmere family.) In each spandrel is a shield. .That on the dexter side bears the arms of *Roos, Holland, Tiptoft,* and *Badlesmere,* quarterly; that on the sinister bears *Lovell* and *Muswell,* quarterly, impaling *Roos, Holland, Tiptoft,* and *Badlesmere.* The arms of *Lovell* are—Or, a chevron azure between three squirrels sejant, gules. Those of *Muswells* Vert, two chevrons argent, each charged with 3 cinquefoils, gules.

This monument has lately been restored at the expense of the Duke of Rutland, who is the representative of the Roos family.

From the other daughters of Lady Tiptoft, Joan and Joyce, are descended many noble families in the peerage. Margaret died a nun.

In the north chancel aisle, near the vestry door, is a large and richly-decorated marble monument to Sir Nicholas Raynton, of Forty-hall, who died in 1646, at the age of 78, and of his wife Rebecca, who died six years previously. He is represented in armour, reclining under a canopy supported by two columns of black marble, in his robes as Lord Mayor, with collar and badge, his head resting on his right hand, and in his left hand a sword, of which the blade is gone. Below him is the figure of his wife in a similar posture, holding a book in her left hand. Below this again are the figures of his son and his son's wife, · also Nicholas and Rebecca kneeling at a desk, with books open before them; behind the man two sons, and behind the woman three

MONUMENT OF SIR NICHOLAS RAYNTON.

daughters, all kneeling. A son, Thomas, who had died before his parents, is represented as an infant lying at the foot of the desk. In shields at the top of the monument are the arms of Raynton impaling Moulton, and of Raynton and Moulton separately. On the wall above is a shield, with those of Wolstenholme.

In the same aisle are brass plates on the east wall, commemorating Robert Rampston, A.D. 1585, and Jasper Nicholls, A.D. 1614, both of whom left money for the poor of the parish.

In the south chancel aisle is a very fine bust, under the drapery of a tent, all in Italian marble, of Thomas Stringer, son of Sir Thomas Stringer, of Durants, who served with great distinction under William III, and died at Bruges in 1706. He was buried in the Durants vault.

Against the south wall of the same aisle is another monument of coloured marble, in memory of Dorothie, wife of Robert Middlesmere, of Enfield, who died in 1610, leaving a son and daughter, who are represented as kneeling below at a desk.

Above it, on the same wall, is another larger monument with the figure of a man praying at a desk. It is that of Francis Evington, who died A.D. 1614.

On the floor are brasses of William Smith and Jane, his wife, "who served King Henry VIII., Edward VI., Queen Marie, and now Queen Elizabeth." He died in 1592, leaving £4 out of his land "to be given to the godlie poore of Enfield."

Against the north chancel pier, by the altar steps, is a brass plate with an epitaph on Dr. Joseph Gascoigne, who died in 1721, aged 80, having been for 40 years vicar of the parish, composed by his friend, Dr. R. Uvedale, Master of the Grammar School. Above this is an oval monument of white marble, supported by female figures—

"Sacred to the revivinge memory of Mrs. Martha Palmere," who departed this life to her owne gaine and the world's losse in the year 1617.

"Whose vertew did all ill so over swaye,
That her whole life was a communion day."

Against the north wall of the north aisle, partly concealed by the gallery, there is the figure of a man, kneeling at a desk, under an arch, in memory of Robert Deicrowe, citizen of London and grocer, who died in 1586, leaving money for bread to be distributed to the poor. Other monuments of interest are those of Henry Dixon, 1696, founder of Dixon's charity; Sir Charles Rich, Baronet, 1677; Stephen Riou, 1740; Elizabeth Green, granddaughter of Sir Hugh Myddleton; Rev. Thomas Brattell, 1703, to whom Enfield Court belonged. John Abernethy, the celebrated surgeon, 1831; James Meyer, Esq., 1826; Rev. H. Porter, 1823.

Previous to the last restoration there was a brass plate on the chancel floor with the arms of Gery, and this inscription:

"Here lies enterr'd
One that scarce err'd;
A virgin modest, free from folly,
A virgin knowing, patient, holy,

A virgin blest with beauty here,
A virgin crown'd with glorie there.
Holy virgins, read, and say
We shall hither all one day.
Live well, yee must
Be turn'd to dust.
To the precious memorie of Anne
Gery, daughter of Richard Gery, of
Bushmead in ye coun. of Bedford, Esquire,
Who dyed the 31st of August. Aº. Dm. 1624,"

but it has now disappeared.

### THE CHURCHYARD

was enlarged in 1778 by the addition of part of a field, purchased of Mr. Clayton, which was consecrated by Bishop Lowth, on August 13th. In 1822 the present fence on the side of the Market-place was erected at a cost of £90. In 1846 an additional piece of ground towards the north was purchased and enclosed. In 1858 the old portion of the churchyard was closed by the Secretary of State for all burials except in vaults and brick graves belonging to the family. Notwithstanding these additions it was found necessary in 1871 to take measures for providing still further ground. Accordingly, a Burial Board was elected in October, and nine acres of land belonging to the parish (part of the 100 acres), were set apart for a cemetery, a portion of which was consecrated in July, 1872, by Dr. Jackson, Bishop of London.

Amongst the tombs worthy of notice are those of Lord and Lady Napier, of Murchiston, and Rev. Dr. Cresswell, vicar, both near the door leading to the Vicarage.

## THE RECTORY.

If the materials for the architectural history of the church are scanty, those for the early ecclesiastical history of the parish are more than usually abundant, from its connexion with two monastic foundations—Hurley and Walden.

The monks, as is well known, were excellent chroniclers, and many of their chronicles have been preserved to us. Amongst others, there is in the British Museum a Register or Cartulary of Walden Abbey, written by order of Abbot Pentelowe, A.D. 1387—a magnificent folio of 270 pages on vellum. This contains a complete collection of charters, bequests, leases, and other documents relating to the affairs of the abbey from its foundation, with notices of its founders and benefactors. We have already seen that, at the time when Domesday Book was compiled, Goisfrid or Godfrey de Mandeville was in possession of the Manor of Enfield. This, with many others, had been granted to him by the Conqueror, as the reward of his prowess in the war against Harold. With the manor he received the advowson or patronage of the church.

It may be as well here to say a few words in explanation. The old rule of law* was that if any lord of a

---

* Si quis cum assensu Diocesani ecclesiam construxerit, ex eo jus advocationis acquirit.

manor built or endowed a church for the benefit of his demesne, he acquired the "jus advocationis," or advowson—*i.e.*, the right of presenting to the Bishop of the Diocese a fit clerk for institution to the benefice. This right was appendant to the manor, and passed with it.

Lords of Manors, also, at that period claimed and were allowed great latitude in the disposal of the tithes of their demesnes, so as to appropriate them to whatever religious purpose they chose, and there was a growing disposition to transfer the endowments of parochial churches to monastic institutions. So it was with Godfrey de Mandeville. He founded a religious house at Hurley, in Berkshire, well known to many_as lying on the Thames between Henley and Great Marlow. To this, at the time of its consecration by the famous Osmund Bishop of Sarum, he made by charter large grants of tithes from all the manors of which he was lord, and amongst others that of Enfield, assigning to the Church of S. Mary of Hurley one-third of the tithe of corn, two-thirds of the tithe of cattle, and the whole tithe of all other things, including vineyards, which could rightly and properly be tithed. Further, he granted them a rustic, or serf, with eight acres of land, in each one of his manors, and in his park (at Enfield), a swineherd with a swineherd's land.

The following is the original charter:—

Sciant universi quod ego Goisfredus de magnâ villâ dedi predicte ecclesie eâ die quâ feci eam consecrari Osmundo Episcopo Sarisburg : pontificali auctoritate presente, in omnibus maneriis que in dominio meo eo tempore erant tertiam partem decime totius pecunie omnium maneriorum meorum in vivo et mortuo et totam decimam pannagiorum meorum in parcis et denariis sine parte, et totam decimam caseorum, lini et lane, pullorum, equorum, vitulorum, pomorum, vinearum, et totam decimam aliarum rerum mearum de quibuscunque juste et recte debet deo decima reddi. Insuper dedi predicte ecclesie in unoquoque manerio totius dominii mei unum rusticum qui octo acras terre habeat et in parco meo unum porcarium cum terrâ porcarii.

The monks of Hurley, also, had from him the right of pannage in the park and woods at Enfield—*i.e.*, of turning in their swine to feed on the acorns, beech masts, &c. This, in those days, was a very important right. In the Domesday Book there is said to be pannage in Enfield for 2,000 swine. For several generations, the church continued to own a swineherd in the park.* In a subsequent charter we find that their swineherd at that period was called Serbo.

The grandson of the founder of Hurley, another Godfrey Earl of Essex, by a charter in the reign of Stephen, gave to the monks of Hurley a rent of 100 shillings ('solidatæ'), charged on his own estates in several places in Berkshire, in exchange for all the tithes which they held by their Founder's Charter in Edmonton and Enfield, with the exception of the tithe of pannage, and the right of pannage for the monks' swine in his park.

These tithes he restored to the Churches of Edmonton and Enfield " that each church might have its own rights

---

* The reader may be reminded of Gurth, in Sir W. Scott's *Ivanhoe.*

for the support of the priests who there perform God's service," and also in part as a provision for the Hermitage at Hadley.*

This, however, seems to have been done with an eye to the interests of the monastery which he was founding at Walden, in Essex, for when this was dedicated, A.D. 1136, he assigned to it 14 churches, and amongst others those of Enfield, Edmonton, and South Mymms, with all their tithes and other revenues, all their rights and privileges, and transferred to the Prior and monks his own advowson or right of patronage.

The original, from the MS. (Harleian, 3697) in the British Museum, is as follows :—

Carta domini Gaufridi de Mandevilla, Comitis Essexiæ.

Monasterii fundatoris.

Ad universitatis vestre notitiam volo pervenire me fundasse quoddam monasterium in usum monachorum apud Waldenam in honorem Dei et S. Marie et beati Jacobi Apostoli, quibus devote contuli et hac presenti carta confirmavi, omnes ecclesias inferius annotatas tam de dominio meo quam de emptis et purchasiis meis scilicet ecclesiam de Waledena . ecclesiam de Enfelda ecclesiam de Edelmeton ecclesiam de Mymmes ecclesiam de Northalâ (and 10 others). Has autem ecclesias concedo et confirmo monasterio S. Jacobi de Waldena et monachis ibidem in servitio Dei constitutis in liberam puram et perpetuam eleemosinam cum omnibus ad easdem ecclesias pertinentibus in decimis et obventionibus, in terris et redditibus, in hominibus, et eorum servitiis, in pratis et pascuis in

---

* —— de reliquo fratribus de Hadlega ibi canonice viventibus victum et vestitum.

bosco et plano in aquis et stagnis, in vivariis et piscariis, in viis et
semitis, in omnibus libertatibus et liberis consuetudinibus.

Et ne aliquis heredum aut successorum meorum aliquam donationem
vel presentationem in prescriptis ecclesiis ulterius se habere estimet
concedo et confirmo predicto monasterio et predictis monachis omne
jus et omne dominium quod egomet vel aliquis antecessorum meorum
melius et liberius in prefatis ecclesiis habuimus vel habere debuimus.
Quare volo et firmiter precipio quod prelatus predicti monasterii et
monachi habeant et teneant in perpetuum ecclesias jam supradictas
cum omnibus earum pertinentiis et libertatibus, ita quidem ut, si quis
aliquam illarum ecclesiarum aliquando tenuerit, de prelato et
conventu teneat.   Duo autem molendina, unum scilient apud Wale-
denam et alterum apnd Enefeldam, cum omnibus pertinentiis et
libertatibus suis in aquis et stagnis et piscariis, et cum multura*
ambarum villarum sc. de Waledena et Enefelda."   Another MS.
(*Vesp. E. vi.*), adds " Cum dimidia virgata terre arabilis."

The monks of Hurley, however, retained their right of
pannage in Enfield, including, as we have seen, a swineherd and his piece of land, and to this William de Mandeville, the next earl, A.D. 1181, added the whole tithe of
nuts in his park at Enfield.   A charter of William de S.
Maria Bishop of London, A.D. 1219, confirms to them,
" totam decimationem pannagii in parco de Enefeld et
decimationem nucum ejusdem parci."

But in the year 1258, with the laudable object of
avoiding any ground of discord or litigation unbefitting
the servants of God, which might arise from joint owner-

---

* " Multura"—the exclusive right of grinding corn.

ship, the prior and monks of Hurley gave up to the abbot and monks of Walden all their tithes, &c., in the parishes belonging to the latter, and received in exchange the church of Strattley or Stretley, in Berkshire. Thus ended all connexion between Enfield and Hurley, after lasting nearly two centuries.

The mill assigned by Godfrey to his monastery at Walden, with the right to grind the corn of Enfield, was, without doubt, the same mentioned in Domesday Book, then producing 10s. per annum rent. It gives its name to Mill Marsh and Mill Field, both still belonging to the Rectory. The right of fishing also brought in a rent, paid in styches of eels—*i.e.*, eels strung on sticks, 24 on each.

We find confirmations of the Founder's Charter by every successive Sovereign and Bishop of London.

Stephen, in his Charter, more particularly defines the liberties of the Abbey, as consisting in "Sacna et socna et toll et theam et infangenatheofe."

Henry II. confirms to them the view of frank pledge.

Accordingly, the abbots exercised certain manorial rights in Enfield, and, when in the 22 Edward I. 1292, they were called on by a writ, "quo warranto," to prove these rights, they showed to the satisfaction of the King's Justices that they and their predecessors from time out of mind had held without molestation, "quendam visum per annum de tenentibus suis in predicta villa de Enfeld, capiendæ emendas panis et cervisiæ fractæ"—*i.e.*, inflicting fines for fraud in the sale of bread and beer.* A note in the year-book of xx Edward I. (a collection of law cases), states that this belonged ·to the view of frank pledge. "Amendement de payn e de serveyse est apendant a vewe de franc plegge."

At the same time it was decided that the abbots had not the right to use the pillory or tumbril as punishments,† and that penalties for shedding of blood belonged not to the abbots, but to the bailiffs of the Counts of Hereford and Essex.

This would seem to show that they had not the right of "infangenetheof" mentioned in Stephen's Charter, for in the same Year-book, which has been referred to, we read " Amendement de payn e de service e pyllory e tumbril e fourches sy est apendant a infangenetheof."

It may be observed that the manorial rights of the abbots have passed on, with the Rectory, to Trinity College. A court-leet is held for the Manor of Surlowes or the Rectory.

In the Cartulary to which reference has been made we find a record of numerous gifts of land or houses in Enfield. Amongst others, Humphrey de Bohun, Earl of

---

* Dr. Robinson translates cervisia fracta—broken victuals ! but cervisia is beer, and frangere assisam, means to sell short weight or measure. " Si quis Brassiator assisam fregerit."—*Liber Albus.*

† Et dicunt quod predictus abbas nee aliquis antecesstorum habueruni pillorium nee tumberellum ad judicia de hujusmodi transgressionibus facienda.

Hereford and Essex, Constable of England, gives to the Abbey, " All that virgate of land which Walter held of us in the vill of Enfield." There is nothing to identify the land, but it doubtless still belongs to the Rectory.

The son of Serbo (the swinehead, as we may presume) follows the example of the Constable of England, and gives a house.

In a subsequent survey of the churches belonging to the Abbey of Walden, it is said that Enfield was appropriated to the use of the monks, with all the tithe, both of demesne and other lands. The monks received half a mark out of the Vicarage, three marks from a mill, twenty shillings from the tenants of the glebe, and kept six acres of meadow in their own hands.

In the Taxatio Ecclesiastica of Pope Nicholas IV., A.D. 1291, we find under the head of

TEMPORALIA : ' bona Abbatis de Walden

de redditibus terre et pratis    ...        £3  11  8

SPIRITUALIA { Ecclesia    ...    ...    ... £40  0  0

Vicaria ejusdem ecclesie   £6  0  0

At the dissolution of monasteries, the Rectory of Enfield, with the advowson, was granted by Henry VIII., in May, 1538, to Thomas Audley, who, in November of the same year, was made Lord Audley of Walden. He presented in 1540, "ratione donationis et concessionis temporalium dissoluti monasterii de Walden eidem domino Thomæ." By exchange with Lord Audley, the Rectory came again into the King's hands, and he presented in 1545. Soon afterwards, in 1548, he granted this, with many others which had belonged to different religious houses, to the Master, Fellows, and Scholars of Trinity College, Cambridge, which he was then founding, and with them it has ever since remained.

In the King's books it is thus valued :—" Valet in terris et tenementis necnon decimis granorum et feni ac omnibus aliis decimis oblationibus et proficuis dicte Rectorie pertinentibus. xxviii. lib.

It was then let for this sum, as appears from the following entry in the Register of Benefactions made by Henry VIII. in the College Library :—

> " Firma Rectorie de Enfeld predicte, in com. Midd. cum omnibus decimis acaliis proficuis et advantagiis eidem Rectorie spectantibus dimissis Johanni Butte per indenturam pro termino annorum, reddendum inde per ann. xxviii. lib."

At the end of the Register there is the following note :—

MEM.—"The premmissez doe not lye nigghe to any the King Majestie's howssez, except the parsonage of Enfelde, which lyethe adjoynynge to the King's howse of Enfelde."

In 3 Edward VI. the Rectory was let to Sir R. Wroth for 40 years. In 1631—to Earl of Pembroke, for 16 years.

In 1647 it was let to Sir Roger Langley ; the
fine paid for renewal was, for 7 years   ... £200
The reserved rent was £18 13s. 4d., and a
corn rent of 14 quarters of wheat and 18 qrs.
5 bus. 1 peck of wheat.
In 1666—to the Duke of Albermarle, for 7 years   180
In 1718—to Sir R. Nightingale           „        350

In 1726—to J. Gascoigne Nightingale, Esq. for 7 years £320

| | | | |
|---|---|---|---|
| 1785—to Wilmot, Earl of Lisburne, (who married Miss Nightingale) ... | | „ | 1,400 |
| 1806—to Sir John Eden and Sir L. Palk | | „ | 3,500 |
| 1813—to Sir L. Palk (in trust) ... ... | | „ | 4,200 |
| 1820—to Colonel Vaughan (afterwards Lord Lisburne) ... ... ... | | „ | 4,200 |
| 1827-34—to Lady Elizabeth Palk and Lady Malet Vaughan ... .. | | „ | 3,400 |
| 1855—to Lady Malet Vaughan... ... | | „ | 3,720 |
| 1862—to Robert S. Palk, Esq., and Rev. Wilmot Palk ... ... ... | | „ | 3,925 |

In 1869 the College refused to renew, consequently, as the lease is for 20 years, renewable every 7, the lease will expire in 1882, and the rectorial estates will fall directly under the management of the College.

In 1650 the Parliamentary Commissioners reported as follows :—" The Parsonage and Glebe lands be worth £30 per annum, and the tythe of corn and grass be worth £230 per annum, which is now received by Sir W. Langley. The said Parsonage House hath belonging to it, one greate barne with outhouses and fish ponds, two small orchards, and four closes of pasture thereto adjoining, containing eight acres or thereabouts. Also, 24 acres of arable land in the Common Field, and 5 acres and 1 rood of meadow in the Common Marshes being lammas ground."

w

The great increase in the value of the Rectory arose from the Enclosure Acts in 1777 and 1801, by the former of which 279 acres (after deductions for the Vicarage), by the latter 950 acres were allotted to Trinity College in lieu of tithes.

## THE RECTORY HOUSE.

There is no record of the building of the Parsonage House, but it was in existence before the time of Henry VIII.'s grant to Trinity College. In a survey (6 James I.) it is thus described:—"One mansion house, one barn and stable and other buildings with a yard and garden, one pigeon house, one pigeon house close with a pond therein, situated in Parsonage-street (now called Baker-street), on the east side, and next a little lane called Parsonage-lane, on the south, and the orchard of T. Meddows, and two closes of pasture, belonging to the said Rectory, on the north and west."

It has been generally occupied by the lessees of the college, but is at present sublet to F. Hasluck, Esq.

The arms over the iron gates at the entrance, are those of the Nightingale family, who came into possession as lessees in 1718. In the grounds, which on the side of Parsonage-lane are enclosed by a very picturesque old wall, are some remarkably fine trees, especially two accacias. The old fish ponds still remain.

## THE VICARAGE.

We learn from Domesday Book that the Parish Priest of Enfield held a virgate of land, of course in addition to tithes and offerings, which are seldom, if ever, mentioned in that book, as the record is one of land.

We have seen that in 1136 Godfrey de Mandeville granted the Church of Enfield, with all its tithes and other revenues, to his newly-founded Monastery at Walden. The effect of this here, as in other cases, would be to make the Monastery collectively responsible for the cure of the parish. They received all the revenues, and sent one or another of their body, as they thought fit, to discharge the duties. But, after a time, it was more usual to appoint some one priest permanently to serve the cure, who thus became a "perpetual vicar," and had assigned to him a certain portion of the tithes and other offerings, with the sanction of the bishop. We are told that Reginald, Prior of Walden, afterwards first Abbot, appointed vicars to his churches in 1190. Consequently, we may assume that the first vicar, properly so called, of Enfield, dates from that year. There does not appear to be any record of the composition made with him by the abbot and monks ; probably he received the small tithes, subject to certain payments to the abbey, as was usually the case. In the Taxation of Pope Nicholas, the Vicarage was valued at £6 per ann.; in the time of Henry VIII at £26. In the report to the Parliamentary

Commissioners in 1650, preserved in the Lambeth Library, it is stated that—

"The Vicaridge House, with the barns, outhouses, and two orchards, with one close of pasture adjoining, and two acres of arable land in the Common Field are worth 8 pounds per annum. And the petty tythes, oblations, and other dutyes thereto belonging, are worth about £50 per ann." They further report, "that Mr. Walter Bridges, the present incumbent, an able and painful preacher, was presented to the said lyving by the Master and Fellows of Trinitye Colledge, and re-ceiveth for salary the said tythes and proffitts belonging to the said Vicaridge. And that our parish (having no chapel), is of a large extent. Butt our church is conveniently situated, and none of the parishioners are far distant therefrom except some few scattering houses."

In 1777, when the Chase was enclosed, 80 acres out of 519 allotted in lieu of tithes, were appropriated to the Vicar of Enfield. At the same time power was given by the Act (17 Geo. III. c. 18) to Trinity College further to augment the Vicarage by an endowment of 160 acres out of their tithe allotment, on the condition that any Fellow accepting the living should vacate his fellowship. By the award of the Commissioners under the Enclosure Act of 1801, a further allotment was made to the vicar of 382 acres 3 roods 20 perches of land, in lieu of all vicarial tithes in the parish, with the exception of a corn rent, charged on certain houses, &c. where land could not be allotted, to be valued every 21 years, if required.

This, when the Commissioners made their award in April, 1806, was valued at £43 6s. 11d.

The greater portion of the Glebe land, which lies on the Chase, has never been properly brought under cultivation, and is of comparatively little value. The rental of the glebe was less in 1870 than in 1840.

### THE VICARAGE HOUSE.

Between Silver-street and the Churchyard, enclosed within a wall, are the Vicarage House and grounds, occupying about 1¾ acres.

In the reign of Edward I., Godfrey de Beston gave a piece of land near the Churchyard, with the buildings on it, to Bartholomew, Vicar of S. Andrew's, Enfield, and his successors, subject to a rent of 12 pence, as appears from the following deed—(Harleian MS. 3697) :—

"Carta Godefridi de Beston de toto messagio suo dato ecclesiæ S. Andree de Enefeld.

Sciant præsentes et futuri quod ego Godefridus de Beston concessi dedi et hâc plenâ cartâ meâ confirmavi Deo et ecclesie Sancti Andree de Enefeld et Bartholomeo ejusdem ecclesie vicario cum omnibus vicariis ibidem eidem succedentibus totum messagium meum quod emi de Ricardo de Plesseto situm prope cimiterium dicte ecclesie cum domibus desuper edificatis et omnibus aliis pertinentibus habendum et tenendum illi et successoribus suis libere quiete pacifice integre per servitium duodecim denariorum annuatim solvendorum Ricardo de Plesseto et heredibus suis ad quatuor terminos, videlicet ad Pascha, iij. den^m.: ad nativitatem S. Johannis, iij. den^m.

ad festum S. Michaelis Archangeli iij. den^m: et ad nativitatem Domini, iij. denariorum: pro omni servitio consuetudine exactione et demanda.

".Ut autem hac mea concessio donatio et carte mee confirmatio perpetuum robus obtineat, presentum paginam sigilli mei munimine duxi roborandum His testibus. Ricardo de Plessito, &c., &c."

To this gift, Richard de Plessito, of whom Godfrey had purchased the messuage, subsequently added 18 perches of garden ground, between the churchyard and the King's Highway, called Ernygstrate, now Silver-street.

" Noverit universitas me pro salute anime mee et animarum patris et matris, &c., concessissee et dedisse et hâc plenâ cartâ meâ confirmasse, Deo et ecclesie S. Andree de Enefeld et ejusdem ecclesie Vicario Bartholomeo et successoribus suis, 18 perticatas gardini mei cum pertinentibus, incipientes a messagio predicti Vicarii quod tenet de me per servitium xii. denariorum annuatim et extendentes se in longitudinem versus Austrum in totam latitudinem ejusdem gardini quod jacet inter cimiterium predicte ecclesie et viam regalem que vocatur Ernygstrate habendum et tenendum."

Richard de Plessito died in 1289, so that the Vicarage must have occupied its present site for nearly six centuries. A great part of the house is extremely old, built of timber, and only cased with brick in 1845, when new kitchens and offices were built. Great alterations had previously been made in 1801 by Mr. Porter, who took down the old chimneys.

In the windows of the dining-room are two diamond-shaped quarries of stained glass, evidently taken out of some older window, with Henry VIII.'s badges of the Red Rose and the Portcullis.

The wall between the garden and the churchyard, 362 feet in length, was built by the parishioners in 1800, as stated in a stone tablet over the door.

### THE VICARS.

The first vicar, as we have seen, was appointed in 1190, but his name is not preserved. One Bartholomew was vicar, when the vicarage house was given in the reign of Edward I., and an Absolom is mentioned in a later deed, but there is no complete list till the early part of the 14th century, when, for the first time, we can avail ourselves of the Bishop of London's register, which furnishes the following names and dates of presentation (with the exception of those in italics).

| VICARS. | DATE. | PATRONS. |
|---|---|---|
| Henry de Chippenham, | February 18, 1333. | |
| Thomas Cradock, | July 14, 1391. | |
| Thomas Exeter, | September 1, 1408. | Abbott |
| John Westland, | | and |
| William Appleby, | September 29, 1435. | Monastery of |
| Edmund Causton, | November 2, 1466. | Walden. |
| John Hobil, M.A. | November 18, 1491. | |
| Thomas Thompson, B.D. | January 7, 1504. | |
| Henry Lockwood, D.D. | October 4, 1540. | Thos. Lord Audley |
| Robert Stringfellow, | October 27, 1545. | Henry VIII. |

| | | |
|---|---|---|
| Christopher Downes, D.D. | April 7, 1550. | ⎫ |
| Thomas Segeswick, B.D. | March 12, 1555. | ⎪ Trinity College, |
| John Malham, M.A. | November 11, 1556. | ⎬ Cambridge. |
| Richard Clapham, | February 9, 1557. | ⎪ |
| Robert Thacker, M.A. | April 7, 1576. | ⎭ |
| Philip Jones, | August 18, 1579. | ⎰ Archbishop of Canterbury, by lapse. |
| Leonard Chambers, | February 3, 1579. | ⎫ |
| Samuel Heron, D.D. | October 10, 1598. | ⎪ |
| Thomas Prowde, B.D. | December 23, 1601. | ⎪ |
| William Roberts, D.D.* | July 12, 1616. | ⎪ |
| *Walter Bridges,†* | *August 27, 1646.* | ⎪ |
| *Daniel Manning,* | *May 6, 1659.* | ⎪ |
| John Hawkins, B.D. | October 3, 1662. | ⎪ |
| Henry Dearsley, B.D. | January 15, 1663. | ⎪ |
| Benjamin Young, M.A. | October 8, 1672. | Trinity |
| Joseph Gascoigne, M.A. | October 29, 1681. | College, |
| Robert Uvedale, D.D.‡ | August 11, 1721. | Cambridge. |
| John Hackett, D.D. | 1732. | ⎪ |
| James Whitehall, | 1734. | ⎪ |
| William Smelt, B.D. | April 29, 1758. | ⎪ |
| Richard Newbon, B.D. | June, 1767. | ⎪ |
| Harry Porter, M.A. | July, 1801. | ⎪ |
| Daniel Creswell, D.D. | March, 1823. | ⎪ |
| John Moore Heath, M.A. | July, 1844. | ⎪ |
| George Hewitt Hodson, M.A. | January, 1870. | ⎭ |

* William Roberts was turned out of his Vicarage in 1642, by the Parliamentary Commissioners, but lived some years. Walker, in his "Sufferings of the Clergy," mentions that the Vicar of Enfield was sent for as a delinquent, and his estate sequestered, but he apparently mistakes the name.

† Walter Bridges, called by the Commissioners an able and painful preacher, is said by them to have been appointed by Trinity College, but we must bear in mind that at that time the Master and the majority of the Fellows had been expelled as Royalists. He was of S. John's College, B.A. 1635. He left the parish in April, 1658, and was succeeded after some interval by Daniel Manning (of Cath. Hall, Cambridge, B.A. 1649) who was deprived at the restoration.

‡ Son of Dr. Robert Uvedale, who was Master of the Grammar School, and a distinguished botanist.

In the first leaf of the volume of the Parish register, which begins in 1666, is the following entry by Mr. Gascoigne, vicar :—

" Ministers of this parish that can now, in the year " 1717-18, be remembered.

" Dr. Roberts, formerly fellow of Trinity Coll. in Cam- " bridge, who continued for many years, till turned out " in the late times in 1642. After him in those times " succeeded several, as Mr. Bridges, Mr. Manning, which " latter was turned out by the Bartholomew Act in the " year 1661. After him came Mr. John Hawkins, " Fellow of Trinity Coll., in Cambridge, who stayed not " much above a year, and returned to the College.

" Mr. Henry Dearsley, Fellow of Trin. Coll., came in " the year 1663, and continued till the year 1672, when " he dyed. After him succeeded Mr. Ben. Young, Fellow " of Trin. Coll., in the year 1672, who lived till July in " the year 1681, and in the same year after him came " Mr. Jos. Gascoigne, Fellow of Trin. Coll., in the month " of October, 1681, who, by the mercy of God, is still " alive, and in very good health."

With the exceptions, already referred to, of Mr. Bridges and Mr. Manning, the College has always presented one of its Fellows to the Vicarage.

## LECTURER.

In the year 1631 Henry Loft gave £4 per annum for a lecturer, who was to preach in the Parish Church on the afternoon of the Lord's-day, not omitting above one month in the year. This magnificent endowment was for many years augmented by the Vestry, but their liberality has ceased. The present lecturer is the Rev. E. H. Egles, M.A., Emmanuel College, Cambridge.

The Rev. J. M. Heath, shortly after he became vicar, instituted a third service on Sunday evenings, at which the whole church is free and open to all parishioners ; the service being entirely voluntary on the part of the clergy. This is still continued. There is also an early service at 8 a.m. on Sunday for the celebration of the Holy Communion, and daily service morning and evening.

### THE CHURCHWARDENS

Are elected annually on Easter Monday. There were originally four (as appears by the oldest vestry-book remaining, of the date April 13, 1691), one for each of the four quarters of the parish, which were then called—Enfield-greene, Bull's-cross, Greene-street, and Ponder's-end, and such was the practice till 1696, when one churchwarden was chosen to represent both Greene-street and Ponder's-end Quarters, and, with the exception of the year 1699, when four were again chosen, three has continued to be the number to the present day, Greene-street and Ponder's-end being considered as one quarter.

The churchwarden for Enfield-green (now called the Town) Quarter, is nominated by the Vicar. The others are chosen by the Vestry.

The division of the parish into four quarters, for other purposes, continued till 1810, when the Vestry, on September 22, agreed "that the three divisions, now "called Bull's-cross, Greene-street, and Ponder's-end "Divisions be reduced into two divisions, the one to be "called Bull's-cross, to commence at Mr. Duncan's, at "White Webb's-gate, and to extend to Carterhatch-lane, "at Enfield-highway; and the other to be called Green- "street and Ponder's-end Division, to commence at, and "to include Carterhatch-lane, and to extend over " Ponder's-end and South-street."

The Churchwardens, in former times, were zealous in the extermination of vermin. In the year 1780, as appears by the Vestry-book, they paid for the destruction of three otters, at 1s. each; twelve polecats, at 8d. each; sixty-five hedgehogs, at 4d. each.

No church-rates have been collected in the parish since the year 1853, so that the Churchwardens are entirely dependant on voluntary contributions to supply funds for the repairs of the church and maintenance of the services.

Easter offerings have also been discontinued for some years past, though the Vicar's claim to them was reserved by the Enclosure Act of 1801.

### PARISH REGISTERS.

The registers of baptisms, marriages, and burials, all extend back to 1550, and with the exception of an interval between January, 1556,* and August, 1557, are complete to the present day, though they were kept very irregularly during the times of the Rebellion and Commonwealth.

The Act by which parochial registers were enjoined was not passed till 1536, and was not at once generally observed, so that the registers, which we have, are probably the first kept in the parish.

The oldest volume is on paper, and extends from 1550 to 1588. The succeeding volumes, as now bound up, from 1588 to 1639; 1639 to 1666; and 1666 to 1704, are on parchment.

It is curious to observe the uncertainty in the beginning of the year. The years 1550, 51, 52, 53, begin with the Feast of the Annunciation, March 25. The years from 1554 to 1577 with the Feast of the Circumcision, January 1. After that they return again to March 25 and so continue till the New Style came into use, in January, 1753.

There is a curious mode of registering baptisms to be noticed during the years between 1576 and 1586. In the case of a boy it is " baptizatus est," or sometimes " baptizabatur" (the force of which is somewhat difficult to explain) ; in the case of a girl " renata fuit."

---

* Where there is this note:—" Memorandum : that I found this nexte leaf or leaves cut out at my receiving the book from Mr. Hall ; as witnesseth Robert Wilbro."

The Register has this entry, Sept. 18th, 1653 :—" Be it remembered that Walter Bridges, Vicar of the Parish of Enfield, was this day and year above written, elected and chosen Registrar, and was approved and sworn by Edwyn Rich, Esq., J.P., according to a late Act of Parliament," and the following in April, 1658 :—

" Mr. Walter Bridges, min. of the parish, who for some few years before-mentioned, as it doth appear from ye beginning of this book, left the books in good order, and sett downe the baptizings exactly, but he leaving the parish about the beginning of Aprill, 1658, the parish being destitute of a minister was constrained to hire one or other to preach on the Lord's Days. Mr. Bridges, above-mentioned, being gone, and strangers preaching here for some time till Mr. Manning; minister, came, the names of children, for a short time, could not exactly be registered."

There are many indications, in the registers of the preceding years, of the disorder prevailing in church matters.

It will be remembered that in 1645 the use of the Book of Common Prayer, either in public or private, was forbidden by the Parliament, under heavy penalties of fine and imprisonment ; and the Directory substituted for it. All religious services at the burial of the dead were forbidden —the dead body was to be " interred without any ceremony."

In 1642, as we have seen, the Vicar, Dr. Roberts, was

ejected. Between September, 1642, and September, 1644, only one marriage is registered. Afterwards we find such entries as these, in 1653 :—" All these three couples were married by Thomas Hubbert, Esq., and by him declared man and wife," and in 1655, " The truly worthy John Bernard, of Huntingdon, Esq., single man, and Mrs. Elizabeth St. John, daughter of the Right Hon. Oliver St. John, Lord Cheefe Justice of the Comon Pleas, were married before her said father, and by him declared man and wife, February 26, 1655. Coram testibus non paucis venerabilibus egregiis et fide dignis."

In August 1, 1678, the Act, for burying in woollen, came into operation, and accordingly in every case of burial the parish register records that an affidavit was made and delivered to the Vicar, as required by the Act, within eight days, but on September 18 of that year, we find a memorandum regarding Dennis Younge, " No affidavit. Information given of her being buried in linnen, and the moiety of five pounds was paid to the poor, according to the Act for burying in woollen." And again, in November, when Mary, wife of Nicholas Raynton, was buried in a vault in the vestry, there is the same memorandum.

After a few years the practice seems to have become more lax, as there are many burials, where no affidavit is mentioned.

The number of nurse-children registered as buried is very remarkable, and also the number of foundlings baptized. The neighbourhood of the Chase will, in some measure, account for both, as also for the number of "strangers unknown " who are buried.

With the year 1569 begins mention of those who died, or were suspected to have died, of the Plague :—

Between August and December in that year, 29 deaths are recorded.

Between June and December, 1578, 50 deaths.

In three months of 1603, September to November, 103.

In the year 1625, 67 died ; in 1665, the year of the great plague, only 55.

It is said that some of those who died of the plague were buried in the churchyard, some in other places. In the original survey of the Chase, made in 1658, a site on the Green, now occupied by an isolated house and garden, known as "the Limes," is marked as "the Pest House," and in the presentment to the jury of the Manor in 1636, it is described as "a cottage erected by the " appointment of His Majestie's Justices of the Peace, for " the harbouring of infected people the last great infec- " tion."

A small pond at the back of these premises has pro- bably been caused by the subsidence of the ground, and indicates the site of the "plague pit." De Foe mentions that a similar " mark was to be seen on the surface, parallel with the passage between Houndsditch and Whitechapel," where a pit had been dug 40 feet in length, 15 feet in breadth, and 20 feet deep.

This house is again presented " at a Court of the " Mannor and Chace of Enfield, held the eighth day of

"October, in the first year of the reign of our Sovereign,
"Lord James the Second," &c.

"(19.)  An house formerly ordered by the Justices for
"a pest-house erected on the said Chace, and now in the
"tenure of John Boone, which we desire may continue
"for a pest-house still, if there should be an occasion."

At a vestry had of ye most part of ye ancient parishioners aforesaid, 21st Jan. 1620, the "duties for buryalls
in the churchyard," were fixed for parishioners, "un-
coffined" 2d., strangers, 4d.

For one hours knell of ye 1st Bell ...   6d.,  strangers 12d.
  „      •    „      2nd Bell...   8d.,      „      16d.
  „           „      3rd Bell...  10d.,      „      18d.
  „           „    ye great Bell... 12d.,     „      24d.

To ye Vicar, for his office of bury-
ing a child    ...    ...    ...   7d.,     „      24d.
To him for a communicate person 10d.,      „      24d.
To Clerk for a child    ...    ...   4d.,     „      12d.
More to him for a communicate
person   ...    ...    ...    ...   6d.,     „      12d.

Duties for buryalls coffined—double the above.

The fee for a person churched at church, was sixpence.
The fee for a person churched at home, was one shilling.

The Clerk's duty was "to attend ye Vicar and Curate
at divine service, marriages, churchings, sac. visiting of
sick, burying of dead, to lay up ye books, to write ye
burrialls in a book."

"The Sexton's office is to keep ye clock and church
clean, to ring and toll ye bells, to make the graves five
foot deep."

## DISTRICT CHURCHES.

### S. JAMES'S, HIGHWAY.

Notwithstanding the increase in the population of the parish, no provision was made for increased church accommodation till the year 1831, when a Chapel-of-ease was built by subscription, on ground given by Woodham Connop, Esq., and consecrated on 15th of October, by Dr. Blomfield, Bishop of London.

A district was assigned by Order in Council, Dec. 9, 1833, comprising the whole of the parish of Enfield east of a line drawn at a distance of 150 yards to the west of the Turnpike-road from Edmonton to Cheshunt. The church was licensed for marriages by the Bishop of London in 1845, May 26th.

An addition to the churchyard was consecrated in 1861.

The present chancel, added at the expense of the Rev. J. Harman, in memory of his wife Elizabeth (who died April, 1859), was consecrated in November, 1864. The east window is filled with stained glass in "Memory of Ezekiel and Sarah Harman, of Theobalds, Cheshunt, and of Mary Wright, sister of Sarah Harman." The windows of the chapel are memorials respectively to Mary Harman, and the wife of Henry Parry, Esq., of the Limes, Ponder's-end.

x

A vicarage house has since been built opposite to the church.

The Vicar of S. Andrew's, Enfield, is the patron.

*Incumbents.*
- T. W. Thirlwall, M.A., 1834.
- Charles Warren, M.A., 1835.
- J. R. Nicholl, M.A., 1838.
- J. Fuller Russell, B.C.L., 1841.
- John Harman, M.A., 1854.

### JESUS CHURCH, FORTY HILL.

This church was erected in 1835 at the sole expense of Christian Paul Meyer, Esq., of Forty Hall, and endowed by him with £4000 conveyed to trustees, and with a house and 7½ acres of land adjoining the church. A district was assigned by Order in Council, December, 1845. It is now a vicarage. The Vicar of S. Andrew's is patron. In 1871 an additional endowment of seven acres of land was given by Trinity College. The first incumbent was the Rev. C. W. Bollaerts, M.A., who died in 1863, and was succeeded in the same year by Rev. Archibald Weir, D.C.L., Trin. Coll., Oxford.

### CHRIST CHURCH.

Christ Church, situated at Cock Fosters, at the western extremity of the parish, was built in 1839 at the sole expense of R. C. L. Bevan, Esq., of Trent Park, who is the patron, who also built a parsonage. A district has been assigned by the Bishop of London. The present incumbent is the Rev. James Swinbourn, who, in 1865, succeeded the Rev. Claremont Skrine.

### S. JOHN'S, CLAY HILL.

This church was built in 1857, from the designs of Mr. P. St. Aubyn, as a chapel-of-ease to the mother church, on land belonging to the Vicarage, which had been bought with the proceeds of the sale of a portion of glebe to the New River Company. The greater part of the cost of the building and endowment was borne by the Vicar, the Rev. J. M. Heath. The church was opened by license in November, 1858, but not consecrated till July 31, 1865. It did not become a district church till March 19, 1867.

The Rev. G. B. P. Viner has since that time been incumbent. There is a vicarage house adjoining the churchyard.

### NEW CHURCH OF S. MICHAEL AND ALL ANGELS.

Notwithstanding these district churches, the accommodation at the mother church of S. Andrew's had been for some time found quite inadequate to the wants of a population rapidly increasing. A new church was consequently determined on, of which the first stone was laid on May 7th of this year (1873), on a portion of what was formerly the Gordon House Estate. The site and £2,000

were given by George Batters, Esq., of Brigadier Hall.
The church, when complete, will consist of a chancel
with aisles and a groined apse, a nave of five bays, with
aisles, and a western tower ; two bays of the nave and the
tower are left for completion hereafter. It is built of
Kentish rag, with Bath stone dressings, from the designs
of Messrs. Slater and Carpenter, of London, under the
superintendence of Mr. Hill, of Enfield. It will be a
chapel-of-ease, served by the clergy of the parish church.

---

### THE CEMETERY.

The cemetery occupies a very beautiful and commanding
site, of about nine acres, between Lavender-hill and Clay-
hill, at a distance of 1¼ mile from S. Andrew's Church,
to the north-west. The cemetery was laid out and
the buildings erected from the designs and under the
superintendence of Mr. Hill, architect, of Enfield, at
a total cost of about £9,000. It was opened July
27th, 1872.

## THE FREE GRAMMAR SCHOOL.

On the west side of the churchyard stands an old red-brick building, with dormers in the roof, and a turret staircase, which, for nearly three centuries, has been the Free Grammar School. Modern sash windows have been inserted in the wall facing the churchyard, and two bay windows, one at each end of the building, have been bricked up, so that the original effect is very much destroyed. A "school-house" is mentioned in 1557, but in 1586, William Garratt left the sum of £50 by will, towards building a school-house in Enfield, and a deed of 1598 speaks of "the Schole House now of late new built there." It stands on part of an estate called Prounce's, belonging to the parish.

In the different trust deeds from 1623 to 1717, inclusive, the chamber and garret over the school were reserved to such uses as the trustees and vestry should direct,* the schoolmaster then residing in Prownce's house, also in the churchyard, known as the Old Coffee-house, now the School of Industry, but about 1739 or 1740 the chamber and garret were divided into several bedrooms, and a wing was added to the school-house as a residence for the master. The passage to the chamber and garret was by a circular staircase in a tower erected outside the

---

* *e.g.*, for the meeting of the trustees and vestry. See *p.* 323.

school-house, but the building of the wing, by enclosing within itself the foot of the staircase, completely shut out all access to the chamber and garret, unless by passing through the master's house. The trust deed of 1740 put the master into possession of "the school-house, with the improvements lately made thereto," and no further mention is made in that, or any subsequent deed, of the chamber and garret, so that the whole has been in the possession of the master for more than 130 years ; and in 1825 the Court of Chancery decreed, "That the master should have the school-house for his residence."

It has been already mentioned that in the reign of Edward IV. a licence was granted to found a Chauntry in Enfield Church, called "Blossom's Chauntry," which might be endowed with 10 marks per annum. It was apparently with this intent that in 1471 (11 Edw. IV.), Robert Ingleton conveyed to Edmund Causton, Vicar of Enfield, John Bristowe, and others the Manor of Poynetts or Poynants, which had belonged to R. Blossom, but there is no delaration of trusts.

It is clear that an estate described as consisting of three messuages and 740 acres of land, must have been worth far more than 10 marks per annum, but there is no mention in the deed of the Chauntry, nor anything to indicate the purposes to which the remaining rents were to be applied.

In 1491 (7 Hen. VII.), on the death of Edmund Causton, the vicar. John Bristowe and others conveyed

Poynetts to fresh feoffees.   In 1500 (16 Henry VII.),
John and Agnes Spottell conveyed it to John Hobel,
Vicar of Enfield, and others.   In 1501 John Hobel con-
veyed to Thomas Sawyer and Margerie his wife, John
Honesbie and Agnes his wife, and William Spottell.
From them it passed to Roger Carewe or Crowe (as
appears by record of the Court of King's Bench, 15 Henry
VII.), and from him to his son John Carewe or Crowe.

In 1506 (21 Henry VII.), John Carewe or Crowe
conveyed the Manor of Poynetts (which is still described
as three messuages and 740 acres of land)* to Wm.
Ockburn, John Goddard, William Woodam, Robert
Alford, and others, but there is no trust declared or
schedule appended, and as far as the documents in the
possession of the trustees are concerned, there is nothing
to support the statement that John Carewe founded a
school or did anything but convey the estate to new
feoffees, on the same conditions as before.   There can be
no doubt but that Poynetts was charged originally with
the payment of ten marks for a chauntry priest, though it
is somewhat remarkable that in a presentation,† made by
the Churchwardens of Enfield early in the 16th century,
of "the chauntries, &c., within the Church," no mention
is made of Blossom's Chauntry amongst the rest.   At any

---

* The present estate is by survey 273 acres.

† See p. 132 supra.

rate, the surplus rents were at the disposal of the Churchwardens. An indenture made in 1520 records that "the
"Churchwardens, with the assent of all the inhabitants of
"the said parish, and to the use and profit of the said
"parish church have bargained and sold to Avery Rawson
"and Thomas Geffery, the wood belonging and apper-
"taining to the said Churchwardens, in right of the parish
"church of Enfield, growing in a wood called Ship-
"wrights of xxvii acres," part of the Poynett's estate, and
there is a similar indenture made in 1532.

In the 1st Edward VI., 1547, Chauntries were
abolished by statute, and the lands, &c., belonging to
them granted to the king, partly with a view to founding
schools. Accordingly in 1548, the King sold Poynetts
to Walter Farr and Ralph Standish for £200, but as the
Court of Augmentations decreed, July 8, 1549, that the
king's title was doubtful, the purchase-money was
returned. This was probably on the ground that Poynetts belonged to the parish, not to the chauntry, and
that the king could claim at most the ten marks assigned
to the Chauntry Priest. Meanwhile, the parish continued
in possession of Poynetts, and by a deed, January 7,
4 and 5 Phillip and Mary, 1557, John Goddard, William
Woodham, and Robert Alford three of the feoffees named
in John Carewe's deed of 1505, convey the estate to
John Butte and many others in trust for the purpose of a
school according to a schedule annexed. This deed was
never executed, and Robert Alford having died in April,

the two survivors, John Goddard, maltman, and William Woodham, yeoman, in May of the same year, after a recital of title extending back to Thomas Sawyer and others in 1501, conveyed to Simon Potter, John Butte and 18 others, " pro et in consideratione cujusdam schole pro eruditione et instructione puerorum pauperum inhabitantium in Enefield in Litteris Alphabeticis et Arte Grammaticali, and pro aliis considerationibus in quadam schedula expressis et significatis."

" This schedule indented and made in the yeare of our Lorde God, according to the course and reckeninge of the Churche of Englande, a thousande fyve hundrede fiftee and eight, and in the fourthe and fiveth yeares of the raines of our Soveraigne Lorde and Ladye Phillipe and Marye," declares the intent of the deed of feoffement to be that the feoffees shall " gyve and paye yearlie to a schole master to teache within the sayde towne of Enfielde the children of the poor inhabitants to knowe and read their alphabet letters and to read Laten and Englyshe, and to understand grammar and to wrigt their Lateines according to the trade and use of grammar scholes, the summe of six poundes thirteen shillings and foure pence." The Churchwardens of the parish church were to be authorised to act as bailiffs of the feoffees to collect and gather the rents.

In 40 Elizabeth, 1598, the estate was conveyed by John Taylor, Simon Potter, and others, to new feoffees, Sir Robert Wroth, of Durants, his son Robert Wroth, Esq., Vincent Skinner, Esq., and others,

with the same directions as to the schoolmaster **and**
children, and also to " give and distribute unto the poor
impotent people from time to time, inhabiting in the
parish of Enfield, or unto such other good and godly
deeds, intents, and purposes, as the said feoffees should
think meete and convenient, all the residue of the rents
and proffitts of the said messuages, lands, &c., after
providing for repairs of the said messuages and of the
" schole house in Endfield now of late new built there."

If the rents improved, the feoffees might at their
discretion deal more liberally with the schoolmaster in
respect of stipend, always, however, having regard and
consideration of the other good and godly uses and purposes expressed.

In 1619 Sir Nicholas Salter, Nicholas Raynton, and
Benjamin Deycrowe purchased for £100 1s., the claims
of the crown upon Poynetts, which, after lying dormant
for some time, had been revived, and by letters patent of
James I., 1615, sold to Edmund Duffield and John
Babington, and which from them had passed to Thomas
Kenethorpe, of London. Though the terms of James'
grant were much more extensive, it seems tolerably certain
that what he really did grant was " the sums of money
issuing out of certain lands, tenements, or hereditaments
in the parishes of South Benfleet and given for the
maintenance of the singing chaplain or priest in the parish
church of Enfield," belonging to the king, " by reason of
the Statute of Colleges of Singers, 1st Edward VI."

Some years before, in 1596, 38 Elizabeth, the then feoffees, John Taylor, Simon Potter and others, had let all that messuage at South Benfleet, &c., exclusive of wood and underwood, and reserving to themselves "all rights of hawkinge, huntynge, fishinge, and foulinge," for twenty-one years, at a yearly rent of £35 for eleven years, and of £37 for the remainder of the term. It is hardly credible that an estate of this value could have been sold for £100, nor is there anything to show that it had ever passed out of the possession of the parish, or that the school was not kept up continuously from 1558. Bradshawe is mentioned as master in 1600, and Richard Ward in 1606-7.

Shortly after the purchase from Thomas Kenethorpe, by a new trust deed of 1st September, 1621, Hugh Mascull and thirteen other feoffees are directed to pay £20 yearly to a learned, meet, and competent master to teach the children of all the inhabitants of Enfield the cross-row or alphabetical letters, and the arts of writing, grammar, and arithmetic, and to employ the residue, after providing for repairs, for the relief of poor orphans, and other poor and impotent people of the parish, and for any other good and charitable purposes.

The feoffees were to do nothing, with regard to the property of the school, or the appointment or dismissal of the master, except in a vestry, at which ten at least of the parishioners, not being feoffees, must be present, to be held in the *chamber above the school*, after public notice in the church on the preceding Sunday. Whenever the number of feoffees was reduced to five, four, or three at the least, fourteen new ones were to be chosen by the vestry.

The school continued to be managed according to the provisions of this trust till the year 1825, when a new scheme was established by the Court of Chancery on the termination of legal proceedings between the master and trustees, which had lasted seven years. This provided, " inter alia," " That the master be required to teach and instruct the children of the inhabitants in the school-house, in the arts of reading, writing, grammar, and arithmetic, on every day in the week (except Sunday), from 9 a.m., to 12, and from 2 p.m. to 5 p.m., except in the afternoons of Wednesday and Saturday, and except one month in the summer and one in the winter ; and the same master or the usher shall attend the scholars to and during Divine service at the parish church ot Enfield on Sundays and prayer-days."

When the number of scholars reached 60, on the average of five months, the master was to receive a salary of £120 per annum, and might appoint an usher, subject to the approval of the trustees, who were to pay him £50 per annum.

The Inspector under the Schools' Inquiry Commission says, in his report, " The history of this school, during one-half century, affords a notable example of the disastrous results of ill-defined relations and consequent conflicts between the masters and governing bodies of endowed schools. Since the year 1818, the Trustees have been continually engaged in litigation, the result of which has been to saddle the charity with a debt of £650, incurred for costs, and to paralyse the action of the school." In 1873 the Trustees having no funds for the repair of the school premises, which were reported to be unfit for school use, and having no power under the Trust Deed to levy capitation fees, determined, with the consent of the Vestry, to close the school for a time and apply to the Endowed School Commissioners for a new scheme, which has been prepared and is now under the consideration of the parish.

The income of the school arising from the Poynett's Estate, at Benfleet, of 273 acres, and from 90 acres, part of the Edward's Hall Estate, bought in 1817, with the accumulations from sale of timber at Poynetts, has amounted of late years to about £280, but is likely to increase.

The following is a list of the masters of the Free School :—

— Bradshawe was master in 1600, at a salary of £20 per annum.

Thomas Taylor was appointed master in the same year, on the death of Bradshawe.

Richard Ward, in 1606-7, and was put into the deed of 1621, and continued master until 1647.

William Holmes was the next master. He died in 1664, and was succeeded by

William Nelson, clerk.

Robert Uvedale, L.L.D., Fellow of Trin. College, Cambridge, was master in 1670.

— Harper in 1700.

John Allen in 1732.

Daniel Shipton, in 1761.

Samuel Hardy, M.A., was appointed in 1762; he resigned in 1791, and died in 1793.

John Milne (Member of the University of Aberdeen), was appointed in 1791. He died in 1836.

James Emery succeeded in 1831, and was called upon to resign in 1846. This led to a trial in the Court of Common Pleas, in which a verdict was returned for Emery.

Charles Chambers was elected 14th December, 1846, but as Emery would not vacate the school-house till a compensation of £450 was paid him, Chambers did not enter upon his duties till the following year.

An attempt to remove Mr. Chambers from the mastership in 1858, after a public inquiry by authority of the Charity Commissioners, led to a Chancery suit, which left Mr. Chambers in possession. The costs were paid by a mortgage upon the estates.

## PAROCHIAL SCHOOLS.

(1.) THE NATIONAL SCHOOLS for boys and girls in London-road, were built by subscription, without any Government aid, in 1839. In 1868, a Class Room and Infant's School-room were added. They are now attended by 120 boys, 70 girls, and 70 infants, who are taught by a master, mistress, and infant school mistress, all certificated, together with an assistant master and two pupil teachers.

They are annually examined by one of H. M. Inspectors, and have for many years received the most favourable reports.

They are under the management of a committee of gentlemen and ladies, of which the Vicar is chairman, and P. Twells, Esq., treasurer.

(2.) The S. MICHAEL'S SCHOOL, Gordon Estate, was built in 1870, as the small room previously used, was not found sufficient. About 150 children are taught by a certificated mistress, assistant, and two pupil teachers.

(3.) A NEW SCHOOL-ROOM for 60 infants was built in 1872, in Gordon-lane, Baker-street, on ground given by Trinity College.

(4.) Another INFANT SCHOOL, also in connection with the Parish Church, is held in Love's-row, in a hired building, formerly used as a dissenting chapel.

(5.) The CHURCH SCHOOL OF INDUSTRY, established in 1800, under the management of a committee of ladies, for the industrial training of 30 girls, is carried on in a building in the Churchyard, belonging to the Free School, formerly known as the Old Coffee-house.

In the district of S. JAMES', Highway, there are,—

(1.) A SCHOOL FOR 160 BOYS, with a master's house, built in 1872, near the Church, under a certificated master and three pupil teachers.

(2.) GIRLS' AND INFANTS' SCHOOL, at the Highway, for 260 children, taught by a certificated mistress, and four pupil teachers.

(3.) A MIXED SCHOOL, in South-street, for 120 children, under a certificated mistress, assistant, and two pupil teachers.

(4.) A SCHOOL-ROOM at the end of Lock-lane, not yet opened.

(5) SCHOOLS at the ROYAL SMALL ARMS FACTORY, for boys, girls, and infants, with three certificated teachers and seven pupil teachers, supported by the War Office. They supply accommodation for more than 500 children.

In the district of JESUS CHURCH, Forty-hill, are boys' and girls' schools, built in 1851, and enlarged in 1868, so as to accommodate 140 children, with a certificated master and mistress. There is also a school for infants near Maiden's-bridge, built and supported by James Meyer, Esq.

In connection with S. JOHN's, Clay-hill, is a school for 60 children, built in 1859, near the Church.

In the district of CHRIST CHURCH, Cockfosters, are girls' and infant schools, built by D. Bevan, Esq., in 1840, and a school for boys, built by subscription, in 1859, providing altogether for 180 children.

## POPULATION.

| | | | The No. of Inhabited Houses. |
|---|---|---|---|
| The population of the Parish of Enfield by the Census of 1811 was... | | 6,636 | 1,115 |
| „ | 1821 | ... 8,227 | 1,309 |
| „ | 1841 | 9,367 | 1,706 |
| „ | 1851 | 9,453 | 1,817 |
| „ | 1861 | ... 12,410 | 2,308 |
| „ | 1871 | ... 16,053 | 2,895 |

Previous to 1811 we can only approximate to the population. In 1793 there were said to be about 920 houses ; in 1801, 926. The average of burials during the last 20 years of the eighteenth century (144), was somewhat larger than during the first 20 years of the present (136), but it is clear that the mortality was much greater in proportion to the population.

According to the return of the Registrar of Births, Deaths, and Marriages, there were in the parish of Enfield,

| | | | MARRIAGES. | |
|---|---|---|---|---|
| In the year ending | BIRTHS. | DEATHS. | In Church. | In Registered Buildings. |
| March 21, 1869... | 548 | 221 | 60 | 8 |
| „ 1871... | 482 | 373 | 52 | 7 |
| ., 1873... | 657 | 244 | 60 | 6 |

In the two first quarters of 1873 there were registered 276 births, and 113 deaths.

The population in 1871 was thus divided amongst the several districts :—S. Andrew's, 5,087 ; S. James', Highway, 8,027 ; Jesus, Forty-hill, 1,213 ; S. John's, Clay-hill, 997 ; Christ Church, Trent, 730.

Y

Enfield belongs to the Edmonton Poor Law Union, and has eight elected guardians.

The rateable value of the parish was in 1821, £32,599 ; in 1871, £68,981.

The rate levied for the relief of the poor was, in 1821, 2s. 1d. in the pound ; in 1871, 2s. 3d. in the pound.

The whole control of the draining, lighting, paving, &c., of the parish is vested in the Local Board of Health, which was constituted August 19, 1850, under the provisions of the Public Health Act (1848). There are twelve members, of whom four retire every year. James Meyer, Esq., has been chairman from the beginning. The rate was, in 1873, 3s. in the pound.

# DISSENTING PLACES OF WORSHIP.

### BAKER-STREET CHAPEL.

A congregation of Presbyterian Dissenters was established in Enfield as early as 1687, by Obadiah Hughes, an ejected minister, and son of George Hughes, Vicar of Tavistock. At that time they held their meetings in a barn, but on the passing of the Toleration Act a meeting-house was built in Baker-street, and Mr. Hughes was chosen pastor in 1688-9. The society took a lease of the ground in 1702, when the meeting-house was rebuilt. In 1752 the freehold was purchased for £200, and conveyed to trustees. In 1771 it underwent considerable repairs and alterations, and was newly floored and pewed. The present chapel is the third erected upon the same site, and is capable of holding about 400 people. School-rooms adjoining were built in 1860, at an expense of £350. The present minister is the Rev. S. J. Smith, B.A.

### PONDER'S-END CHAPEL.

This chapel was opened in 1768. The first minister was the Rev. Mr. Alliston, of London ; he was succeeded by the Rev. John Knight, who continued for 20 years. In 1825 the Rev. G. Clarke, of London, was chosen, and remained till his death, a period of seven years.

The original Congregational Chapel at Chase-side, known as Zion Chapel, was built in 1780, and opened on the 7th of June. The ground was purchased by Matthias Peter Dupont, landlord of the Castle and Falcon, in Aldersgate-street, who erected the present building, with the assistance of contributions amounting to £240. Tavern-keepers are so seldom · church-builders, that his name deserves to be recorded. Messrs. Woodgate and Midley opened the chapel by two sermons, each being an hour and a half in length. Yet abundant as was the mental fare, it was supplemented by a no less substantial repast at the George Inn, where an item of £3 for coach-hire, and another of £4 12s., " expenses of ministers at the George," bear witness to the hospitality of the genial and pious founder. The events of the day are duly chronicled in the Gentleman's Magazine, p. 295. The first minister appears to have been a Mr. Whitefoot, on whose induction a similar liberality was exercised, the earliest entry in the chapel books being " chaise for ministers to attend the ordination of Mr. W. Whitefoot, £1 10s.—expenses at the George, £2 13s."

### CHASE-SIDE CHAPEL.

In the year 1793, in consequence of a schism among the brethren, the seceding party built the adjoining Chase-side Chapel. The present structure was erected in 1832.

In December, 1871, at a united meeting of the two congregations, called for the purpose, a resolution was passed " that the members and office-bearers of Zion and Chaseside Churches do hereby unite to form one church," after which the Rev. H. S. Toms was chosen to the united pastorate, the venerable Mr. Stribling retiring on his full stipend, after 40 years of faithful service.

It is now in contemplation to build a new chapel large enough for the accommodation of the two congregations, which have been so long dissevered.*

### HIGHWAY CONGREGATIONAL CHAPEL.

The Congregational Chapel at the Highway, with school-rooms adjoining, was opened in 1854.

### PRIMITIVE METHODIST CHAPEL.

This congregation took its origin from itinerant preachers, who some twenty years ago collected a number of hearers on Chase-green, and afterwards took a barn at the Holly-bush, which they fitted up as a temporary chapel, where they continued to meet till on the receipt of a liberal donation from Mrs. Tolputt (the wife of a clergyman of the Church of England), they raised by additional subscriptions a sufficient amount for the erection of the present chapel, a neat, unpretending building, which was opened on the 28th October, 1858.

---

* From a paper by Rev. H. S. Toms.

## WESLEYAN METHODIST CHAPEL.

The Wesleyan Methodist Chapel, in Cecil-road, was built in the year 1864. The land was given for the purpose by Mr. Cave, of Enfield, who also contributed liberally towards the cost of the building, the amount of which, £1,030, was raised by subscription. It is calculated to accommodate 230 sitters. There is no settled minister.

## BAPTIST TABERNACLE.

The Baptist congregation in Enfield was formed on the 10th June, 1867, and for a short time held its meetings in the Assembly-room at the " Rising Sun," but receiving notice to quit from the landlord, and being unable to obtain any other room for the purpose, they erected the present iron building in the London-road, which was opened on the third of December the same year.

## BAPTIST CHAPEL, TOTTERIDGE ROAD.

The Baptist chapel in the Totteridge-road was opened in 1872.

There are also chapels at BOTANY BAY and WHITE WEBBS, chiefly supplied from Lady Huntingdon's College at Cheshunt.

Religious services are held at the MISSION ROOM, Baker-street, conducted by the London City Missionary.

Services are also held in a room on CHASE GREEN, near the river, by the PLYMOUTH BRETHREN.

Some years ago a Roman Catholic gentleman purchased
a commodious site, with ample space for church and
presbytery, and having a frontage to the London and
Cecil-roads. Upon this ground a building was erected,
in which, for the present requirements of the Roman
Catholic residents, numbering about 50, mass is said by
the priest from Waltham Cross on Sundays and holy days
of obligation, by the direction of the Archbishop of the
Roman Catholic Diocese.

## BRITISH AND OTHER SCHOOLS.

The BRITISH SCHOOLS, at Chase-side, were built, with
the assistance of a Government grant of £200, at a cost
of £1100, in the year 1838, when the first stone was laid
by Lord Brougham. At this time there was no school
for boys in Enfield, except the Grammar School. The
building was opened on the 19th November in the same
year, on which day 80 boys and 30 girls were entered on
the books. The adjoining houses for the master and
mistress were built in 1857. During the 34 years that
the schools have been in existence, above 1,400 boys,
and 1,050 girls have been admitted. The education is
wholly unsectarian, no creed or catechism being used, and

the only text-book for religious instruction being the
Bible. The children are expected to attend the Sunday
services at whatever place of worship may be selected by
their parents.

Mr. Wakley, who has been the master from the commencement of the school, received a Government certificate last year (1872). The mistress has since obtained
one, and both schools will now participate in the advantages offered by the Education Act.

The present number of children on the books is, 98
boys and 74 girls.

The joint secretaries are Rev. S. J. Smith, Baker-street
Chapel, and Rev. H. S. Toms, Chase-side Chapel.

The BAKER STREET INFANT SCHOOL was established
in 1846. It is conducted by a committee of ladies, who
are elected yearly by the subscribers. The average
number of children who attend is about 50.

Schools have lately been opened in connection with the
BAPTIST CHAPEL in the Totteridge-road.

There is also an INFANT SCHOOL at Ponder's-end.

# The Charities.

THE following account of the Enfield Charities is taken from that drawn up in 1789 by the Vicar and Churchwardens and Overseers, and published by their authority. As this is the original document from which all subsequent statements have been adopted, it has been thought best to reprint it *verbatim*, with the addition of "NOTES," which have been supplied by Mr. Purdey, the Vestry Clerk, and of an appendix containing gifts of a later date, thus completing the record down to the present time.

---

A PARTICULAR of the several charitable gifts, rents, and revenues belonging to the parish of Enfield, in the county of Middlesex ; with the names of the donors, for what uses to be disposed of, according to the wills of the donors, and constitutions of every respective gift and settlement.

Abstract of deeds of trusts, wills of the donors, and orders of Vestry.

A2

ii.

## First Gift.—Poynet's.

A farm, called Poynet's, in South Benfleet, Hadleigh,
and Thundersly, in the county of Essex, formerly lett at
£55 per annum (now on lease from Michaelmas, 1786,
for fourteen years, at £80 per annum), which the feoffees
in trust shall from time to time for ever dispose and pay.
as followeth—viz., £20 part of the rents, issues, and
profits thereof yearly, for and towards the maintenance
of a learned, meet, and competent schoolmaster, to keep
a free school for the teaching and instructing of the
children of all the inhabitants of the said parish of Enfield,
in the cross-row, or alphabetical letters, and in the art of
writing, and in the arts of grammar and arithmetic, within
the town and parish aforesaid, in the new-built school
there (which school, and house for the schoolmaster to
dwell in, the parishioners purchased and built at their own
proper costs and charges), to be paid quarterly—viz., at
Lady-day, Midsummer-day, Michaelmas-day, and Christ-
mas-day, or within twenty-eight days next after any of them;
and all the residue thereof for and towards the relief of poor
orphans, and other poor and impotent people of the said
parish for the time being, and to any other good and
useful uses, to be done and performed within the said
parish, except so much thereof as shall be sufficient to
pay and discharge all such other charges and expenses as
shall from time to time grow to be due and payable, or
upon any other meet or reasonable occasion to be laid

out for, upon, about, or by reason of the said premises.
When the feoffees are dead, to five, four, or three at the
least, this feoffment to be renewed.

N.B.—There has been received several sums for timber
cut on this estate.

Particular of the annual receipts and disbursements of
each gift.

| Annual Receipt. | £ | s. | d. | Annual Application. | £ | s. | d. |
|---|---|---|---|---|---|---|---|
| A Year's Rent... ... | 80 | o | o | To the Schoolmaster* | 20 | o | o |
| | | | | To the Lecturer* ... | 26 | o | o |
| | | | | Land Tax, about ... | 3 | o | o |
| | | | | Quit Rent to the Manor of Hadleigh | 1 | 2 | 6 |
| | | | | Ditto to South Benfleet ... ... ... | 1 | 2 | 8 |
| | | | | Charges of repairing marsh walls, on a medium ... ... | 1 | o | o |
| | | | | To be applied in repair of the schoolhouse, or to such uses as contained in the abstract ... | 27 | 14 | 10 |
| | £80 | o | o | | £80 | o | o |

[NOTE.]

| | £ | s. | d. |
|---|---|---|---|
| Farm-house and Land of Poynetts, containing 270 acres in South Benfleet and Hadleigh, let on 21 years lease from 29 September, 1853 ... ... ... | 150 | o | o |
| Edward's Hall, let on yearly term ... ... ... ... | 80 | o | o |
| Two cottages and Field ... ... ... ... ... | 8 | o | o |
| Dividend on £21 14s. 4d. 3 per cent. consols *exparte* Tilbury and Southend Railway ... ... ... ... | 9 | 9 | o |
| | £247 | 9 | o |

* The duty of schoolmaster and lecturer is performed by one
person.

## Second Gift.—Ramston's.

Robert Ramston, of Chinckford, in the county of Essex, gent., by a codicil annexed to his will, bearing date the 1st of August, 1585, gave, for the comfort and relief of the poor people of the parish of Enfield, the sum of 40s. to be paid in the month of November, yearly, for ever, to the Churchwardens for the time being.

N.B.—This gift is paid by Mr. Patrick, of the Dividend Office in the Bank of England.

---

[NOTE.]

It is now paid by Lord Maynard.

| Annual Receipt. | £ | s. | d. | Annual Application. | £ | s. | d. |
|---|---|---|---|---|---|---|---|
| A Year's Gift Money of George Howland, Esq., due yearly on the 12th of November ... | 2 | 0 | 0 | By an allowance for Land Tax ... ... | 0 | 6 | 0 |
| | | | | Bread given away every other Sunday | 1 | 14 | 0 |
| | £2 | 0 | 0 | | £2 | 0 | 0 |

[NOTE.]

This money is now given in clothing to the poor at Christmas.

---

## Third Gift.—Wilson's.

Thomas Wilson, of London, brewer, by will dated the 30th of October, 1590, gave all the rents, issues, and

profits of three houses, with the appurtenances, being in
Whitechapel, in the county of Middlesex, on the south
side of the High-street there, near the Bars, to be yearly
for ever bestowed on six poor men of the parish of
Enfield, to be paid to them quarterly, or within one
month, which said houses are now lett on lease for 21
years from Lady-day, 1786, at £82. 10s. per annum,
clear of deductions ; and that the same poor men shall
from time to time be chosen and appointed by the
Churchwardens and six parishioners of the said parish of
Enfield, always at a Vestry ; and if any of the said poor
men shall go to dwell out of the parish, or decease, or
any such so chosen to have a part of the said rents
happening to be wealthy, or able to live without the
same, then, from time to time, one other poor person or
persons of the said parish to be chosen in form aforesaid,
in the room of such person so dying, or dwelling out of
the said parish, or of ability to live without it. When
feoffees reduced to three, the feoffment to be renewed to
six.

---

### [NOTE.]

One of these houses was sold under Act of
Parliament (42 Geo. III. c. 101), to the trustees of the
Commercial-road, and the purchase-money, £2,091 5s. 8d.
(invested in consols), may be applied to the purchase of
any real estate.

| *Annual Receipt.* | | | | *Annual Application.* | | | |
|---|---|---|---|---|---|---|---|
| | £ | s. | d. | | £ | s. | d. |
| Of Mr. Daniel Lawrence, for No. 1 ... | 28 | 10 | 0 | To six poor men, at £12 12s.* per annum each ... ... | 75 | 12 | 0 |
| Of Mr. Wm. Wright, for No. 2 ... ... | 28 | 0 | 0 | To re-pay the parish £16 0s. 5d., advanced for insuring the premises for seven years, from August, 1788 ... | 4 | 11 | 6½ |
| Of Mr. Bendahan, for No. 3 ... ... ... | 26 | 0 | 0 | Towards a fund for keeping the premises insured ... | 2 | 6 | 5½ |
| | £82 | 10 | 0 | | £82 | 10 | 0 |

\* From Michaelmas, 1795, this sum will be increased.

† This insurance cost £32 0s. 10d., the half of which was paid out of the rents of the estate, the other £16 0s. 5d. was advanced by the parish, to be repaid by annual payments at £4 11s. 6½d. per annum, which expires at Lady-day, 1792, from which time to Michaelmas, 1795, when the present insurance expires, it is to be added to the above £2 6s. 5½d., to raise a sufficient fund to keep the premises always insured, as under :—

| | | £ | s. | d. |
|---|---|---|---|---|
| Three years and a-half to Lady-day, 1792, at £2 6s. 5½d. per annum ... ... ... ... ... | | 8 | 2 | 6¾ |
| Three years and a half from Lady-day, 1792, to Michaelmas, 1795, at £6 18s. per annum | .. | 24 | 3 | 0 |
| | | £32 | 5 | 6¾ |

### [NOTE].

| | | £ | s. | d. |
|---|---|---|---|---|
| Two Messuages in High-street, Whitechapel ... | .. | 160 | 0 | 0 |
| Dividend on £2091 15s. 8d. 3 per cent. Consols | ... | 61 | 8 | 7 |
| | | £221 | 8 | 7 |

## Fourth Gift.—Smith's.

WILLIAM SMITH, of the parish of Enfield, in the county of Middlesex, yeoman, by will dated the 26th of September, 1592, gave £4* per annum for ever, to be paid to the Vicar and Churchwardens of the Parish Church of Enfield aforesaid, for the time being, by four even portions, viz., at Christmas 20s.; at Lady-day 20s.; and at Midsummer and Michaelmas, 20s. each; which said money in such sort paid, the said Vicar and Churchwardens, calling unto them some four other men of the same parish, shall, within six days after every such receipt, distribute it among the poor inhabitants where most need is. And if it shall chance that the said sums of money, or any of them, shall be in the whole or in part unpaid by the space of two months after any of the feasts wherein they should be due, he did will then that his house, with all and every the parcels of land hereafter named, should be demised or lett out from time to time, by the said Vicar and Churchwardens, and in case no Vicar, the Churchwardens and four other men, at such price as they, or the greater part of them, shall think good, and pay the rent as aforesaid, viz., the house where John White did dwell, with five acres of pasture adjoining to the same, and four acres of pasture near Phipps Hatch Gate, and three acres of arable in Broadfield, and two.

---

* There is now only received £3 13s. 4d.; the other 6s. 8d. has been lost to the parish many years.

acres in Maypleton-field, and one acre called a five-rod
acre, at or near Bullock's Stile.

| Annual Receipt. | £ | s. | d. | Annual Application. | £ | s. | d. |
|---|---|---|---|---|---|---|---|
| Of the Overseers of the town quarter, for the workhouse | o | 6 | 8 | To one poor woman, at 18s. 4d. per quarter ... ... ... | 3 | 13 | 4 |
| Of Mr. Shroder one year ... ... ... | o | 10 | o | | | | |
| Of Mr. Maurer ... | 1 | 13 | 4 | | | | |
| Of ditto, for late Jenks | 1 | 3 | 4 | | | | |
| | £3 | 13 | 4 | | £3 | 13 | 4 |

[NOTE].

The full amount of this charity is now received, viz.—

| | £ | s. | d. |
|---|---|---|---|
| One year's rent charge, C. Walford ... ... ... ... | 2 | 16 | 8 |
| S. L. Lucena ... ... ... ... ... ... ... | o | 10 | o |
| Overseers for Workhouse Premises ... ... ... ... | o | 13 | 4 |
| | £4 | o | o |

## FIFTH GIFT.—DAVID'S.

JOHN DAVID, of Enfield, Middlesex, yeoman, by will
dated the 20th of November, 1620, did will and devise
that the rents, issues, and profits, from time to time
coming, growing, and arising of and in all that his messuage or tenement, with the barns, stables, yards, and
outhouses whatsoever thereunto belonging, situate, lying,
and being on the left side of the Market-place at Enfield-
green, should be yearly employed and bestowed to and

upon the relief of four poor, aged, and well-disposed widows of the said parish of Enfield for ever, to be paid unto them at the four usual feasts, or within 21 days next after, by even portions ; and that the same poor widows should, from time to time, be chosen and appointed by the Churchwardens and six parishioners of the said parish, always at a vestry to be holden at the said parish ; and if any of the said poor widows should go and dwell out of the said parish of Enfield, marry or decease, then, from time to time, one other poor widow or widows of the said parish should be chosen in manner and form aforesaid, in the room of her or them so dwelling out of the said parish, marrying, or deceasing. There are six feoffees, and when reduced to three the feoffment to be renewed to six.

N.B.—The estate is now lett on lease for 99 years, from Midsummer, 1788, at £40 per annum.

| *Annual Receipt.* | | | | *Annual Application.* | | | |
|---|---|---|---|---|---|---|---|
| | £ | s. | d. | | £ | s. | d. |
| Of Mr. John Ostlife, the lessee ... ... | 40 | 0 | 0 | To four poor women, at £10 per annum each .. ... ... | 40 | 0 | 0 |
| | £40 | 0 | 0 | | £40 | 0 | 0 |

N.B.—This estate used to be lett to different tenants at £48 10s. per annum, but great part thereof being so old and decayed as to make it necessary to be re-built, the same was lett to Mr. Ostlife at the above rent, he covenanting to expend £500 in repairing or re-building the same.

[For Note to David's Gift, see next page.]

[NOTE.]

| | £ | s. | d. |
|---|---|---|---|
| Rent of Public Offices and Houses in Market-place (£40—less loss of Common right, £2 11s. 0d.) | 37 | 9 | 0 |
| Allotment of Chase let on yearly tenancy | 6 | 12 | 0 |
| | £44 | 1 | 0 |

### SIXTH GIFT.—DEYCROWE'S.

JOHN DEYCROWE, by will dated the 25th day of May, 1627, gave a moiety of his messuage or farm, situate at or near a street in Enfield, called Green-street, and of all barns, stables, houses, outhouses, gardens, orchards, lands, tenements, and hereditaments thereunto belonging and appertaining, as the same are mentioned in a certain presentment or survey made by a jury at a court holden for the Manor of Worcester, to be held freely of the said manor, to Thomas Sone, his heirs and assigns for ever, and requires him and them for ever to pay thereout to the poor of the parish of Enfield £4 yearly, by 20s. quarterly, to be paid on every of the four most usual quarter days of payment in the year, or within eight days next following, to the Churchwardens and Overseers of the said parish of Enfield; and they calling and taking unto them two others of the inhabitants of the said parish, such as they shall think well of, do and shall give and bestow, dispose and distribute the said 20s. quarterly to and amongst the poor people of Enfield aforesaid for the time being, for ever.

| Annual Receipt. | | | | Annual Application. | | | |
|---|---|---|---|---|---|---|---|
| | £ | s. | d. | | £ | s. | d. |
| Of Mr. Boddam ... | 4 | 0 | 0 | To two poor women, at 10s. per quarter each .. ... ... | 4 | 0 | 0 |
| | £4 | 0 | 0 | | £4 | 0 | 0 |

### SEVENTH GIFT.—LOFT'S.

HENRY LOFT, of Enfield, Middlesex, yeoman, by will dated March the 3rd, 1631, gave to the parish of Enfield the sum of £20 per annum for ever—viz., £12; part thereof to be paid to the Minister and Churchwardens for the time being, to and for the only use, benefit, and behoof of six poor widows, to be chosen after his decease by the said Minister, Churchwardens, and six others of the vestrymen of the said parish of Enfield, at a vestry, equally to be divided amongst the said six poor widows, at the four most usual feasts or terms in the year, or within 14 days next ensuing every of the said feast days, by even portions; and if any of the said poor widows shall depart this mortal life, or go to live out of the said parish to dwell, or happen to be married, that then one other poor widow to be chosen in her stead or room by the said Minister, Churchwardens, and six others of the vestrymen of the same parish for the time being, at a vestry as aforesaid; and £4, another part thereof, to the said Minister and Churchwardens, at the days and times aforesaid, to and for the use and only benefit and behoof

of a preacher or lecturer, which shall preach in the afternoon of the Lord's-day, in the said Parish Church of
Enfield (the said preacher or lecturer for the time being
not omitting preaching above one month in the year in
the said Parish Church); and £4, the other part thereof,
at Midsummer-day, or within 14 days then next following,
to the Minister and Churchwardens as aforesaid, to be
bestowed by them for and towards the cloathing of the
poor of the said parish of Enfield, or providing of them
such necessary apparel as they shall think fitting; which
said sum of £20 is to be paid out of the premises hereafter named—viz., one messuage, three barns, one garden,
one orchard, and 39 acres and a half of land, with the
appurtenances situate, lying, and being at Horsepool
Stones, in the parish of Enfield aforesaid; also one
cottage and one acre of land, in Baker-street, then in the
occupation of Robert Morphew; and also one close of
pasture, called Bullocks Stile, and two acres and a half of
land, then in the occupation of Henry Hunsdon, the
elder; and also of and in two and twenty acres of land,
with the appurtenances, lying and being in Chigwell, in
the county of Essex, then in the tenure of Abraham
Fuller.

| *Annual Receipt.* | | | | *Annual Application.* | | | |
|---|---|---|---|---|---|---|---|
| | £ | s. | d. | | £ | s. | d. |
| Of Benjamin Crew ... | 20 | 0 | 0 | To six poor women, at 10s. per quarter each ... ... ... | 12 | 0 | 0 |
| | | | | To the Rev. Samuel Hardy, as lecturer . | 4 | 0 | 0 |
| | | | | To the Minister and Churchwardens, to cloathe the poor ... | 4 | 0 | 0 |
| | £20 | 0 | 0 | | £20 | 0 | 0 |

[NOTE].

The lands in Enfield from which this sum is paid are numbered on the parish map—1292, 1293, 1362, 1374, 1608, and 1894.

---

### Eighth Gift.—Cock's.

GEORGE COCK, of the parish of St. James, Clerkenwell, in the county of Middlesex, brewer, by will dated the 16th of September, 1635, gave to the poor of the parish of Enfield the sum of £30 for a stock for the increase of profit thereof to be yearly given to the poor of Enfield in bread, with which said sum the parishioners purchased a tenement, with a little close of pasture ground adjoining to the same, at Clay-hill, in the said parish of Enfield, and it is disposed of for bread given to the poor on Sundays.

N.B.—The tenement is in the possession of Thomas Richardson, as one of the paupers of the said parish; the close of pasture is on lease to Mrs. Ann Schroder for 31 years, from Michaelmas, 1762.

---

[NOTE.]

In the year 1829 the late Mr. Harman agreed with the parish to exchange the above property for premises in Enfield Town, adjoining the Greyhound Inn, which exchange was accordingly made by deed, and the premises conveyed to trustees.

| Annual Receipt. | | | | Annual Application. | | | |
|---|---|---|---|---|---|---|---|
| | £ | s. | d. | | £ | s. | d. |
| Of the Overseers of the town quarter, for the tenement ... | 1 | 8 | 0 | By bread given away every other Sunday in the year ... ... | 2 | 11 | 4 |
| Of Mrs. Schroder, for the close .. ... | 1 | 4 | 0 | Quit Rent to the Manor of Worcester | 0 | 0 | 8 |
| | £2 | 12 | 0 | | £2 | 12 | 0 |

[NOTE.]

| 1871. | £ | s. | d. |
|---|---|---|---|
| One Year's Rent of Commissioners of Police ... ... | 15 | 0 | 0 |
| E. Letchworth, Esq. ... ... ... ... ... ... ... | 12 | 10 | 0 |
| One Year's Rent of Allotment of Land on Enfield Chase ... ... ... ... ... ... | 2 | 2 | 0 |
| | £29 | 12 | 0 |

## NINTH GIFT.—RAYNTON'S.

SIR NICHOLAS RAYNTON, Knt., and Alderman of the City of London, by will dated May the 2nd, 1646, gave to the parish of Enfield £10 per annum for ever, to put out three poor children, born in the town of Enfield, apprentices ; which said sum is to be paid to the Churchwardens for the time being, at Michaelmas in every year, by the Master and Four Wardens of the fraternity of the art and mystery of Haberdashers in London, out of some houses in the parish of St. Edmond the King, in Lombard-street, London.

N.B.—Since the dreadful fire of London in 1666, the Churchwardens never received the full sum of £10.

---

[NOTE].

In July, 1813, the attention of the Vestry was called to the subject, when an application was made to the Haberdashers' Company for the full payment, and also for the arrears for the last 35 years, to which the Company assented, and accordingly paid over the sum of £70, which was invested in the purchase of £100 three per Cents., in the names of trustees.

| Annual Receipt. | | | | Annual Application. | | | |
|---|---|---|---|---|---|---|---|
| | £ | s. | d. | | £ | s. | d. |
| Of the Haberdashers' Company | 10 | 0 | 0 | Binding three children apprentice, at £2 13s. 4d. each | 8 | 0 | 0 |
| | | | | Land Tax, at 4s. in the pound | 2 | 0 | 0 |
| | £10 | 0 | 0 | | £10 | 0 | 0 |

| | £ | s. | d. |
|---|---|---|---|
| Annuity from Haberdashers' Company | 10 | 0 | 0 |
| Dividend on Stock | 3 | 0 | 0 |
| | £13 | 0 | 0 |

### Tenth Gift.—Billings'.

William Billings, of Enfield, Middlesex, yeoman, by will dated June the 11th, 1659, gave 20s. per annum for ever, to be paid to the Minister and Churchwardens at Bartholomew-tide, every year, for and towards the cloathing of poor children of the said parish of Enfield ; which said money is to be paid out of one messuage or tenement, with the appurtenances, and the closes of several pasture grounds thereunto adjoining and belonging, situate, lying, or being near unto Cole's Bridge, near Clay Hill, in the parish of Enfield aforesaid.

This, and Ann Osbourn's Gift, being now disposed of together, the account is stated in No. 16.

### Eleventh Gift.—Grave's.

Roger Grave, of Enfield, Middlesex, yeoman, by will gave 40s. yearly for ever, to the Schoolmaster of the Free School of the parish of Enfield for the time being, for and towards his recompence for teaching and instructing the poor children of the inhabitants of the parish of Enfield aforesaid ; to be paid out of the issues and profits of a certain tenement, with the appurtenances, situate, lying, and being by the New River, near Forty-hill, in Enfield aforesaid ; which said 40s. is to be paid half-yearly, by even and equal portions.

| Annual Receipt. | £ | s. | d. |
|---|---|---|---|
| Of Richard Gough, Esq., for his late house at Patten's Ware ... ... ... | 2 | 0 | 0 |
| | £2 | 0 | 0 |

| Annual Application. | £ | s. | d. |
|---|---|---|---|
| To the Rev. Sam. Hardy, the Schoolmaster ... ... ... | 2 | 0 | 0 |
| | £2 | 0 | 0 |

## Twelfth Gift.—Wroth's.

Sir Henry Wroth, in consideration of his inclosing part of Stonard Field, near Ponder's-end, in the parish of Enfield, agreed to pay the parish of Enfield £1 7s. 6d. per annum, at Michaelmas, yearly, to one or more of the Churchwardens for the time being, and whosoever enjoys the same are to pay the said sum, which the said Churchwardens are to distribute amongst the poor people of the said parish of Enfield, as they at their discretions shall think fit.

| Annual Receipt. | £ | s. | d. |
|---|---|---|---|
| Of Mr. Chapman, for Durance Estate ... | 1 | 7 | 6 |
| | £1 | 7 | 6 |

| Annual Application. | £ | s. | d. |
|---|---|---|---|
| This gift is usually received and distributed by the churchwardens of Greenstreet and Ponder's-end quarters... ... | 1 | 7 | 6 |
| | £1 | 7 | 6 |

## Thirteenth Gift.—King James's.

King James the First gave to the parish of Enfield a sum of money in consideration for his taking some part of Enfield Chace to enlarge Theobald's Park, with which money the parishioners of Enfield purchased an estate called Marches and Devises, in the parish of North Mimms, in the county of Hertford, and which is now lett on lease at £18 18s. per annum, for 21 years from Michaelmas, 1784, which rent is at the disposal of the parish. When the feoffees are reduced to five, four, or three at the least, the feoffment to be renewed.

| *Annual Receipt.* | | | | *Annual Application.* | | | |
|---|---|---|---|---|---|---|---|
| | £ | s. | d. | | £ | s. | d. |
| Of John Philips, the tenant | 18 | 18 | 0 | Land Tax | | 2 | 9 | 0 |
| | | | | To be disposed of at the discretion of the Vestry | 16 | 9 | 0 |
| | £18 | 18 | 0 | | £18 | 18 | 0 |

[NOTE.]

This estate was sold under Act of Parliament (48 Geo. III. c. 156), and the purchase-money invested in Consols, till in the year 1816 the trustees, under the sanction of the Court of Chancery, purchased that part of Edwards' Hall lying south of the road which passed through the estate, containing 94a. 2r. 34p., for the sum of £1700, which was raised by the sale of the said stock, added to the sum of £341 13s. 7d., at that time owing to this gift from the Benfleet Estate. The rent of this estate is "at the disposal of the vestry for any general use that doth concern the town and parish of Enfield or the poor thereof."

The rental of Edward's Hall is £50.

## FOURTEENTH GIFT.—NICHOLS'

JASPER NICHOLS, of St. Sepulchre's, London, yeoman, by will dated the . . . . . . . gave £50 to the poor of the parish of Enfield, with which money, and a benevolence of his executors, the parishioners, with the consent of Thomas Coats, gent., and Robert Curry, citizen and cordwainer of London, executors of the said Jasper Nichols, have purchased an estate, lately lett at 52s. per annum (besides the quit rent), which is a messuage or tenement, lately called or known by the name of the Bull and Bell, situate, lying, and being at Horsepool Stones in the parish of Enfield, with several parcels of land thereunto belonging, lett to Thomas Hill on lease for 30 years, from Michaelmas, 1781; 52s. whereof is to be paid for bread, at 12d. per week, and thirteen loaves to the dozen, and given to the poor on Sundays, according to the will of the said Jasper Nichols, deceased. When the feoffees are reduced to five, four, or three at least, the feoffment to be renewed.

| *Annual Receipt.* | £ | s. | d. | *Annual Application.* | £ | s. | d. |
|---|---|---|---|---|---|---|---|
| Of Thomas Hill ... | 4 | 0 | 0 | Bread given away every other Sunday in the year ... ... | 2 | 12 | 0 |
| | | | | Towards the paying of a forty shilling gift ... .. ... | 1 | 8 | 0 |
| | £4 | 0 | 0 | | £4 | 0 | 0 |

[NOTE].

This land was let on building leases by order of the
Charity Commissioners in 1860, for terms of 80 years,
and now produces ground-rents to the amount of £58.
A part is still not built upon.

---

### FIFTEENTH GIFT.—MARKET PLACE.

A messuage or tenement called the KING'S HEAD, and
the MARKET PLACE thereunto adjoining ; also a close of
pasture to the same, with the market, and all liberties,
free customs, tolls, stallage, pickages, fines, amerciaments,
and all the shambles, shops, and stalls, for the use of the
market, with the market-house there, together with all
the ground and soil, and all other profits whatsoever,
formerly lett at the yearly rent of £40 per annum, now
divided as follows—viz., the King's Head and close of
pasture, now a garden and bowling green, is lett to David
Walker, as tenant at will, at £20 per annum. The
houses on the west side of the Market-place, and the
market, &c., are lett to Thomas Vaughan on lease for
57 years, from Christmas, 1789, at £12 per annum, and
the messuage in the Churchyard lett to George Skegg on
lease for 21 years, from Lady-day, 1772, at £5 per
annum. And whereas by one indenture of feoffment,
dated October the 24th, in the year of our Lord 1691,
and inrolled in the Court of Common Pleas at West-

minster, in that Michaelmas Term, it is therein particularly mentioned and expressed that the feoffees shall and
will permit and suffer such person or persons as the
Minister, Churchwardens, and other parishioners of the
parish of Enfield shall nominate and appoint to receive
the rents, issues, and profits of the said premises ; the
same to be distributed to the only proper behoof, use,
and benefit of the poor of Enfield, from time to time,
inhabiting and residing in the said town of Enfield, in
such manner and form as the Minister, Churchwardens,
and others the parishioners of the said parish shall from
time to time appoint. The Free-school house, and small
garden thereto belonging, is occupied by the Rev.
Samuel Hardy, as schoolmaster and lecturer.

| *Annual Receipt.* | | | | *Annual Application.* | | | |
|---|---|---|---|---|---|---|---|
| | £ | s. | d. | | £ | s. | d. |
| Of David Walker, for the King's Head ... | 20 | 0 | 0, | By Window and House Tax, for the School-house .. ... | 10 | 8 | 4 |
| Of Thomas Vaughan | 12 | 0 | 0 | To be disposed of by order of Vestry ... | 26 | 11 | 8 |
| Of Geo. Skegg ... | 5 | 0 | 0 | | | | |
| | £37 | 0 | 0 | | £37 | 0 | 0 |

[NOTE].

| | £ | s. | d. |
|---|---|---|---|
| King's Head, now let on yearly tenancy to George Baldwin ... ... ... ... ... ... | 58 | 0 | 0 |
| Allotment on Chase ... ... ... ... ... | 4 | 1 | 0 |
| | £62 | 1 | 0 |

## Sixteenth Gift.—Billing's and Osbourn's.

Ann Osbourn, of the parish of St. Saviour's, Southwark, in the county of Surrey, widow, by her will dated February the 23d, 1666, gave to the parish of Enfield, Middlesex, the sum of £100 to purchase land, which shall remain for ever, the profits thereof arising yearly to be bestowed and employed every year for the relief of poor widows that are of good report, and of setting to school one or more poor child or children that are either fatherless or motherless, in the said parish of Enfield, and to be converted to no other use ; and the parishioners did add, out of the parish rents, £20 more, and purchased with the said money* one messuage or tenement, since pulled down, a garden, and two acres of land, in the parish of Enfield aforesaid, at or near Cole's-bridge, and one acre and a half of meadow in Wild-marsh, and one acre of land in Dung-field, and two acres of land in the same Dung-field, called Locker Croft, and five roods of land in Long-field.

---

[NOTE.]

At the time of the Enclosure Act (41 Geo. III. c. 143), a part of the property of this Charity was exchanged by

---

* These are the same premises as were charged by the will of William Billings with the payment of 20s. per annum to the parish of Enfield.

the Commissioners for 3a. 12r. 10p. of land at the back
of the Workhouse, numbered 1641 on the parish map,
and now rented by the Edmonton Union.

| *Annual Receipt.* | £ | s. | d. | *Annual Application.* | £ | s. | d. |
|---|---|---|---|---|---|---|---|
| Of Richard Connop, one year ... ... | 3 | 10 | 0 | Quit Rent to the Manor of Chapless | 0 | 7 | 6 |
| Of Jos. Jennis, ditto . | 4 | 0 | 0 | To four poor widows, at 7s. 6d. a quarter each ... ... ... | 6 | 0 | 0 |
| | | | | To the Minister and Churchwardens, to be bestowed at Bartholomew-tide, for cloathing poor children ... ... ... | 1 | 2 | 6 |
| | £7 | 10 | 0 | | £7 | 10 | 0 |

#### [NOTE].

| | | £ | s. | d. |
|---|---|---|---|---|
| One year's rent of Edmonton Union ... ... ... ... | | 15 | 0 | 0 |
| Ditto of Mr. Lucena ... ... ... ... ... ... | | 2 | 2 | 0 |
| Ditto of Mr. Jennings ... ... ... ... ... ... | | 4 | 0 | 0 |
| Interest on £100 lent to the Market-place Charity ... | | 4 | 0 | 0 |
| | | £25 | 2 | 0 |

### SEVENTEENTH GIFT.—DIXON'S.

HENRY DIXON, citizen and draper of London, and
inhabitant of the town of Enfield, in the county of
Middlesex, by will dated November the 9th, 1693, did
give and bequeath all his messuages, lands, tenements,
and hereditaments, situate in the towns or parishes of

Benington or Munden in the county of Hertford, and
Enfield, in the county of Middlesex, and in the parish of
St. Mildred in the Poultry, London, to the Company of
Drapers, London, and their successors for ever, upon
trust that the said Company of Drapers and their
successors (after deducting all charges incident to the said
lands and premises, and other payments, in his will
mentioned), should dispose of the residue to the use
hereinafter mentioned, that is to say, in, for, and towards
placing apprentices to handicraft trades. In the first
place, of such poor boys, wheresoever born, as bear his
Christian name and surname, and are of the age of 15
years or more, the sum of £5 for each boy; and for the
payment of the like sum of £5 to every such boy so
placed out apprentice as aforesaid, that shall duly and
truly serve his said apprenticeship, within a month after
he shall be made free of the city of London, for the better
enabling him to set up and follow his trade; and in the
next place, in, for, and towards placing apprentices to
handicraft trades, such poor boys, wheresoever born, as
bear his surname only, and are above the age of 15
years, the sum of £4 for each boy; and for the payment
of the like sum of £4 to every such boy so placed out
apprentice, that shall duly and truly serve his said
apprenticeship, within a month after he shall be made
free of the City of London, for the better enabling him
to set up and follow his trade; and for want of such, then
in and for placing out apprentices to handicraft trades,

of such and so many poor boys born and resident in the
several parishes of Benington and Enfield aforesaid, and
of the parishes of Saint Katherine Coleman and Saint
Mildred, in the Poultry, London, that are above the age
of 15 years, the sum of £4 for every such boy, and for
the payment of the like sum of £4 to every such boy of
the said several parishes so placed out apprentice that
shall duly and truly serve his said apprenticeship, within
a month after he shall be free of the City of London,
for the better enabling him to set up and follow his
trade ; and for want of such, then, in the next place,
in and for the placing out apprentices, to the trades
aforesaid, of such of the sons of the tenants which now
are, or hereafter shall be, tenants of the hereby devised
lands, or any part thereof, whose parent or parents shall
desire the same, and are of the age of 15 years, the sum
of £3 for each such son, and for the payment of the like
sum of £3 to every such son of a tenant so placed out
apprentice, within two months after he shall have served
the term of seven years as an apprentice, and shall
produce a certificate of his serving such apprenticeship,
under the hands of the Churchwardens for the time being
of the parish in which he shall have served his said
apprenticeship, and also a certificate of his having been
above the age of 15 years at the time he was
bound apprentice as aforesaid, from the hands of the
Churchwardens for the time being of the parish in which

he was born, for the better enabling him to set up and follow his trade ; and, for want of such, in the last place, to and for the placing out apprentices, to the trades aforesaid, of any poor boys as the Court, commonly called the Court of Assistants, of the said Company of Drapers, for the time being, shall from time to time nominate, think fit and appoint, and are above the age of 15 years, the sum of £4 for each such boy ; and for the payment of the like sum of £4 to every such boy so placed out apprentice that shall duly and truly serve his said aprenticeship, within a month after he shall be made free of the City of London, for the better enabling him to set up and follow his trade. And he desired that immediately after his decease a copy of so much of his will be delivered to the respective ministers of the said several parishes as shall concern each parish, and to be entered in their respective vestry books, for their parishioners (for the time being) respective better information and observation of his said bequest, and gave to each minister of such respective parish the sum of 20s. as a legacy, and for his care in causing such clause of his will to be entered in the vestry book of his respective parish.

The method of applying for this gift is by producing a certificate under the hands of the Minister and Church wardens of Enfield, for the time being, in the form following, viz.:—

*To the Worshipful the Master, Wardens, and Assistants
of the Company of Drapers, London.*

We, whose names are hereunto subscribed, the Minister
and Churchwardens of the parish of Enfield, in the county
of Middlesex, do hereby certify the Company above-
named that A.B., the son of C.D. by E. his wife, is a
poor boy of this parish, and was baptized the  . . . .
.day of  . . . .  17  . as by the register appeareth ;
and having first made due enquiry, we like and approve
of G. H. of the parish of  . . . . . .  in the City of
London, citizen and          , to be a fit master for the
said A.B.  And we do, therefore, desire your worships
consent for Mr. Henry Dixon's gift, for him to be put
out apprentice to the said G.H. for the term of seven
years, according to the last will and testament of the said
Henry Dixon, deceased.

Witness our hands this  . .  day of  . . . . .

R. N., *Vicar.*

K. F.  
J, W.  } *Churchwardens.*
J. A.

N.B.—The boy must be presented at Drapers' Hall on
a Court-day, being the first Monday in every month, by
one of the Churchwardens who signed the certificate for
the Company's approbation, before he is bound, otherwise
the gift will not be paid.

[NOTE.]

The Company has now increased its payment to £10 and upwards.

---

### EIGHTEENTH GIFT.—PIGOTT'S.

THOMAS PIGOT, by his will bearing date February the 25th, 1681, gives to the parish of Enfield, yearly for ever, 10s. to the poor of Ponder's-end quarter, to be laid out in bread and distributed to them on St. Thomas's Day, and if default shall be made in payment of the said 10s. he gives a power of distress and sale in any of his lands given to his kinsman, Thomas Pigot and his heirs, on which the same is charged.

☞ This gift has not been paid many years, nor is it known for any certainty which are the lands.

### NINETEENTH GIFT.

A messuage or tenement, with the garden and premises, situate at the Chace-side, in Enfield, purchased by the parish of Enfield in the year 1740, and now used as a workhouse for the poor of the said parish.

☞ This is part of the premises charged with the payment of Smith's gift.

---

[NOTE].

At the time of the enclosure in 1801, sixteen poles of land were added to the garden at the back of the workhouse, and an allotment of 35 poles was awarded in lieu of common rights, the rent of which is paid to the Overseers.

## TWENTIETH GIFT.—NICHOLS'.

MRS. MARY NICHOLS, of Enfield, by her will dated May the 22nd, 1751, left to the parish of Enfield £900, part thereof to be laid out in the purchase of an organ, the other part thereof to be deposited in Government Securities, the interest thereof to be applied towards paying an organist. When the organ was compleatly built and erected, there remained as much money as purchased £319 8s. 10½d. 3 per cent. Consolidated Bank Annuities, which stands in the name of the Accomptant General of the Court of Chancery, and placed to the credit of a cause intitled the Attorney General against Patteshall, the interest whereof is £9 11s. 8d. per annum, and paid to the organist for the time being.

☞ The parish pays the organist an additional salary, £14 11s. 8d.

The said Mary Nichols also left £50 to the said parish, to be laid out at interest, the interest to be distributed yearly in bread amongst the poor for ever, on the day she was buried, which was on June the 12th, 1751. This £50 purchased £46 10s. Old South Sea Annuities, subscribed, the interest of which is £1 7s. 10d per annum.

| Annual Receipt. | £ | s. | d. | Annual Application. | £ | s. | d. |
|---|---|---|---|---|---|---|---|
| Interest on £319 8s. 10½d. 3 per cent. Consolidated Bank Annuities ... ... | 9 | 11 | 8 | Cash received at the Bank by the Organist, by warrant from the Accomptant General .. ... | 9 | 11 | 8 |
| Interest on £46 10s. Old South Sea Annuities, subscribed | 1 | 7 | 10 | Bread given annually to the poor on June 12th ... ... ... | 1 | 7 | 10 |
| | £10 | 19 | 6 | | £10 | 19 | 6 |

N.B.—When a new organist is appointed, an affidavit of the appointment must be made either by one of the Churchwardens or the Vestry Clerk of the parish, of such appointment, and the new organist produced at the Accomptant General's Chambers by the person making such affidavit, to identify his person.

### TWENTY-FIRST GIFT.—MAURER'S.

FREDERICK MAURER, of Enfield, Esq., left, by his will dated March the 22nd, 1772, £50 to the poor of the parish of Enfield, to be distributed amongst them, at the discretion of the Ministers and Churchwardens of the said parish.

*₄* With this sum the parish, by consent of the executor, purchased £57 10s. 3 per cent. Consolidated Bank Annuities.

| Annual Receipt. | £ | s. | d. | Annual Application. | £ | s. | d. |
|---|---|---|---|---|---|---|---|
| Interest on £57 10s. 3 per cent Consolidated Bank Annuities ... ... ... | 1 | 14 | 6 | Bread given to the poor, every other Sunday in the year | 1 | 14 | 6 |
| | £1 | 14 | 6 | | £1 | 14 | 6 |

In the year 1813 the parish added to this gift several small balances of different charities, which arose from returned property tax, and therewith purchased £100 more of the same stock, making the whole income £4 14s. 6d.

---

## TWENTY-SECOND GIFT.—DARBY'S.

RICHARD DARBY, of Gray's Inn, in the county of Middlesex, Esq., by will dated January the 12th, 1735, gave to the poor of Ponder's-end quarter, in the parish of Enfield, £100 to be distributed to such persons, and in such proportions, as his wife should think proper.

The said Sarah Darby never distributed the above legacy; but, by order of the Court of Chancery, the same was, on the 2nd September, 1776, paid, together with the interest thereof to the 5th of August, 1776, making together £278 6s. 3d., with which, and £3 9s. 5d. out of the Benfleet Rents, the then Overseers purchased £333 6s. 8d., 3 per cent. Consolidated Bank Annuities; the interest whereof is to be paid by half-yearly payments, at Midsummer and Christmas, in every year, to four poor persons of Ponder's-end quarter, in equal proportions, such poor persons to be nominated and appointed by the inhabitants of the said parish of Enfield, in vestry assembled, by giving notice of such vestry in the Church on the two Sundays next preceding the same.

| Annual Receipt. | £ | s. | d. | Annual Application. | £ | s. | d. |
|---|---|---|---|---|---|---|---|
| Interest on £333 6s. 8d. 3 per cent. Consolidated Bank Annuities ... ... | 10 | 0 | 0 | To 4 poor persons of Ponder's-end quarter by Half-yearly payments, at Midsummer and Christmas | 10 | 0 | 0 |
| | £10 | 0 | 0 | | £10 | 0 | 0 |

### TWENTY-THIRD GIFT.—TURPIN'S.

MARY TURPIN, of Enfield, spinster, by will dated June the 30th, 1775, directed her executors to lay out £200 in the purchase of 3 per Cent. Bank Annuities, in the names of the Vicar of Enfield and the Churchwardens and Overseer of the town quarter, for the time being, in trust, to apply the interest towards teaching and instructing three poor girls of the said parish and quarter, (whose parents do not receive alms of the said parish) in reading, writing, and needle work. Messrs. John Cradock and John Fenton, the executors, laid out the said sum of £200 in the purchase of £240, 3 per cent. Consolidated Bank Annuities, in the names of the Reverend Richard Newbon, John Ostlife, and Robert Thorne.

| Annual Receipt. | £ | s. | d. | Annual Application. | £ | s. | d. |
|---|---|---|---|---|---|---|---|
| Interest on £240, 3 per cent. Consolidated Bank Annuities ... | 7 | 4 | 0 | A Year's Pay to the School Master and Mistress, for teaching 3 girls .. ... | 7 | 4 | 0 |
| | £7 | 4 | 0 | | £7 | 4 | 0 |

## Twenty-fourth Gift.—Benfleet Timber Money.

Out of the monies received for timber, felled on the Benfleet Estate, being No. 1 of the Gifts, there has been purchased £400, 3 per cent. Consolidated Bank Annuities.

| *Annual Receipt.* | | | | *Annual Application.* | | | |
|---|---|---|---|---|---|---|---|
| | £ | s. | d. | | £ | s. | d. |
| Interest on £400 3 per cent. Consolidated Bank Annuities ... | 12 | 0 | 0 | Bread given away every other Sunday in the year, at the Church Door ... ... | 7 | 6 | 8 |
| | | | | Towards three Forty Shilling Gifts to 2 poor men and 1 poor Woman ... | 4 | 12 | 0 |
| | | | | At the disposal of the Vestry ... ... | 0 | 1 | 4 |
| | £12 | 0 | 0 | | £12 | 0 | 0 |

N.B.—The above £4 12s. and Nichols Gift . £1 8s. ⎫
—————— ⎬ makes the three 40s. Gifts, called Bread Gifts.
£6 0 ⎭

| | £ | s. | d. |
|---|---|---|---|
| By the foregoing state of the Gifts it appears that the annual amount of the same is ... ... ... | 357 | 18 | 10 |
| That the annual outgoings of the same are ... ... | 287 | 3 | 4 |
| Remains to be disposed of, at the discretion of the Vestry... ... ... ... ... ... ... ... ... | 70 | 15 | 6 |
| ☞ Out of this the assistant School-master is paid annually ... ... .. ... ... ... ... ... | 40 | 0 | 0 |
| Undisposed of | 30 | 15 | 6 |

Particulars of the several Gifts in the foregoing account said to be disposed of in bread.

| | £ | s. | d. | | £ | s. | d. |
|---|---|---|---|---|---|---|---|
| Robert Ramston ... | 1 | 14 | 0 | Forty-nine 3d. loaves distributed to the poor every other Sunday in the year | 15 | 18 | 6 |
| George Cock ... ... | 2 | 11 | 4 | | | | |
| Jasper Nichols ... | 2 | 12 | 0 | | | | |
| Mary Nichols ... ... | 1 | 7 | 10 | | | | |
| Freder. Maurer ... | 1 | 14 | 6 | | | | |
| The Surplus of the Interest of the £400, 3 per cent. Consolidated Bank Annuities, bought with the money received for timber cut on the Benfleet estate | 7 | 6 | 8 | Bread given to the poor annually on the 12th of June, being the burial day of Mary Nichols ... | 1 | 7 | 10 |
| | £17 | 6 | 4 | | £17 | 6 | 4 |

RICHARD NEWBON, *Vicar.*

KANDS FORD,  
JOSEPH WELCH, } *Churchwardens.*  
JOHN ALLEN,  

JOHN DELL,  
CHRISTOPHER STROTHOFF, } *Overseers.*  
THOMAS WOOD,          1789.

## WRIGHT'S ALMHOUSES.

On the west side of Enfield-highway are six almshouses, bearing the following inscription :—

"These almshouses were erected and endowed by Mr. Charles Wright, of Enfield-highway, for the support of six poor widows, A.D. 1847."

Mr. Wright was for many years a resident at Enfield-highway, where he died Aug. 19, 1851, aged 83 years.

A few years before his death he built these almshouses, and placed six poor widows therein, and by deed dated Oct. 4, 1848, conveyed them and a perpetual rent-charge of £80 a year, chargeable upon nineteen freehold houses in the parish of St. Luke's, to trustees, for the benefit of six poor widows,—not possessing an income exceeding £10 a year, and not receiving parochial relief, or being under 60 years of age,—who had for 12 months preceding election lived in Enfield-wash, Enfield-highway, Green-street, South-street, or Ponder's-end.

The said widows are to be elected by the trustees, and to occupy the almshouses, and to receive a sum of £10 yearly, by quarterly payments, and one ton of good coals before Christmas in every year ; and if there should be any surplus remaining after providing for the repairs and insurance of the almshouses, it is to be disposed of for their benefit.

The present trustees are :—Mr. Ellis Hall, James Pateshall Jones, Esq., the Rev. John Harman, Mr.

William Mitchell, and Mr. William Walker. The appointment and the filling up the trust when a vacancy occurs, are vested in the trustees for the time being absolutely.

## CROWE'S ALMHOUSES.

Mrs. Ann Crowe, of Enfield, by. will dated Feb. 26, 1763, gave to her brother, Matthew Kenrick, £500 three per cent. red. stock, in trust, to apply the dividends towards repairing her almshouses in Turkey-street, and to buy the four inhabitants thereof three chaldrons of coals yearly, to be divided along with the remainder of the income, if any, equally between them.

———

# APPENDIX.

———

## ELLSOM'S GIFT.

JOSEPH ELLSOM, of Enfield, butcher, by his will dated
March 6th, 1797, left the sum of £200 five per cent.
stock (now £210 new three and a half per cent. stock),
the interest thereof to be given in equal portions every
half year, within one month after it becomes due, to two
poor widows, or single women, of the age of sixty years
and upwards, born in the parish of Enfield ; to be elected
by the Trustees and the Churchwardens, or the majority
of them. He also gave the residue of his five per cent.
stock, and of his effects, to be laid out in the same stock,
which being done, produced together £312 12s. stock
(now £328 4s. 7d. new three and a quarter per cent.
stock ;) the interest thereof to be given in the same
manner, and in case either of the said four poor women
depart this life, then another poor woman to be elected
in manner aforesaid in her room ; and in the event of the
death of either of the three trustees, another trustee to be
appointed by the survivors, within three months ; if they
neglect to do so, then the Churchwardens are to make the
appointment.

### EATON AND MEYER'S GIFT.

MRS. ELIZABETH ANNE EATON, of London, by will dated
August 24th, 1806, gave all her estate at Enfield for the
benefit of six poor widows ; but as the will was not legally
executed, so as to pass real estates, and as no heir-at-law
could be found, an inquisition was held at Enfield, on
July 3rd, 1815, when it appeared that fourteen acres of
land, in Broadfield, were within the Manor of Enfield,
and therefore escheated to the Crown, in right of the
Duchy of Lancaster ; three houses, and ten acres of land,
being within the Manor of Worcesters, fell to James
Meyer, Esq., as Lord of that Manor—who, having sold
part thereof for as much money as produced £1700, three
per cent. consols, added thereto £300 of the same stock,
being the value of that part of the estate, which he himself retained ; and acting upon the original intention of
the said Mrs. Eaton, he made over the whole £2,000
stock to trustees, by a deed dated November 16th, 1816,
enrolled in Chancery ; the interest to be disposed of
according to the intentions of the said Mrs. Eaton.  The
trustees are the Lord of the Manor of Worcesters for the
time being, the Vicar of Enfield for the time being, and
others.

Any vacancy in the trust to be filled up by the survivors, but if the survivors be less than three, then the
vacancy to be filled up by a Vestry, whereof notice shall
have been given in the church on two Sundays preceding.
Two widows are chosen by the Lord of the Manor of

Worcesters for the time being, one by the Vicar of Enfield for the time being, and three by the majority of the trustees ; the said Lord of the Manor to have the casting vote ; and in case either of the said widows die, or remove out of the parish, or marry, or cease to be poor, then another to be elected in her stead.

There is a proviso in this deed, that if the said James Meyer, Esq., his heirs, or assigns, shall at any time be evicted, or turned out of possession, or interrupted in the quiet enjoyment of a certain piece of land belonging to Osborn's gift, lying in his park, containing 1 rood and 28 poles, then the said £2000 stock shall be transferred to the said James Meyer, his executors, administrators, or assigns, for his and their own proper use and benefit.

The Duchy Court of Lancaster, in 1828, at the intercession of Dr. Cresswell, agreed to pay the annual rent of the 14 acres above mentioned, amounting to £32 13s. 8d. per annum, to the Vicar and Churchwardens of Enfield every year, Mr. Sawyer having given up a claim which he had to a beneficial lease thereof ; and the Vicar and Churchwardens have agreed to divide the same equally between three poor widows, being parishioners of Enfield, of unimpeachable characters.

### DICKASON'S GIFT.

THOMAS DICKASON, of Enfield, Esq., by will dated December 31st, 1813, bequeathed to the Vicar and Churchwardens of the parish of Enfield for the time being

the sum of £200, to be laid out in the joint names of the
Vicar and Churchwardens of Enfield aforesaid, for the time
being, in the purchase of Government Stocks ; such Vicar
and Churchwardens, on the 25th day of December, in
every year for ever, to divide the interest of such stocks
between such poor persons residing within the parish
of Enfield as they in their discretion shall think proper
objects of charity, and the most deserving ; the widows
of housekeepers (not having usually received alms of the
parish), to be always preferred.

The sum of £285 3s. reduced three per cents., stands
in the names of the trustees.

### CLAXTON'S GIFT.

MRS. FRANCES CLAXTON, of Enfield, by will dated May
19th, 1817, gave to the Vicar of Enfield, for the time
being, £333 6s. 8d. three per cent. consols ; the interest
of which is to be applied in keeping her tomb, in Enfield
churchyard, in repair ; and if anything remain, the same
to be given to some poor widow above 60 years of age.
The legacy duty reduced this to £305 stock.

### MESTURAS' GIFT.

JAMES FRANCIS MESTURAS, of Enfield, Esq., by will
dated August 27th, 1817, gave £50 to the Churchwardens
of Enfield, for the use of the poor, with which was purchased £50 three per cent. reduced stock, in the names
of the trustees, and the interest given yearly to one
widow.

## THE TWO HUNDRED ACRES.

Enfield-chase, previous to its division in 1777, was wholly within the parish of Enfield, and as the Act dismembered that parish, by annexing the allotments of Edmonton, South Mimms, and Hadley, to their respective parishes, two hundred acres were awarded to Enfield, in satisfaction of the said dismemberment; the rent of which said two hundred acres was directed by the Act to be applied, one-half thereof in aid of the land-tax of the parish, and the other half in aid of the poor rate. In 1800, Enfield sold a moiety of the above two hundred acres, and with the produce redeemed the land tax; the remaining half, applicable to the poor rate, is let on leases for 99 years, from Michaelmas, 1778 (excepting lot 36, containing three roods and eighteen perches, which is in the occupation of the Workhouse).

## THE TIMBER MONEY.

The Act of Parliament, passed in the year 1801, for dividing and enclosing the Common-fields and Chase-allotment in this parish, directed that a certain part of the timber then growing on the said Chase-allotment, should be sold, and the produce placed in the Government funds, and the interest thereof applied in aid of the poor-rate of Enfield parish. Accordingly the Commissioners placed £15,131 10s. 4d. three per cent. Consols, in the name of the Accountant General of the

Court of Chancery, exparte the Churchwardens of the parish of Enfield, the annual interest whereof, being £453 18s. 10d., is yearly applied in aid of the poor rate of Enfield.

## CONDUITS.

In the Enfield Inclosure Act of 1777, it is directed— That Sir Thomas Halifax, and his assigns, should continue at his and their costs and charges, a pipe and cock from the main of the conduit on the top of the hill, opposite his house, at Chase-side, "for the use and benefit of the inhabitants of Enfield, in the manner the same is now, (in 1777) or hath been used and enjoyed."

In the award of the Commissioners of the Inclosure Act of 1801, it is directed, "That the well at the northeast corner of the allotment of David Miles (1810) shall for ever after be continued, and kept open as a public watering place; and that all persons shall and may, at all times hereafter, have free access, on foot, to the said well, along the footpaths herein before awarded over the allotments of Mary May, and David Miles, to the said well, and that the stiles which cross the said footpaths shall at all times hereafter be made commodious and convenient for the persons using the said well, by and at the expense of the owners of the allotments through which the said footpaths are directed to pass."

## MRS. ANNE GOUGH'S GIFT.

MRS. ANNE GOUGH, widow of the late Richard Gough, of Forty-hill, Esq., by a codicil dated June 26th, 1830, left the sum of £200, to be distributed amongst poor persons, of the parish of Enfield, at the discretion of her executors, Humphrey Hall, and John Farran, Esquires; who, in order to perpetuate her memory, and to make her benefaction a source of permanent good to the poor, invested, on the 11th day of April, 1834, the above mentioned sum in the three per cent. Consolidated Annuities, purchasing thereby £220 1s. 8d. stock, in the names of the then Vicar and Churchwardens of the said parish, and directed that they, and their successors, should lay out the dividends thence accruing, in the purchase of articles of clothing, and distribute them yearly, on the day after Christmas day, amongst the deserving poor of the said parish, for ever. The stock stands in the names of the trustees.

## KELHAM'S GIFT.

MRS. AVICE KELHAM, of Enfield, by her will, dated the 12th day of December, 1829,* gave the sum of £1260,

---

* *Extract from the Will of Mrs. Avice Kelham.*

.. "I give and bequeath to the said Robert Kelham Kelham and William Belt, of Bedford-row, in the County of Middlesex, their executors, administrators, and assigns, the sum of one thousand pounds, 3½ per cent. Reduced Bank Annuities, upon trust from three per cent. Consols, the interest of which is to be applied for the benefit of the Girls' Sunday School, and also the sum of £1000 in the same Stock, the interest of which is to be applied in purchasing coals for the poor (chiefly aged widows) of Enfield.

The dividend annually arising therefrom is thus distributed, viz.,—£29 12s. for coals, and £37 6s. for the benefit of the school, which sums are paid by the official trustees of Mrs. Kelham's will, and are applied as directed, the former by the Vicar and Churchwardens, and the latter by the Treasurer to the said school.

---

time to time for ever hereafter, to lay out and expend the annual interest, dividends, and proceeds thereof in the purchase of coals, and to distribute the same in the months of December, January, and and February in each and every year, to such poor persons residing within the said Parish of Enfield, as they, the said Robert Kelham Kelham and William Belt, or the survivor of them, or the executors, administrators, or assigns of such survivor shall think fit. And it is my will, and I do hereby direct that in the distribution of the said coals, aged widows shall always have the preference.

I give and bequeath to the said Robert K. Kelham and William Belt, their executors, administrators, and assigns, the further sum of £1400, 3½ per cent. reduced Bank Annuities, upon trust from time to time for ever, hereafter to receive the annual interest, dividends, and proceeds thereof, and to pay the same as the same shall become due and be received, into the hands of the treasurers for the time being, of the Girls' Sunday School, now held at the Free School, at Enfield, aforesaid, to be applied by the committee of management of the said school, in manner hereinafter mentioned, that is to say, as to the annual sum of eight pounds, part thereof in paying salary

The Sunday School, herein mentioned, was originally held at the Free School, in the Churchyard, but has since been combined with the National Schools in London-road.

The fund (£37 6s.), according to the will of the testatrix, is directed to be disposed of entirely for the benefit of the said school,—viz., in educating and clothing the children, and including a salary of eight pounds per annum, paid to the school mistress, for giving the girls religious instruction and taking them to church on Sundays.

of eight pounds per annum to the school mistress for the time being of the said school, and as to the remainder thereof in clothing the scholars of the said school, and for and towards the instruction of the said scholars, or any other purpose for promoting the interest of the said school that the said committee of management thereof for the time being shall think fit.

But in case the said Sunday School shall at any time hereafter be discontinued to be attended by ladies, as a committee of management thereof, then it is my will, and I do hereby direct that from thenceforth, the annual sum of £20, part of the said last mentioned annual interest, dividends, and proceeds, shall be paid as a salary to the schoolmistress of the said school, to be from time to time chosen by the Vicar for the time being, of Enfield, and the remainder of, shall be from time to time applied in or towards clothing the children of the said school, in such manner as the said Vicar for the time being shall think fit. And I do hereby direct that the receipt and receipts of the treasurer for the time being, of the said Sunday School, shall be a sufficient discharge to the person or persons paying the whole or any part or parts of the annual interest, dividends, &c." Mrs. Kelham died 27th July, 1841.

### THE GREEN AND ENCROACHMEETS.

The Enfield Inclosure Act (41 Geo. 3, c 143) directed—
That the Commissioners should set out and allot to the
Vicar, Churchwardens, and Overseers, for the time being,
to be held by them and their successors for ever, such
part of the Chase, called the Enfield Allotment, as is
called Enfield Chase Green, not exceeding 20 acres,
as the said Commissioners should think proper, to be
inclosed in such manner as the said Commissioners, by
their award, should direct and appoint; and as soon as
the same should be assigned, set out, allotted, and inclosed as aforesaid, the said Vicar, Churchwardens, and
Overseers for the time being, and their successors,
should from time to time stand seized thereof, with the
majority of freeholders and copyholders in vestry assembled, which vestry should be called in the usual manner,
and under the same regulations as the Chase vestries are
by law directed to be held in the parish of Enfield; and
that they should have the sole and exclusive management
thereof in any way they, at such vestries, should direct for
the benefit of the poor.

The Commissioners never did assign, set out, allot, or
inclose any part of this Green, nor have they, by their
award, given any directions, or made any appointment,
relating thereto; therefore the Vicar, Churchwardens,
and Overseers, with the freeholders, and copyholders in
vestry, do not stand seized thereof under the Act.

It may therefore be considered that the Chase Green is still vested in the Churchwardens for the time being (who were incorporated) by the 17 Geo. 3, c. 17 an Act for dividing the Chase of Enfield, in trust for the owners and proprietors of freehold and copyhold property, within the parish, and their tenants, entitled to rights of common, &c.

The sum of three pounds is paid by the occupier of the Shrubbery on Chase-hill for encroachments, and disposed of in clothing for the poor.

### NEW RIVER COMPANY'S GIFT.

The sum of two pounds is annually paid by the New River Company, to the Churchwardens of Enfield for the time being, for a certain privilege in respect of drainage, at Chase-side, granted by the parish, which sum is disposed of in clothing for the poor.

# NAMES OF SUBSCRIBERS.

Abbiss, James, J.P., The Shrub-
berries, Enfield.
Adams, F. C., Chase-park.
Adams, H. J., Chase-park.
Alexander, W. D., J.P., Summit-
house.
Arabin, Mrs., 36, Grosvenor-square.
Austin, Walter, Juglans-lodge.
Baird, Rev. James, The Vicarage,
Southgate.
Balfour, H. T.; The Clock-house,
East Barnet.
Bangs, William, Bow.
Barclay, J. Gurney, Knott's-green.
Barker, W. Nutter, B.A., The Palace.
Barry, Horace, Bush-hill House.
Batters, George, Brigadier-hill.
Baxendale, Lloyd, Totteridge.
Beadle, Edmund, Winchmore-hill.
Bell, Mrs., Hole-park, Kent.
Bell, Mrs. Spencer, Devonshire-
place.
Bell, Miss, Borovere, Alton.
Bentley, James, Wood-green Park.
Bevan, R. C. L., J.P., Trent-park.
Bevan, F. A., Prince's-gate.
Bevan, W. A., West Farm.
Bevan, R. Y., Trent Park.
Bird and Carpenter, Misses, Chase-
side.

Booth, E., Trent-park.
Bond, Mrs., Elm-bank, Hampstead.
Bosanquet, J. W., J.P., Claysmore.
Bosanquet, Mrs. Augustus, Osidge.
Bosanquet, Bernard T., Enfield.
Bosanquet, Percival, D'Acre Lodge.
Bowles, H. C. B., J.P., Myddelton-
house.
Brading, T., Ponder's-end.
Braikenridge, Geo. J., Bush-hill.
Braikenridge, The Rev. G. W.
Clevedon, Somerset.
Bunnell, Peter, Penge.
Burrell, Sir Percy, Bart., M.P.,
West Grinstead-park.
Burrell, Lady.
Burnett, George R.; Kensington.
Busk, Mrs., Ford's-grove.
Butler, Mrs., Observatory, Armagh.
Butler, Charles, Warren-wood.
Buszard, William, Enfield.
Carr, William, Brunswick-square,
Brighton.
Cass, Rev. F. C., M.A., The Rectory,
Hadley.
Cater, J. White, West-lodge.
Cater, F., Durants.
Cattarns, R., Enfield.
Cave, Henry, Enfield.
Challis, Alderman, Enfield.

Challis, William H., Enfield.

Child, Miss, Gough-park.

Christy, Alexander, Stanley-hall, Salop.

Church, H., Lawn-house, Southgate.

Collyer, Jas., L.R.C.P., Oak-house.

Cooper, G., The Clock-house, East Barnet.

Copleston, Rev. R. E., Vicarage, Edmonton.

Cotton, Alderman, Theobald's-park.

Cundall, Arthur, Enfield.

Curtis, Thomas, The Hall, Berk-hampstead.

Curzon, Hon. Edward C., J.P., Scarsdale-house.

Curzon, G.A., Capt. 2nd Life Guards.

The Bishop of St. David's

Dawson, W. I., Bush-hill Cottage.

Duncan, T., New-cottage, Potter's-bar.

Durant, R. jun., J.P., High Canons.

Lord Enfield, M.P., Penerley-lodge.

Edelsten, P., Manor-house, Bull's-cross.

Egles, Rev. E. H., Enfield.

Fairhead, Allen, Enfield.

Ford, H. R., Morecambe-lodge, Lancaster.

Ford, Edward, J.P., Enfield Old-park.

Ford, J. Rawlinson, Adel Grange, Yorkshire.

Ford, J. W., The Cottage, East Barnet.

Ford, A. L., Liverpool.

George, A. G., Southgate.

Gibbons, Ebenezer, Enfield.

Gilbert, Josiah, Marden-ash.

Graham, G. J., East-lodge.

Grey, Sir William, Bohun-lodge.

Lord Geo. F. Hamilton, M.P., Hertford-street, Mayfair.

Hall, Ellis, Enfield-highway.

Hankey, George, Frant, Tunbridge.

Harman, Rev. J., Vicarage, Enfield-highway.

Harman, John, Portman-square.

Harnett, Wm. J., M.D., L.R.C.P.E., L.M., L.R.C.S.I., M.B.

Harrison, Daniel, J.P., Chase-hill.

Harrison, T. Haydn, Broxbourne.

Heath, Rev. J. M., Milland.

Heath, H. G., Clay-hill.

Henry, David, Forty-hill.

Herbert, J., Birmingham.

Heseltine, J., Grosvenor Lodge, Upper Clapton.

Hills, T. Hyde, 45, Queen Anne-street.

Hobbs, William, Enfield.

Hobbs, Thomas, Enfield.

Hodson, Rev. Geo. H., Vicarage, Enfield.

Hunter, John R., Enfield.

Hunter, Edward, The Glebe, Black-heath.

Ingersoll, R. T., Enfield-highway.

Jack, Charles, Beech-hill-park.

Jackson, Mrs. James, River-house.

Jackson, Joseph, Enfield.

Jones, Rev. Thomas, M.A., Green-
street.

Jones, J. Pateshall, Roselands.

Kemble, Mrs., Oakmere, Potter's-bar.

Kempe, Rev. E. W., Chase-side.

Kemp, C. F., Foxbush, Tunbridge.

Kent, Rev. Charles,

Knight, Thomas, Enfield-highway.

Knott, J., London-road, Enfield.

Knott, T., London-road, Enfield.

Langton, Walter, Southgate.

Law, J. S., South-lodge.

Letchworth, Edward, 88, St. James'
street.

Lewis, Capt. Henry, R.N., Devon-
shire-street.

Lister, Mrs., Hampstead.

Lock, William, Enfield.

Lucena, S. L., Windmill-hill.

Luck, Mrs., Hampstead.

Maclagan, Rev. W. D, Rectory,
Newington.

Malcolm, Mrs., Bush-hill.

Mann, Thomas, Winchmore-hill.

Mansel, R. S., Everley-lodge.

Maple, John, Tottenham Court-road.

Mathison, R., Enfield.

Meyer, James, J.P., Forty-hall.

Meyers, J. H., Enfield.

Micholls, H. L., Southgate-house.

Miles, John, Friern Barnet.

Milne, E., Hadley.

Mitchell, John, South-street, Ponder's-end.

Mitchell, William, Enfield-highway.

Monro, M. M., Bury-farm.

Moore, W.W., Leggatts, Potter's-bar.

Morgan, E. L., Wildwood.

Morison, Miss, Markyate-street.

Mugliston, G. T. W., M.D., Enfield.

Muir, H. B. Little-park.

Murray, John, Albemarle-street.

Nash, Henry, J.P., Bury-house.

Naylor, W. B., Ponder's-end.

Ollier, J., Beauchamp-lodge.

Owen, Arthur, Enfield.

Paris, Miss, Trent-lodge.

Parker, Mrs., White-lodge.

Parker, Henry, jun., Parkfield,
Potter's-bar.

Parker, F. S., The Grange, East
Barnet.

Parker, W. S., White Lodge.

Parry, H., The Elms, Ponder's-end.

Parrott, T. M., Churchbury-house.

Patman, Messrs., Enfield.

Paulin, T., Beaulieu, Winchmore-hill.

Pearson, George, Bolt-court.

Peet, Henry, Cockfosters.

Pitman, — Newgate-street.

Riddell, John R., Bycullah-house.

Richardson, T. S., Broomfield-park.

Ridge, James, M.D., Carlton-house,

Roberts, E. C., Southgate.

Robins, J. Y., J.P., Myton-house,
Warwick.

Sawyer, Arthur A., Enfield.

Sheppard, Edgar, M.D., Colney-hatch.

Short, Alfred, Clay-hill.

Sidney, Alderman, Bowes-manor.

Smart, R. W., Llanover-lodge.

Smith, Charles, Enfield.

Smith, E. Cozens, F.R. Hist. Soc., Chase-side.

Somerset, Col. A. P., J.P., Enfield-court.

Somerset, Mrs.

Somerset, Captain Aylmer, Rifle Brigade.

South Kensington Museum.

Stearns, Edward, Forty-hill.

Stearns, F., Clay-hill.

Stern, S. J., Little-grove.

Stocks, Herbert W., Enfield.

Taylor, J. Donnithorne, Grovelands.

Taylor, J., Baker-street, Portman-square.

Tennant, C. R., 10, West Kensington Gardens.

Thomson, James, Colney-hatch.

Thompson, Julius H., The Lindens.

Tindal, Admiral, Chase-lodge.

Tipping, William, M.P., Brasted-park.

Trinity College, Cambridge.

Tremlett, Rev. Dr., Parsonage, Belsize park.

Trenchard, J. A., Nynn-house, Northaw.

Trotter, Capt., Dyrham-park.

Todd, Mrs., Winchmore-hill.

Twells, Philip, J.P., Chase-side House.

Upward, W., Clay-hill Lodge.

Earl of Verulam, Gorhambury.

Walford, Cornelius, Belsize-park.

Walker, John, Arno's-grove.

Walker, Mrs. Edwin, Chase-cottage.

Walker, Mrs. Francis, Elm-hall.

Walker, C. H., Crouch-hill House.

Walker, Rev. Henry Aston.

Walker, Capt. Albert, Hongkong.

Walker, Henry, Bayswater.

Warren, James, Capel-house.

Watkins, Rev. H. G., Vicarage, Potter's-bar.

Weir, Rev. Arch., D.C.L., Vicarage, Forty-hill.

Whitaker, Joseph, Enfield.

White, Edward, Brook-house, Southgate.

White, Rev. Geo. W., Enfield.

Wigan, Mrs., Eversley.

Wilkinson, H. White-webb's-park.

Williams, Miss

Williams, R., Walbrook.

Willis, J. W., Grove-house.

Wilson, Rev. Alex., Vicarage, Tottenham.

Wilson, John Richard.

Withers, Joseph, Burleigh-house.

Young, C. Baring, Oak-hill.

Young, John, jun., Bush-hill.

Lord Zouche, Parham-park.